SECTION ONE

1.1
INTRODUCTION

Limitless, then, in His glory is He in whose hand rests the mighty dominion over all things; and to Him you will be returned [Holy Quran, 36:83]. I start in His name, and to Him all praise is due. May His Glory be Glorified. Although true love itself is bound by no religion, knows no caste, no language, nor does it constrict itself to any limitations, boundaries or barriers, the love that I know and believe in is what I have learned through my understanding of Islam, and the benevolence of its Lord. It is at this point that I would like to assert that I am not a religious scholar, nor claim to be one. In understanding what love is, and describing the indescribable, Sufis have come the closest in their attempts to define love (both human love and Divine love). However, I am no Sufi, for any association as such is a commitment that is currently beyond my ability to ascribe to. I am no more than a man who has loved, and strived to maintain its purity. Therefore, this book is not to be mistaken as a Sufi manual of any sort, but it is a gift of knowledge to my readers and a humble reminder of the timelessness of the love that is prescribed in the Holy Quran, and the importance of striving to honor the inclination of your heart towards another.

On many occasions I've been referred to as a "hopeless romantic" due to my ideologies on eternal love, until I reflected and came to terms with what I am and what I am not. I am not hopeless, for all I have ever had is hope. If optimism could have been exhausted to its death, I'm sure I've raised it back from the dead more than a few times, for someone truly in love never loses hope. Perhaps I was a "hopeful romantic," but I wasn't happy with that either. There had to be another name for people that refuse to give up on love, no matter how difficult it may seem. Until quite recently, I came across someone named Asma, who referred to herself as, "a disciple of true love's forgotten creed." It was in that moment that it all made sense to me. True love, in all its sacredness and beauty, has been forgotten, and perhaps I am another one of its few disciples. One may believe that disciples of true love's forgotten creed have been around since the beginning of time, from civilization to civilization, as true love has thrived throughout the centuries. Surely it has never known the bounds of religion, or caste, skin color or language, for it has penetrated the hearts of men and women from generation to generation indiscriminately. However, I have learned what true love is through my love for Allah ﷻ (May His Glory be Glorified), and my understanding of Islam. I believe love to be at the center of Islam, and intrinsic to the heart of a Muslim, just as it is in mine.

Islam is an Abrahamic monotheistic religion comprised of a religious text known as the Holy Quran which is considered by its adherents to be the verbatim word of God. In Arabic, the word for God is Allah ﷻ which is contracted from 'al', meaning 'the' and 'ilah', meaning 'diety, god' to al-lah meaning "the God." It is said that the variants of the word Allah ﷻ occur in both pagan and Christian pre-Islamic inscriptions. The followers of Islam are known as Muslims, who believe that Islam is the original, complete and universal version of a primordial faith that was revealed to Prophet Muhammad ﷺ (Peace be upon him) by God through the angel Gabriel and many times before to previous Prophets including Adam, Noah, Abraham, Moses, and Jesus, Peace and Blessings be upon them all. The Holy Quran is considered to be both the unaltered and the final revelation of God. Along with the Holy Quran, an integral part of Islam consists of the teachings and example of Prophet Muhammad ﷺ called the Sunnah which is composed of accounts called Hadith.

It is important to point out that along with Hadith, Islam and its practice also includes observance of the five pillars of Islam: Shahada (declaration of faith in the Oneness of God), Salah (five obligatory prayers throughout the day), Zakat (charitable giving based on accumulated wealth), Sawm (fasting), and Hajj (pilgrimage to the holy city of Mecca). There are two main denominations or branches of Islam: the Shia and Sunni, both of which agree on the essential details of the practice of these acts, but the Shia do not refer to them by the same name. Moreover, Islamic Law, known as the Sharia, governs virtually every aspect of life and society from marriage, family relationships, human rights, banking, welfare, peace and security to the rules of war, the social status of both genders, and the environment.

Similar to other monotheist religions, Islam is focused on the existence of one God, or in the oneness of God. Contrary to popular belief, Islam does not denounce any other God, nor does it believe in a hierarchy of Gods. Islam holds that there is simply one God, Allah ﷻ is His name, incomparable is He, and the purpose of existence is His worship. Moreover, Allah ﷻ is beyond all comprehension, He can not be visualized, there is absolutely nothing equal to Him and His Glory, and He has no kin.

With reference to the poem in the opening of this book, according to Hadith, Prophet Muhammad ﷺ, invoked Allah ﷻ by a number of names. There is no universal agreement among Muslim Scholars as to how many names there are, but it has been related by Scholars that Allah ﷻ has three thousand names. Shaykh Nazim Adil al-Haqqani in Volume One of "Liberating the Soul; A Guide for Spiritual Growth", discusses that one thousand of the names are only known by angels, one thousand are only known by prophets, three hundred are in the Torah (Old Testament), three hundred are in Zabur (Psalms of David), three hundred in Injil (the true Gospel, bestowed upon Jesus) and out of the hundred that remain, scholars have said that some of these names appear only in the Holy Quran and others are only in the Hadith, while some appear in both. However, there has been a consensus among Muslims over a list of Ninety-Nine Names. The Holy Quran refers to these names as "al-'asmā' al-ḥusná," which translates to "The Best Names," from the following Ayah:

> Say, "Call upon Allah ﷻ or call upon the Most Merciful. Whichever [name] you call - to Him belong the best names." [Holy Quran, 17:110]

This makes two thousand nine hundred and ninety nine names. Allah ﷻ has specifically hidden one name in the Holy Quran which is called "Is-mul-laa-hil-a'zam" which means The Greatest Name of Allah ﷻ. It is believed that whoever has read the entire Holy Quran must have read the Greatest Name of Allah ﷻ without knowing it.

Allah ﷻ has chosen to hide certain things out of His mercy, and there is divine wisdom behind what Allah ﷻ has chosen to conceal, and what He has revealed. He has hidden the most righteous of people in His eyes, so people should respect one another indiscriminately. He has hidden the night of Qadr (the holy night in which The Holy Quran began to be revealed). Surah Qadr mentions that the night of Qadr is equivalent to a thousand months, and thus it is hidden so believers would worship and obey His orders throughout the month of Ramadan in order to search for the night of

Qadr. Similarly Allah ﷻ has hidden His consent so people continue to please Allah ﷻ by engaging in good deeds. The hour of acceptance on Friday is kept hidden so believers are encouraged to spend their time in worship to their full potential. The time of death is hidden, so one is always aware of the reality of death and strives to remain in a state of purity. Similarly, He has hidden the Greatest Name so people are inclined to search for it in the entire Quran.

Just like atoms are the basic unit of chemical matter, and cells are the basic unit of life, love is the core of the universe, for all of existence is made to love. Islam promotes a very specific definition of love; Halal love. Halal love is the love between two parties that does not transgress the limits set by Allah ﷻ and it strives to save them from committing sin. Halal love's purpose is to find Allah ﷻ through the oneness of two souls. The only way for love to be Halal is for it to be legitimated through marriage.

If a man and woman feel attraction towards one another, and it is permissible for them to marry, there is no better answer to the situation except marriage. Prophet Muhammad ﷺ said: "We do not think that there is anything better for those who love one another than marriage." (Narrated by Ibn Maajah, 1847; classed as Saheeh by al-Busayri and by Shaykh al-Albaani in al-Silsilah al-Saheehah, 624) It is understood that love cannot be increased or made to last longer, without marriage. Marriage is a union that is blessed by Allah ﷻ, and it is only through this blessing that the love increases by the day.

In Islam, the status of marriage is so esteemed that it is narrated by Al-Haakim in al-Mustadrak from Anas (may Allah ﷻ be pleased with him), Prophet Muhammad ﷺ said, "Whomever Allah ﷻ blesses with a righteous wife, He has helped him with half of his religion, so let him fear Allah ﷻ with regard to the other half."

Al-Bayhaqi also narrated in Shu'ab al-Eemaan from al-Raqaashi, "When a person gets married he has completed half of his religion, so let him fear Allah ﷻ with regard to the other half." (Al-Albaani said of these two Hadiths in Saheeh al-Targheeb wa'l-Tarheeb, [1916]: they are Hasan li ghairihi.)

When asked whom a Muslim loves, there are ninety-nine names of Allah ﷻ which provide for ninety-nine attributes to love Him for, all of which can be invoked for one's worldly love to be legitimated through marriage, and for one's beloved to be a blessing in the form of a spouse. In my attempts to pray for my worldly beloved to be bestowed upon me as a spouse, I have appealed to the attributes of my Lord as follows:

Ar-Rahman: Oh Most Beneficent, make my spouse into someone I can love, or grant me my beloved in the form of a spouse. Make my beloved a source of goodness for me, and make me a source of goodness for my beloved. Aid me in fulfilling the duties I owe to my beloved, and allow me to show gentleness and mercy especially when it is most difficult. Allow me to see the good and disregard the negative faults of my beloved and be forgiving of such faults. Allow me to be dutiful, respectful, merciful, and loving towards not only my own parents, and kinship, but as well as the parents and kinship of my beloved.

Ar-Raheem: Oh Most Merciful, make my beloved a source of mercy for me, and make me a source of mercy for my beloved. Moreover, allow me to become continuously and intensely merciful towards my beloved, and make it easy for me to show affection. Allow me to show kindness and compassion, and make me a source of divine blessing and mercy for my beloved and for those connected to my beloved through kinship. Furthermore, make me and my beloved feel compassionate towards, and be attached to, the entire Ummah (entire Muslim population). It is You who, even when we disobey, delays punishment and gives us a chance to turn back to You. I ask You of Your ultimate forgiveness; allow us to turn to You. Show us nothing but Your mercy, and cancel our punishment for You are the only one who can.

Al-Malik: Oh Eternal Lord, The King and Owner of the Dominion of all things, make my entirety faithful to my beloved, and my beloved faithful to me. Make me just and reasonable towards the dominion you have blessed me with, and allow my beloved to become the Kingdom that I reign over, free from the whims of my ego and injustice, for I shall be held accountable on the Day of Judgement for inflicting any wrongs towards whomever I love. Allow me to be patient towards my beloved, and aid both of us in staying away from what is forbidden, and allow us to be content with, and to trust in, Your knowledge and wisdom, as You are the King of all Kings, and the disposer of all affairs, and You know all that which we do not.

Al-Quddus: Oh Most Pure, and the All-Perfect, hide my imperfections and make me faultless in the eyes of my beloved, as the love for my beloved has made her/him faultless in the eyes of my own. You are the All-Perfect, the one who does not do injustice to people, and thus make me as perfect as you possibly can and allow me not to be unjust, nor oppress my beloved. Bless our union and preserve its sacredness from any impurities and imperfections. Allow us to have pure belief in Your command, and enhance and beautify our prayers. Cleanse our bodies and souls and prevent indecency and evil between us and ourselves.

As-Salam: Oh Source of Peace, Wholeness and Well-Being, make my beloved a source of inner peace, wholeness, tranquility and safety for me. Allow us to surrender to You and to be guided by You. Aid us to strive towards doing as many good deeds as possible in order to receive inner peace from You and from each other. Allow us to protect our hearts from diseases such as lying, backbiting, evil speech, hypocrisy, jealousy, showing off, and aid us in seeking a cure from such diseases from the Quran and Sunnah. Moreover, aid us in fulfilling the rights we have over each other, and in protecting each other's honor.

Al-Mu'min: Oh Remover of Fear, Giver of Tranquility, Source of Faith, grant me freedom from the fear of all obstacles that stand between me and my beloved. Aid me and my beloved in strengthening our emaan (faith), as You are the Source of Faith. Provide us with the guidance and enlightenment to have the strongest of emaan to stay away from Your prohibitions and to follow Your command, and allow us both to be a source of guidance and inspiration for each other. Bless us both with emaan until our last breath, and adorn us with the characteristics of Your true believers. Grant us steadfastness and safety in this world and the Hereafter.

Al-Muhaymin: Oh Bestower of Security, The Protector, The Guardian, The Witness and Great Overseer, extend Your wings of love to cover and protect my beloved. You are the one that is ever watchful; I call upon You to watch over and offer security to my beloved in both my presence and absence from whatever has the ability to harm us. Allow us to be constantly reminded that You are the Witness, and the Overseer, the One who sees every deed that we do and observes our reactions to situations, and witnesses our inner thoughts. Let this truth motivate us to stay away from sins and temptations. Allow us to accept that other than You, the Holy Quran is Muhaymin, trustworthy in highness and a witness. Let me and my beloved be elevated with the Quran, aid us in fulfilling the rights of the Quran, and make the Quran a witness for us and not against us.

Al-'Azeez: Oh All Mighty, The Dignified, The Powerful, The Eminent, Your glory and power are overwhelming and cannot be overcome or resisted. Aid me in overcoming the forces that conspire against me and my beloved. It is You who is the Ultimate in honor and nobility. Grant me honor in the eyes of my beloved, and make me worthy of such an esteemed position. Allow us to seek Your pleasure and be confident that You will aid us, for You have the power over all things. Aid us in showing sabr (patience/perseverance) and shukr (gratefulness) for whatever befalls us. Aid me in understanding that my relationships, including the halal relationship that I seek with my beloved, are a source of trust (amaanah) from Al-'Azeez and I should honor each trust that I am given by looking after them according to the guidelines of Al-'Azeez.

Al-Jabbar: Oh Mighty Restorer, Repairer, the All-Compelling. It is You who can restore, repair and reform. It is You who irresistibly compels things to be set aright. Bless me for my beloved, and bless my beloved for me as a spouse. Restore me in the eyes of my beloved, and compel me to honor Your reforms. If I have wronged my beloved, aid me in making repairs to my tarnished reputation in the eyes of my beloved. Repair my relationship to its soundness, wholeness, and righteousness. It is You who mends the broken-hearted by restoring peace of mind as well as offering a reward if they are patient. If I have wronged my beloved, mend the heart that I have broken, and enable me not to be oppressive. Make me obey Your commands willingly, and enable me to reach all the goals which are pleasing to You.

Al-Mutakabbir: Oh Possessor of all Rights, The Perfection of Greatness, the All Supreme and Majestic, it is You who has the rights, privileges, and attributes that are above and beyond the rights of everyone else. Save me and protect me from the evil of pride and arrogance, and guide my heart and its actions with humility towards You. Humble me and aid me in upholding the rights of my beloved, and destroy even the smallest amount of pride that enters my heart which may have the ability to inflict injustice, oppression, or arrogance towards my beloved. Make me and my beloved the kind of believers You are most pleased with. Allow us to respect the differences of others in beauty, knowledge, wealth, fame, status and color, and aid us in the battle against pride and arrogance so we do not transgress the limits set by You.

Al-Khaaliq: Oh Great Creator, and Maker, it is You that brings things into existence from their non-existence, who invents and innovates without a prior model and then bestows upon them their characteristics and other decreed qualities. Allow me and my beloved to accept ourselves as Your perfect creation, made without any flaws in the eyes of You. You are our Creator; let us overcome the fear of the creation and only fear You. Aid us in overcoming the fear of people's opinions, poverty, and failure, and to only focus on pleasing You. Lead us towards having unfaltering faith in You as our sole Creator, and let us never ascribe partners to You. Make us of those who are good in form and good in manners.

Al-Baari: Oh Great Producer, Originator, and Inventor, it is You who has given us distinguished characteristics and knows us best. It is You who evolves and re-creates that which exists, both physically and spiritually. Evolve me and re-create me into the person that is worthy of my beloved. Make me pious and righteous, and deserving of the love and respect that my beloved has endowed upon me. Allow me to maintain my health and take care of my beloved, and keep us away from what is prohibited and has the potential to harm us both mentally and physically. Keep us striving for excellence in all that we do, and evolve us into a believing and practicing couple that is a source of motivation and inspiration for others.

Al-Musawwir - Oh Great Shaper, Fashioner, and Bestower of Forms, it is You that has given all of creation a special inclination or desire, a special form and a special manner. You have shaped and formed all that exists with its own uniqueness and beauty. It is You who has beautified us, and it is only You that can further beautify us in our own uniqueness. It is You who has made me specific to the likes of my beloved, and my beloved for me. Allow us to live up to our potential by helping us care for ourselves. Aid me and my beloved to use our hearing, our sight, our limbs and our hearts to do as many good deeds as we can, as opposed to harming ourselves or others by sinning, oppressing, or causing any other forms of injustice. Verily, our hearing, our sight, our limbs and our hearts shall all be witnesses on the Day of Judgement. Save us from ourselves and allow all of these blessings to be witnesses for us instead of being testifiers against us.

Al-Ghaffaar: Oh All Forgiving, The One Who Veils and Protects, it is You who looks over our faults, over and over again, and veils our faults and mistakes in the eyes of others so that we are protected by the guilt and shameful effects of our misdeeds. It is You who changes our wrong deeds into good deeds. Help me become forgiving towards my beloved, and my beloved forgiving towards me. Aid me in becoming a veil that covers and conceals the faults of my beloved, and allow my beloved to do the same for me. Allow us to seek forgiveness, for indeed You are a Perpetual Forgiver. Make me and my beloved a source of goodness and protection for others, and aid us in putting a veil over, and concealing, the faults and shortcomings of others, and protect us from engaging in backbiting.

Al-Qahaar: Oh Ever Dominating, The Subduer, The Conquerer, and Prevailer, it is You whom all of creation submits before. Protect me from unreasonably subjugating and subduing my beloved, and equally protect me from any unreasonable and unjust subjugation at the hands of my beloved and all that which wishes to subdue me. Aid us in becoming the best of Your creation in willingly submitting to You wholeheartedly, just as the skies, the angels and all of creation obey You. Make me a source of inspiration and motivation for my beloved to follow in Your worship as I willingly surrender my heart, limbs, actions, speech, senses, talents and skills to You against my own whims and desires. Let my submission be a beautiful glorification, one that is not seen as humiliation but as a means of inspiration for my beloved. Moreover, humble us, and allow us to be kind and compassionate to the weak, the orphans and the poor.

Al-Wahhab: Oh Great Giver of Gifts, and the One Who Constantly Bestows, it is You who continually bestows gifts, favors and blessings upon all of creation. It is You who gives freely and endlessly without expectation of any return, I ask of You to make me a blessing for my beloved as opposed to being a trial, and make my beloved a blessing for me instead of being a trial. When You have granted me my beloved as a gift and blessing in the form of a spouse, or if You have granted me a spouse as a blessing in the form of my beloved, allow me to honor You for Your Benevolence, and to honor my beloved for being the best of gifts from You, apart from the endless blessings You have always bestowed upon me.

Ar-Razzaq: Oh Great Provider and Bestower of Sustenance, it is You who creates all means of nourishment and sustenance and provides for all of creation. Bless me in rizq (provision) so I can provide for my beloved. Aid me in fulfilling my part by working hard and trusting in Your benevolence without seeking prohibited means. Allow my beloved to be content with what I am able to provide through what is bestowed by You, and allow us both to be thankful for Your mercy, for You are our sole provider. Our rizq not only includes money, but it also includes knowledge, good manners, security, peace of mind and spiritual enhancement, all of which is created and provided in the way You want. Guide us to use Your provision wisely, and lead us to deeds that increase Your rizq. Allow us to enter into Your gardens by Your mercy and benevolence so we can enjoin the best of Your provisions.

Al-Fattaah: Oh Judge of All that is Opened, The Granter of Success, it is You who opens all the doors of mercy, profit and sustenance to all of Your creation. Open the heart of my beloved to me, and open my heart to my beloved so that no one can come between us, for whatever mercy You bestow, none can withhold nor subdue. Moreover, open our hearts to Your path and to the path of knowledge, and open the doors of mercy, profit, provision, marriage, tranquility and peace of mind for us. Make me into the kind of spouse who is a means of entry through the Gates of Paradise, and make my beloved into such a spouse for me. Allow us to strive in being sincere in trusting Your wisdom, for it is You who opens and closes doors for us as You will, for You know what we do not. Grant us success in our endeavors, and aid me and my beloved in developing skills that would benefit the Ummah and our communities.

Al-Aleem: Oh All-and-Ever-Knowing, and Omniscient, it is You whose knowledge is neither acquired through learning, nor followed by forgetfulness, nor are You ignorant of anything. You are aware of all things, even before they happen. Aid me and my beloved into acquiring the knowledge of all worldly disciplines created by You, and in attaining the most honorable knowledge of You and Your divine names, attributes, and Your religion. Bless our married life, and rid our relationship from ignorance towards You. Make me into a source of knowledge for my beloved, and a source of inspiration in wanting to attain knowledge of You and Your religion. Make me steadfast on Your path, and make my beloved a means of coming closer to You. Moreover, make it easier for us to understand and accept that the trials we go through which cause us pain, stress, and disappointment are only what You have decreed, for it is You who havs designed our destiny by Your divine knowledge and wisdom.

Al-Qabid: Oh Withholder, it is You whose wisdom decides when to withhold something from Your creation, whether it be knowledge or provision, or something physical or spiritual. It is You who contracts our heart which may cause distress or depression, but I ask of You to allow me and my beloved to understand that there is divine wisdom behind every decision that You make, and You know what is best for us. Allow the constriction of our hearts to bring us back to You in order to revive our faith and strength in order to progress in our worldly affairs. Allow us to fear Your wrath, for it is You who bestows us with everything that comes to us as You will, and it is You who can withhold and make scarce for us Your blessings.

Al-Basit: Oh Extender, it is You whose wisdom decides when to extend blessings to Your creation. Increase us not only in blessings and provision, but also in knowledge and faith. Allow me and my beloved to understand that not only the withholding of anything, but the extension of anything can also be a trial for us; therefore, allow us to enjoy our blessings reasonably, and to be thankful to You under all circumstances. Aid us in becoming a source of expansion for others through offering relief by aiding them financially, or spiritually through reminding them of Your blessings and Your promise that after hardship comes ease.

Al-Khafid: Oh Al-Khafid, The Humbler, The One who Softens. It is You who decides and chooses the ones who need to be humbled, whose hearts need to be softened and made gentle. It is You who decides when to weaken someone and whom to diminish. It is You who we call upon in order to humble the proud, and to grant us victory over our unjust enemies. Soften my heart towards my beloved and soften my beloved's heart towards me, and humble us towards each other. Allow us to live in harmony, and at times when one is angry, allow the other to soften and weaken his/her stance in order for both to continue to live harmoniously without any pride in our hearts.

Ar-Rafi: Oh Ar-Rafi, it is You who is the Great Exalter and the Uplifter. It is You who chooses out of His wisdom who to uplift and elevate above petty desires and selfishness. It is You who guides whoever You choose to rise above the differences and distinctions that divide mankind. I ask You to guide me and my beloved to rise above our differences, and to learn to accept one another through times of hardship and ease. Guide me and my beloved to accept the differences between our families, and learn to love each other's families wholeheartedly.

Al-Mu'izz: Oh Bestower of Honor and the Glorifier, it is You who grants invincible strength and honor, and it is You who is the source of all Power. You choose who is glorified in this world and in the hereafter. I ask of You to make me and my beloved worthy of such glory in both worlds. Make us among Your most obedient of slaves, and raise us in honor through our humility towards You. Grant us the strength to face hardships with patience and remain steadfast in fulfilling the obligations towards each other and our religion. Allow us to increase in actions of services and submission that will exalt us and make us among Your most honored people.

Al-Mudhill: Oh Great Humiliator, and Bestower of Disgrace, it is You whose wisdom creates situations that are low and despicable, and who creates the appearance of dishonor and circumstances of humiliation. Protect me and my beloved, our children and our families from facing humility and disgrace in this world at the hands of Your creation. Let our actions and our words increase us in humility and humbleness towards You, for You are our Creator and our Love. Aid us in living lives full of compassion, generosity, respect and justice in order for us to not end up like the people who have been disgraced and left characterless and abased.

As-Samee': Oh All-Hearing and Ever Listening, it is You who hears all sounds and voices without discriminating between languages, and even before things have been said. It is You who hears everything, including our thoughts and all that which is said in public and in private for nothing is beyond Your attention and comprehension. Allow me to understand my beloved and hear what is held back out of fear or respect, for my being oblivious to what is withheld may be a means of oppression or injustice to my beloved. Moreover, allow my beloved to understand me as such, and strengthen our relationship through the aversion of secrets, and an inclination of unfaltering trust in one another. Allow us to use our tongues wisely so that our words do not become something that keep us from the Gates of

Paradise, for on the Day of Judgement our tongues will testify against us. Allow me to be watchful of my tongue towards my beloved, and my beloved towards me. Aid us in learning about the prohibitions of the tongue which include lying, swearing and backbiting, and aid us in learning etiquette of speech for Muslims to please You through Your Dhikr (praise and remembrance), and kind words towards Your creation. It is You who hears every sound and thought. Make me and my beloved of those whose prayers are answered.

Al-Baseer: Oh All-and-Ever-Seeing, and All-Comprehending, it is You who sees everything, including the smallest of acts from the smallest of Your creation, including all that is apparent and all that is hidden; no detail, existence, or circumstance is beyond your sight. Allow me to be preventive and aware towards any injustice or hardship I may cause my beloved, and make my beloved aware and preventive of any injustice or hardship towards me. Allow us both to be aware of Your existence and watchfulness so that we engage in our worldly affairs with honesty and integrity. It is You who grants us favors and blessings, gives life, causes death, guides or leads astray, all in accordance to Your divine wisdom, for You know what is best for us and that which we do not. Allow us to submit to Your will for You are aware of every move we make, and everything decreed to us is a test for our own good. Allow us to guard our gaze and look to each other for all our needs, and to be garments for each other, and let no other come between us.

Al-Hakkam: Oh Giver of Justice and Arbitrator, it is You who delivers justice, and prevents or restrains Your creation from going against Your verdicts, for it is You who makes the final decision in all matters. Aid me in being just towards my beloved, and my beloved towards me. Protect us from the intentions of others that look to our love with evil eyes, and prevent me and my beloved from facing any injustice at the hands of all Your creation. Just as You never wrong Your creation, nor punish them for more than the sins they commit, allow us in being just and not being unfair or unequal in treating one another, or anyone else. Strengthen and bless the spousal relationship between me and my beloved, protect us from lying to one another or to anyone else, and aid us in always speaking the truth, for You are the one judging. In all matters of our lives, let us remember that it is You who has decided all, for Your decree is the ultimate of all decisions. Allow us to accept and adhere to whatever You have legislated for us, for You are the All-Knowing and You know all of which we do not.

Al-'Adl: Oh Al-'Adl, it is You who is Most Just, and Impartial. It is You who rectifies and sets matters straight in a fair, impartial and equitable manner, and who always acts justly and delivers absolute justice. Your wisdom of justice is based on the complete knowledge of the past, present, and the future. Allow me and my beloved to be just towards each other, and aid us in our affairs which require rectification in impartial and equitable manners. Allow us to be just and impartial towards each other's families and to increase love between us all.

Al-Latif: Oh Most Gentle One, the All-Kind, and Most Subtle, it is You who disposes of our affairs in the most subtle and gentlest of ways without us even perceiving it. Your mercy and kindness is beyond our perception and comprehension, for You are in control of all matters. You know what harms Your creation, and You know what benefits Your creation. We are but slaves at the hands of Your infinite mercy and Your kindness. What may seem like a punishment or injustice according to our limited comprehension, or what we may dislike, is always a decision that is most beneficial to us, for You are aware of our situations, our deeds, our thoughts, desires and what we carry in our hearts. Let us be at peace knowing that You show kindness and compassion that we don't notice because it may be too subtle to be seen or felt; in fact, what may seem like a trial may actually be a gift or a favor bestowed upon us, which takes us gently from one situation to another, thereby causing us to benefit without us even knowing it. Allow me and my beloved to submit to Your wisdom, let us enjoy the fruits of Your kindness and gentleness, and make us among Your most thankful believers even during the toughest of our trials and tribulations. Increase us in kindness and gentleness towards one another, and make us a source of gentleness and kindness towards the poor, orphans, widows, the war-torn, the disabled, and anyone else in need. Make all our good deeds, thoughts, intentions, and our desires for the sake of You, for it is You who is the Lord of the Worlds.

Al-Khabir: Oh Knower of All Reality, it is You who knows the internal qualities and meanings of all things and who has perfect knowledge. You understand even the meaning of secrets hidden from us, and the truth in every condition and situation. You understand secret requests and unspoken prayers, and nothing is hidden from Your All-Awareness. Aid me and my beloved in understanding each other and increase telepathy between our hearts. Allow us to understand each other's silence and unspoken desires, and increase comfort between us so that nothing remains hidden between us. Protect us from feelings of loneliness and isolation, and especially those feelings which have the potential of arising out of the discomfort and distance between our hearts. If there are misunderstandings between us, make us aware of them and bring our hearts closer than they were. Verily, it is You who is All-Capable.

Al-Haleem: Oh Most Kind and Serene, The Calm Abiding, it is You who bestows all that is visible, and all that is hidden, the Forbearer of Blessings. We may disobey You, but it is You who continues to bless us. If You chose to, Your wrath could destroy us instantly, yet You give us chances to turn back to You. Allow me and my beloved to be lenient, forgiving and calm towards one another and make us a source of serenity and peace for each other. Protect my beloved from my wrath, and protect me from the wrath of my beloved, for it is You who is capable of all anger and all vengeance, but You delay our punishment and You forgive. It is You who loves your creation, more than a mother loves a child. Make me and my beloved the best of parents with utmost mercy and tenderness towards our children. Protect all our relationships from anger, and allow us to practice forbearance. Allow us to be the best of examples of goodness, and allow us to never take advantage of Your forbearance.

Al-'Azeem: Oh Most Magnificent, and Most Supreme, it is You who is All-Superior, Enormous and Above Imperfection. You are the only One worthy of praise, for your actions are perfect. You are the Exalted, beyond all glory, and Owner of all power, might, and strength, compared to which all of existence is small and insignificant. It is You to whom all honor, glory and strength belongs. Increase me in honor in the eyes of my beloved, and my beloved in the eyes of me, make us worthy of such an esteemed rank and let it do good for us in both worlds. Increase me and my beloved in strength and help us patiently endure all trials and tribulations with ease, and make us glorious in both worlds. The biggest of our trials, and challenges, and the most severe of our hardships are all insignificant compared to Your mercy and ease. Allow us to accept that if it came from You, then You are its only solution. Let our trials, hardships, and challenges bring us closer to You in the most beautiful of ways. You are the King of Kings, the One who the Throne belongs to. Guide us towards practicing your perfect religion in the purest of ways, and grant us a beautiful death with full submission and humility towards Your sovereignty, magnificence, and grandeur.

Al-Ghafur: Oh Allah ﷻ, You are Al-Ghafur, the Exceedingly and Perfectly Forgiving who repeatedly forgives over and over again regardless of how many times we sin, and how large our sins are. You esteem us in the eyes of Your creation by putting a veil over our sins and hiding them so people do not judge us, and protect our reputations and forgive us as if we hadn't engaged in the act of sin at all. The extent of Your forgiveness is beyond what any of us could ever expect and it outweighs and exceeds Your wrath, for You are the Most Merciful. I ask of You to not only put a veil over my sins in front of the world, but to protect me in the eyes of my beloved, and protect my beloved in my eyes. Allow us to be the ones who immediately seek Your forgiveness after we have wronged ourselves, or if we have wronged Your creation. Make us among the people who You are intensely forgiving and merciful towards no matter how large our sin is, and no matter how often we sin. Similarly, allow me to cover the fault of others including the faults of my beloved, and allow my beloved to cover my faults, and aid us in forgiving others who have wronged us in this world.

Ash-Shakur: Oh Allah ﷻ, you are Ash-Shakur the Most Appreciative and Most Grateful. It is You who is the Ultimate Rewarder of all good deeds, and who gives abundantly in response to the smallest of our actions. Always make me and my beloved among those who are able to see clearly and be thankful for all the blessings that You have bestowed upon us out of Your mercy and appreciation of our goodness, and make us equally appreciate each other as being one of the many blessings that have been granted to us. Moreover, allow us to appreciate and recognize all these blessings even during the hardest of trials, and to remember to be endlessly thankful especially when it is hardest. Help us in paying attention to details in our lives and in the world around us to be able to notice the good that other people do; help us recognize their efforts and encourage them to continue doing good.

Al-'Aliyy - Allah ﷻ, You are Al-'Aliyy the Most High, The Exalted, whose greatness and perfection is beyond our comprehension. You are above all, and Your greatness surpasses all that is, all that has ever been, and all that shall ever be! Allow me and my beloved to always be conscious of Your greatness and make us among those who You raise in distinction and rank in the heavens and the earth, for all judgment belongs to You, The Most High. Make it easy for me and my beloved to place no one, and absolutely nothing, above or before You in our lives, and humble us by filling our hearts with humility before You.

Al-Kabir: Oh Allah ﷻ, You are Al-Kabeer the One who is Incomparably Great in might, power, wisdom, mercy, perfection, and in all the attributes that You possess, for nothing could ever be compared to You. Allow us to never submit to anyone or anything besides You, for no one and nothing can ever possess such an attribute of greatness to exceed in rank, size, dignity, nobility, and authority, as You are the Greatest. Your attributes, rights and privileges are above and beyond everyone else, and it is You who distributes these among Your creation as You are the Owner of all sovereignty. Allow me and my beloved to be among those who notice Your greatness in everything that we do, and in everything that we see, touch, hear, and feel. May all our actions be for the purpose of seeking Your pleasure. Allow us to get to know You through everything we do, and through everything we are confronted with in our lives, for everything is from You. Allow us to admire Your perfection and reward us generously as we strive to become among those whom You deem perfect. Make us among those who hear Your name and are able to feel from our hearts how there is nothing greater than You, and when we stand in worship, allow us to put the entire world behind us and focus on nothing but You.

Al-Hafiz: My Lord, you are Al Hafiz. You are the One whose power preserves the heavens and the earth. It is through Your guardianship and preservation that all of existence prospers and is safe from hardships and evil. It is You who guards and protects, it is You who prevents us from perishing and getting lost, and it is You who is attentive to all of us individually. Therefore, allow me and my beloved to strive to live, and to do everything, for the sake of You, for You are always attentive and mindful of what we do. If I begin to get lost and misguided, allow my beloved to be a source of guidance from You. Similarly, if my beloved begins to stray then allow me to be a source of guidance from You. Protect my beloved in my absence, and protect both of us when we are together. Make us among those who are always under your guidance and that of the Holy Quran. It is You who has ordered our guardian angels to preserve all our deeds to be used as witness against us, and it is You who never forgets all that we've done. I ask of You to always guide us in striving to attain Your mercy and forgiveness, for You not only know everything, but You never forget! Make us among those who realize the importance of this, so we never delay in asking for Your forgiveness.

Al-Muqith: Oh Al-Muqith, You are the All-Sustainer, the All-Nourisher and it is You who preserves all of creation. You oversee all that exists, and it is You who takes care of all living things by sending provisions. You not only create what sustains all of creation, but You also makes accessible what is necessary and what is luxury. It is You who either gives us enough for us to survive, or gives us in excess. Moreover, it is You who withholds in order to put an end to life as You will. I ask You to help us even when we forget to ask for Your help, and guide us towards asking in order for us to attain more of Your provisions. I ask You to remove our afflictions and sustain our bodies with provisions, sustain our hearts and souls with the knowledge of Islam, and our consciousness. Make me and my beloved and our families (parents, siblings, and children) be among those who recognize You in every sustenance. If You give us in excess, enable us to become those who sustain others and allow us to inspire people to rely on You for being the source of all sustenance, irrespective of where it comes from. Moreover, protect me and my beloved and members of our families from seeking haram means of sustenance, or doubting in Your power to sustain us.

Al-Haseeb: Oh Al-Haseeb, You are the Accountant, the Reckoner, and the Sufficient. It is You who keeps account of everyone in the world including the smallest and subtlest of deeds. It is You who is sufficient because You are the source of all care, and it is You who rewards and takes special care of Your most pious of slaves. Make me and my beloved among those who are aware of our weaknesses and allow us to work together in order to overcome those weaknesses. Help us in holding ourselves accountable and in repenting for our shortcomings. Moreover, after we have repented for our sins, guide us in asking for more than just Paradise, but in asking for the highest level of Paradise without reckoning.

Al-Jalil: Oh Al-Jalil, You are the One who is Majestic, and above all in rank and dignity. You are above all in superiority and independence, and You are the owner and the source of all attributes of greatness. Aid me and my beloved in loving each other for the sake of You and allow our love to increase us in rank in the hereafter.

Allow me to fulfill my obligations towards my beloved, and allow my beloved to fulfill his/her obligations towards me. Protect us from the dependence upon anyone else except upon You.

Al-Karim: Oh Al-Karim, You are the Most Generous and Most Honorable. It is You who has created the heavens and the earth for us with treasures and bounties beyond our imagination. Make us among those who are truly deserving of honor and of Your generosity on the Day of Judgement. It is You who brought us into existence without an obligation to do so, it is You who gave us the entire world to live in and enjoy, it is You who gave us the Holy Quran not only as a source of guidance, but as a cure. You not only advised us to pray for the sake of worship, but made our prayers into opportunities to attain endless rewards. It is You who not only gave us food, but with an amazing variety of flavors. It is You who has always gone above and beyond in Your love for us, so allow me and my beloved to go above and beyond in our love for You. Allow us to develop a relationship with the Holy Quran and make use of its guidance and allow it to transform our character, mind and heart in order for us to become more esteemed in Your eyes. Allow us to always be conscious of your generosity, and let it inspire us to be equally as generous in our communities towards all of Your creation. Allow me to always be generous towards my beloved and her family, and make my beloved equally generous towards me and my family, and fill our hearts with love and appreciation.

Ar-Raqeeb: Oh Ar-Raqeeb you are the One who witnesses everything, and You are never absent from our lives. You closely watch, hear, see and are aware of what we do and what we intend to do. You are aware of our heart's innermost desires, our thoughts and our feelings. Despite what is in our hearts, it is You who controls and guides us, and it is You who supervises us and protects us from ourselves. Make me and my beloved among those who realize that we are never alone, and allow us to follow Your command in public and in private for Your presence knows no bounds. Allow us to be conscious of You in all our actions, and when we speak. Make our speech the kind that is most pleasurable to You, and when we are tempted to sin, divert our attention and allow us to engage in conduct which is most pleasurable to you.

Al-Mujeeb: Oh Al-Mujeeb, it is You who responds to our needs, answers our prayers,m and fulfills our requests. It is You who disposes of our affairs according to Your wisdom, and it is You gives us more than what we ask for in ways which are best for us. Moreover, it is You who accepts praise. Make me and my beloved among those who realize that since You always answer when called, and respond when needed, we are obliged to listen and attend to Your calls in order for us to remain on the right path. Allow us to respond to Your commandments. Make us confident in You once we have prayed to You, and let us understand that You do not disappoint, and that a delay in Your response is not a denial. Allow me and my beloved to respond to one another in times of need, and make us a source of strength and goodness for each other. Moreover, make us into people who respond to the needs of those in our communities, and are helpful towards Your creation. Verily, all aid comes from You.

Al-Waasi: Oh Al-Waasi, you are the All-Encompassing, and the Boundless. The capacities and meanings of all Your attributes are without limit. Your authority and Your domain is endless. It is You who has promised to ordain good to us in this world and in the hereafter, as long as we turn to You. Allow me and my beloved to guard ourselves against evil so that You ordain Your mercy towards us, and bless us with all that is good beyond our imagination. It is You who responds to every single request in Your tremendous and endless dominion, and are never distracted by anything in Your infinite sphere of activities allocated to all of creation simultaneously. Allow us to understand the beauty of this, and make us among those who strive to please You without being distracted by the world. Moreover, allow me and my beloved to be the best of guardians in our own domains, and help us in raising our children and taking care of our families by enriching our abilities beyond any limit. Verily, You are the source of all enrichment.

Al-Hakeem: Oh Al-Hakeem, You are the One whose wisdom is perfect, for You are the All-Wise. Your divine will is executed with Your divine wisdom, and thus all of creation is subject to the fulfillment of Your will in the most appropriate way and in the best timing. It is You who prevents and restricts us from harming ourselves, and protects us from calamities. It is You who decides and puts matters in correct places, and controls the entirety of the universe to operate according to the best and most accurate timing possible. Allow us to understand this and to be content with Your wisdom under all circumstances by putting our trust in You. Since all wisdom belongs to You, it is only You who can increase me and my beloved in wisdom and knowledge of the world and our religion. Allow us to reflect on Your wisdom and in doing so, increase us in knowledge and consciousness of You and Your attributes.

Al-Wadood: Oh Al-Wadood, You are the source of all love and affection. You are the Most-Loving, and Your love is intense, constant and everlasting. You are the one who loves us endlessly and even though You do not need us in any way, You still choose to be most loving and the most affectionate. Fill the hearts of humanity with love towards You and all of Your creation. In doing so, fill the hearts of me and my beloved with a longing and desire for You. Allow us to never fall short of trying to please You and to ask for Your forgiveness. Let our worship reflect the love we have for You in our hearts, and let us learn to love You above everything and everyone else. Moreover, compel our hearts to yearn and strive for nothing but endless and undying love for each other. Allow us to easily communicate with each other and show our affection, and never be ones who deprive each other of love. Allow us to fulfill the rights and obligations we owe to one another, and in doing so we can ultimately achieve Your pleasure. Bless our marriage, and make our love intense, and continuous. Let our love be contagious so that our children can learn to be as loving towards each other, and towards all of Your creation, through what they learn from us. Allow my beloved to love my family the same as his/her own family, and allow me to love the family of my beloved as my own. Protect me and my beloved from misunderstandings and from evil, and let disputes against us to have no affect on the intensity of our love for each other. Moreover, rid our hearts of hatred and make it easy for us to learn to love for the sake of You. Allow us to learn to love for others what we love for ourselves, and to protect us from being jealous or envying another's happiness.

Al-Majeed: Oh my Lord, You are the Glorious and the Most Honorable. Your glory, dignity, nobility, honor, limitless compassion and generosity to us is without any fault or deficiency. You give beyond expectation and You deserve all praise! Allow me and my beloved to submit to You as slaves, and aid us in staying away from Your prohibitions. Help us in learning, understanding, and living by the way of the Quran so that You may choose to increase us in dignity and honor. Allow us to love you endlessly without ever forgetting to praise You for Your absolute perfection and for the favors that You have bestowed upon us. Aid me and my beloved in being respectful towards Your creation and inspire us to become generous and compassionate towards each other, our families and the rest of Your creation.

Al Baith: Oh Allah ﷻ, You are the Resurrector, the Awakener. It is You who brings Your creation to life; and gives new beginnings. It is You who awakens us from our sleep and gives us chance after chance to serve you. It is You who compels us towards performing certain tasks by creating impulses and through motivation. You inspire determination and plant the will in our hearts to rise up and engage in good, and You remove from our hearts the whisperings of evil. Guide me and my beloved to begin each day and to end each night by glorifying Your name. Allow us to make the best of the time that we have on Earth together, and inspire us to serve you and your Ummah, and to be among the best of the believers. Oh Allah ﷻ, give me and my beloved, our families and our children an honorable end, so that when we are awakened on the Day of Resurrection, we are among those who will be under Your shade.

Ash-Shaheed: Oh All and Ever Witnessing, You observe everything and everyone You have created. Nothing is hidden from You, the seen and the unseen, and even all our actions, thoughts and intentions. You witness our every move, and everything will be accounted for. Allow me and my beloved to always be conscious of You. Allow us to live by our testimony of faith, and let our actions, words, and conduct in private and in public reflect our faith in You. Remind us that we are Your servants; no matter how much glory and honor You bestow upon us, we will always remain Your slaves. You witness every step that we take, and everything that we imagine, therefore, allow all our actions and utterances to be for the sake of Your pleasure. Make the consciousness and awareness of You to be an inspiration for us to increase our good deeds, and allow us into the highest

Paradise.

Al-Haqq: My Lord, You are the Absolute Truth! Your attributes and Your existence are undeniable and all of existence cannot exist without You and Your will. Your words are the truth, Your Messengers are the truth, Your Books are the truth, and Your Religion is the truth. The worship of You alone, with no partners or associates is the truth. Allow us to live by these truths, and protect us from mixing the truth with falsehood. Allow us to abide by the truth even if it is against our personal interests, and let me and my beloved be a source of inspiration for others to speak, and stand up, for the truth. Allow us to always remember that Your promises are true, and allow us to be patient in times of hardship, for You have promised ease. Always enable us to see the truth, give us the ability to follow it, and protect us from betrayal and deception. Make me and my beloved, our children and our families among those who witness the reality of your Paradise.

Al-Wakil: My Lord, You are the Disposer of Affairs, The Trustee, Our Guardian and Administrator who provides the perfect resolution for all our matters. Allow us to always maintain our trust in You, and increase us in our faith, for You are sufficient for us, and there is no other deity except for You. Aid us in always being content with whatever You have decreed for us, because the destiny of those who have You as a Companion is incomparable for You are the Lord of the heavens and the earth. When we are faced with depression and worries, I ask of You, my Lord, to make me and my beloved trust that You will manage our affairs in the way that is best for us. Protect our hearts from ever fearing the power of our enemies, and protect us from going towards unlawful earnings. Make us among those who have entrusted our souls to You, and those who firmly believe that You are sufficient for us as the best disposer of affairs. Let no hardship overcome our faith, and if either of us weakens, let the other be a means of inspiration and guidance back to You.

Al-Qawiyy: You are the One who is beyond all weakness, and Your strength is supreme and inexhaustible. You affect everything, and nothing can affect You. Your power is irresistible, and nothing in the heavens and the earth can help but submit to You. Allow me and my beloved to be just as strong in our belief. Allow us to hasten to what benefits us and in seeking Your help. It is You who strongly detests strength based on tyranny and injustice, therefore, aid us in being just towards one another, and towards Your creation even in the smallest matters. Allow us to be a source of inspiration for others to be just and to stand up for the rights of the weak. It is You, my Lord, who has the power to use the heat of the sun to melt and demolish all of mankind if You choose. It is You who controls the power of the wind which can lift up entire nations and blow them away like feathers. It is You who can use the might of the oceans to swallow us whole. Your strength is unlimited and all is within Your power. Allow us to rely on no one else but You to be our strength against the most tyrant of people. Allow us to take comfort in You as our protector; and as our perfect Beloved in times when we are overcome by difficulties and hardships.

Al-Mateen: My Lord, You are the One who, along with His unconquerable might, is firm in His nature, and nothing can ever object to Your actions or prevent Your will from being carried out. Allow me and my beloved to be just as firm in Your path, and let us be inspired by You to follow our religion at all times. Aid us in applying the laws of the Quran in our lives, and by prohibiting all that You have prohibited. Make the steadfastness of me and my beloved into a source of inspiration for others including our children and families to also stand firm in their belief, and save us all from Your punishment. Allow us to surround ourselves with people who are firm upon Islam, and protect us from those who are transgressors and followers of falsehood.

Al Wali: My Lord, You are the Protecting Friend, the Loving Guardian. It is You who is closest to us, for no one else is as near to Your creation as You. It is You who is at our immediate assistance, to guard and defend us against what seeks to harm us. It is us, Your creation, that distances away from you, and yet you remain ever so close to us. Guide me and my beloved to never stray from You, and to never let the distance between us and Yourself to increase. Allow us to be as near to You, as You are to us. Guide us and protect us from ourselves, and from your creation that seeks to harm and conspire against us. Bring light into our lives, and make us among the best of believers. Take us out of darkness and allow us to wage war among the evil within ourselves and the evil that attracts us externally. Allow us to focus on our obligatory acts of worship. Love us, and guide us in using our limbs righteously. In times of need, allow me and my beloved to look to no one else but You as our friend, our ally, and our only means of support.

Al Hamid - You are the One who is praised and is Praiseworthy; in fact, You are the only one worthy of admiration and praise. Allow me and my beloved to count our blessings, from the most obvious to the most subtle, and be able to thank and praise You for it. Allow us to see clearly, and to thank You when things go in our favor. Most of all, grant us the wisdom to thank and praise You when things do not go in our favor, for we are being protected and steered towards something that is better meant for us. Make me and my beloved, our children and our families of those who praise You as You should be praised. Guide us in praising You often and sincerely, and make us among those who you allow into

Paradise.

Al Muhsi: My Lord, You are the Appraiser and The Accountant who is aware of details of all that has passed, and all that is yet to come. You possess all quantitative knowledge and comprehend everything, either big or small, hidden or apparent. You register and record all our thoughts and all our deeds. You justly reward us for all the good that we do, and You will hold us accountable for all the bad that we do. Allow me and my beloved to always be conscious of this, and allow our consciousness to motivate us into doing good deeds. Enable us to inspire each other, and make us a source of reminder for each other of Your watchfulness over us, so that we seek Your pleasure in all that we do.

Al Mubdi: Oh Great Producer, You are the Originator, The One that Initiates everything. Whether it be peace or war, provision, sustenance or starvation, everything begins at Your will. Just like You have created mankind, everything has a beginning, and its origin is You. You can create things that can dominate us and destroy us; instead You have chosen to love and protect us from Your creation by keeping everything in harmony. Allow me and my beloved to understand Your might, and to look no further than You in times of need, for all good is initiated by You. Allow us to produce the best of children in the eyes of You, and to raise and nurture them with the best of provisions provided by You. Bless our family so nothing but love, peace, and tranquility originates from our homes.

Al Mu'eed: Oh Great Reviver, You are the one that renews and recreates, and restores all at Your will. Just as you created mankind and allowed it to reproduce, you have allowed your entire creation to reproduce; sexually and asexually. Moreover, when we suffer and weaken due to an illness, it is You who restores our health. When our emaan falters and we stray away from You, it is You who guides us, and renews our faith and spiritual essence. When we are wrongfully humiliated, it is You who restores our honor. When we lose ourselves to depression and we have no motivation, it is You who revives our spirit and shows us the light. Allow me and my beloved to be a means of spiritual revival for one another. Allow us to be means of motivation and inspiration for one another. Give us the guidance to ensure that Your religion is practiced in our homes, and that our children and their offspring are keepers of their faith. Ensure that we remain steadfast in practicing Islam generation after generation. Give us confidence at our time of death that we have left the world in good hands, and that our children will honor our name. Do not make our children trials for us, but instead a means of attaining Your mercy and pleasure.

Al-Muhyee: My Lord it is You who is the Giver of Life, who creates us from nothing, through a drop of fluid that grows miraculously into a detailed body clothed with muscles, flesh, veins and skin. Thereupon it is only You who surrounds us with all the right conditions in order for us to survive until You have decreed to end our life. It is You who has the ability to restore life and join the soul and body on the Day of Judgement in order to hold us accountable for our sins in this world. Allow me and my beloved to never lose sight of the truth that You can make anything happen at the command of a single "Kun!" ("Be!") as You have caused us to exist out of nothingness. Allow us to cherish our lives by using our time wisely, and to respect other people by benefiting them with our knowledge, love and support. Make me and my beloved the best of spouses, reminding ourselves and others of our accountability in the hereafter.

Al Mumit: You are the All Mighty, Bringer of Death, the Taker of Life. My Lord, it is You who decrees death from

36

whomever You please, for no one causes death but You. For everyone, there is death in which we become lifeless to be buried away, and there is spiritual death. You are the bringer of both. There is a third death which is the separation from lusts and attachments and the love of this world. My Lord, I ask of you to guide me and my beloved into reaching a state of purity in which we can detach ourselves from the lusts and the love of this world and of material things. I ask You to revive us and ensure that we never attain a spiritual death, a death in which we stray so far away from your religion that we become disbelievers. Protect us from the evils and false enchantments of this world, so that when the decreed time of our death comes, we die gloriously as believers with the shahadah (testimony of faith) on our tongues. Allow us to die beautifully in the state of purity.

Al-Hayy: Oh Ever-Living Lord, it is You who has a continuous life without a beginning or an end, You were before all else, and You will remain after all else without an end. You are the one who has granted us life, and You are the source to which we will all return. Your hearing is endless, Your sight is endless, Your beauty is endless, Your existence is endless, and You are perfect in all Your attributes. It is You upon whom we rely. Aid me and my beloved in trying to come as close to perfection as we can in terms of our actions and our belief. Help us preserve our health, beauty, sight, hearing, and strength. Allow us to be honest in our dealings, and do justice no matter what the reward, for everything will indeed be left on the earth and will perish one day. Make us among those who are most righteous so that when we return to You, You will be pleased with us and grant us an everlasting Paradise.

Al-Qayyoom: Oh Self-Subsisting Sustainer, it is You by whom all things subsist. You sustain, protect and oversee. You provide, preserve and manage all that exists. You are free from any dependence, while all of creation depends entirely on You! Protect me and my beloved from any dependence on anyone else but You, and help us sustain ourselves. Bless us with sustenance and inspire us to give charity from the sustenance You have provided us with.

Al Waajid: You are the All Perceiving, the Resourceful, and the Wealthy. You have discovered and obtained everything. You have no wants, and You lack nothing. All the treasures and resources that one can imagine, you have it all in abundance. It is You who finds us at our lowest, and it is You who has what we need in order for us to be fulfilled. It is You who finds us lost, and it is You who shows us the way. It is You who finds us alone and abandoned, and it is You who claims us as Yours and provides shelter. Allow me and my beloved to become resourceful, and to be able to share our wealth with those in need. Allow us to be kind to the orphans, widows, and the victims of war, and to aid them as all sustenance comes from You; truly, charity does not decrease wealth. Allow us to have a perceiving eye, and to be among those who do not turn a blind eye to those we could assist. Help us become strong members of our communities, and to be a means of support and inspiration for the rest of our Ummah.

Al Maajid: You are the Noble, the Generous, the Magnificent. Whatever You do, You do it out of Your goodness, and it is glorious, dignified, and exceedingly generous. You are the highest and most perfect example of goodness, richness, and generosity. You give without asking for anything in return. In fact, You give without even being asked. You continually observe our needs and wants, and know exactly when to bless us with Your bounties without turning away. Allow me and my beloved to learn from Your highest example, and to engage in goodness around us. Allow us to inspire one another to be a means of goodness and generosity, and to be kind to our families, neighbors, and members of our community.

Al Waahid: My Lord, You are the One who is unique in Your essence, and who has no second, no partner, and no rival. You are the source from which all of creation has come from. You are alone and unique in every single way. You simultaneously manage the affairs of Your entire creation, as there is no one else who creates or sustains, or who sees and listens to all of creation from man to insect. It is You alone who has created the sun, stars and the moon, and arranged everything in perfect orbit. It is You who is solely responsible for the beauty in everything beneath the earth, on the earth, and beyond the earth. Allow me and my beloved to increase our awe and appreciation of Your Oneness. Allow us to look to You for everything in our lives first; when we are surrounded by difficulty, let us think of no one else before You to be able to come to our aid. You are the sustainer of the heavens and the earth. Allow us to never ascribe partners to your Oneness.

Al-Ahad: Oh Lord, You are the Unique One, and the Only One of Your kind. You are unique in Your essence and attributes, and You will forever be unequaled and incomparable to anything else. Protect me and my beloved from ever ascribing partners to You. Let not only our words and our actions, but also our limbs and hearts to be equally reflective of our testimony of Your Oneness. Aid us in raising our children and protect them from ever ascribing partners to You and from falling into falsehood. Allow us and our families to be among those who die by the Shahada so that the fire cannot touch us, and we enter Your everlasting gardens.

As Samad: You are the Eternal, and the Satisfier of needs. You remain unaffected, and unchanged, without any needs. You depend upon no one, while the entirety of existence depends upon You. There are so many circumstances which affect our lives, however You are unaffected by any circumstance. You are the only one able to fulfill all needs in the most perfect way, without ever being in need of anything or anyone. You are eternal, Your goodness is eternal, Your generosity is eternal, and You are the Absolute. When You bless us, You bless us in abundance, and when You give, Your treasure is endless. Allow us to be satisfied with whatever You give to us out of Your generosity, and allow us to trust that all our needs will be met. Allow me and my beloved to aspire to please You, and You alone. Decrease us both in the amount of love we have for this world, and decrease the desire of being praised and acknowledged by Your people; instead replace it with a burning desire to attain Your approval alone.

Al Qaadir: My Lord, You are the All-Capable, the Most Able, the All Powerful. It is You alone who possesses all the power and the ability to measure out anything and everything. It is You who has the capability to make any decree and determine what will be. At the command of a single "Kun" ("Be"), "Faya Kun" ("And it is") becomes inevitable. You say "Be" and it is according to Your will. May You always attend to our prayers, and may You command it to "Be" whenever we make a legitimate request, whether it be a need or a want. For those of us who pray for a partner, My Lord, it is You alone who is capable of fulfilling that prayer. Make it easy for those who wish to marry their beloved, and bless them with their beloved in the form of a perfect spouse. Allow me and my beloved to be an example of Your powers of fulfillment. Aid us in preserving our love, and allow our love to grow stronger within our marriage.

Al Muqtadir: My Lord, You are the Powerful Determiner, the Omnipotent. Your great and overwhelming power controls all of Your existence, and You alone subdue everyone and everything in Your domain. You enforce all our decrees and Your decree prevails in every situation. When we seek to achieve something, it is only carried out into an accomplishment because of Your decree. Our success is by You, as it is You who enabled us to accomplish our deeds. We are often proud of little things such as how we raised our children, and we forget that it was You who enabled us to raise them well; it was Your provisions that allowed them to be nurtured well; and it was Your wisdom that allowed us to make the best of decisions for them. Allow us to always humble ourselves by remembering that whatever we have is from You. No matter what circumstances are brought to us, allow us to never give up, or become overwhelmed against the biggest of our problems, for nothing is comparable to Your Majesty. It is You that can subdue the biggest of our problems. If You can save Prophet Yunus (Peace and Blessings be upon him) from the belly of a whale, and if you can split the sea in half for Prophet Musa (Moses) (Peace and Blessings be upon him), then no matter how impossible it may seem, You will offer a solution to our worldly probelms. Guide me and my beloved to practice our belief in Your Omnipotence, and make us grateful for all aspects of Your decree for us.

Al Muqaddim: You are the Expediter, the One who brings forward and grants advancement. It is You who chooses to esteem us, and grant us honor. It is You chooses which of our prayers are to be answered at which time, and when the time comes it is You who expedites its fulfillment accordingly. Allow me and my beloved to learn and practice patience, and to be steadfast on our belief that Your timing is perfect. Allow us to engage in good deeds, and to ask for forgiveness from our sins, for our sins hold us back while our good deeds allow us to move forward. The more good that we do in our lives, the more advancement will be granted to us. Make us a means of reminder for each other that all that You do is always at the perfect time, so that when one gets impatient the other can inspire patience. Make us a means of purification for one another, so that when one sins, the other motivates and inspires goodness.

Al Mu'akhkhir: My Lord, you are the Delayer. You delay things out of mercy for us, and many times, we do not even realize it; for if You were to immediately advance upon us Your wrath for every sin we committed, we would not be. Thus, it is You who delays out of mercy, and we become anxious and resentful, and forget that everything has the right time. If we have a prayer that is not being fulfilled by You, it might be because delaying the fulfillment will make the blessing last longer, and it may mean more to us than immediate fulfillment. Just as You delay punishing us for our sins so that we may come to repent, there is also similar reason behind delaying goodness to us. Allow me and my beloved to understand this, and to make us reminders for one another so that impatience, anxiety, and resentfulness do not consume us. Allow us to develop a better opinion of You with a deeper certainty in Your power, and more trust in Your timing. Give us the ability to appreciate delay in the fulfillment of our prayers, and make us a means of motivation for the other to ask for forgiveness after committing a sin, while You have delayed Your punishment.

Al Awwal: My Lord, You are the One who was before all; You are the First and the Foremost. Unlike us, You do not have a beginning, which is dependent upon being created. You are self-existent, and You are the source of all that became. Allow me and my beloved to place You first and foremost, before anything and everything else in our lives, and make sure we please You. Allow us to be first and foremost in good deeds and attaining Your pleasure. Make us among those who rush to prayer, and make it easy for us to revolve the rest of our lives around our obligatory prayers. Make me a source of guidance for my beloved, and make my beloved a source of guidance for me in order to help each other prioritize You and Your commandments.

Al Aakhir: My Lord, you are the Last and the Endless. It is You who remains after Your creation perishes, and beyond whom there is nothing. Just as You are the first of Your attributes, You will be the Last of them, with no one or nothing ever comparable to You. It is You who has promised that whomever puts You first will never be last! Allow me and my beloved to always put You first. Allow us to always be conscious of our imminent last moments on the earth, and to remember we will not be able to accumulate any good deeds or rewards after that. May we guide each other towards giving continuous, generous, and ceaseless charity that would help us even after our death. Allow me and my beloved to motivate each other to do good deeds, to resist against our desires, and to prioritize You in all that we do.

Az Zaahir: My Lord, You are the Apparent and the Evident. Your existence and Oneness is apparent through all of the signs in the universe. Everything that we look at around us is testimony of Your existence, for nothing else could have created it. Allow me and my beloved to always be conscious of the apparent and obvious signs of You, and to not be blinded by falsehood. Allow us to look around us and realize that everything is manifested through You. Whenever our faith weakens, allow these signs to strengthen our faith again. Just as You are apparent, everything is apparent to You, such as our intentions. Allow us to check our intentions, and to prioritize even the smallest of our deeds for the sake of You.

Al Baatin: You are the Hidden One, and the Knower of all that is hidden. You remain hidden, and yet You remain everywhere around us. You know the inner state of our hearts, and yet You have veiled yourself from our perceptions. No one has seen You, and yet all of creation is a testimony of Your existence and attributes. Allow me and my beloved to have the ability to find You in all things hidden. It is easy to find You in what is apparent, but only a true lover and believer will be able to find Your signs in what is not easily apparent. When we are alone and scared, let each of us be a reminder to the other that You are the knower of all hidden things, and our inner states; You will protect us and respond to our prayers. Moreover, allow me and my beloved to be a reminder to each other against hypocrisy, as we may seem one way on the outside, and our intentions and agendas may be hidden, whereas You know all that is hidden. Allow us to be true to ourselves, and to praise and thank You for keeping our sins hidden. Allow me to cover the sins of my beloved, and allow my beloved to cover mine, and help us both in purifying our intentions.

Al Waaliy: My Lord, You are the Patron, the Helping Friend, the Supporter when we are in need. It is You who assists us and never abandons us, and it is Your support alone that brings us ease. You are the one that accentuates sovereignty, and protects the universe as a whole. It is You who has set the balance in harmony, and oversees all things in motion, including the orbit of the sun, planets, stars and the moon. You sustain it all. Allow me and my beloved to always praise You and to glorify Your name. Allow us to attain knowledge of all that You recommend, for knowledge is the ultimate light, and the path out of darkness.

Al Muta'ali: My Lord, You are the Supremely Exalted, above all of creation; the Highest, far beyond our imagination and limitation known to us. You are beyond our thoughts and ideals, for we cannot even imagine You having any faults or imperfections. You exceed all of creation in all of Your attributes, and Your Supremacy and Glory is incomprehensible by us. Allow me and my beloved to be conscious of You in all that we do, and in our thoughts, and intentions. The universe was created for the worship of You, and this is why the laws were prescribed; to devote our lives to You, accompanied by love. Allow us to be righteous, and to humble ourselves for we are all subject to Your Supremacy. Allow us to be reminders for one another that You are higher than everything, and yet You are the closest to us. Let us never despair, give us knowledge of the deeds most pleasing to You, and assist us in calling others to You.

Al Barr: You are The Source of Goodness, the one who is gentle towards all of Your creation. Your gentleness and Your goodness do not stop because of the sins and disobedience of Your creation. You are still kind to the wrongdoers, You pardon the transgressors, You forgive the sinners, You turn to the ones that repent to You, and You accept the pleas of those who ask for Your help. You are always just and honest, and Your decisions have regard to our circumstances. You bestow Your bounties on to us in abundance even when we do not ask. Allow me and my beloved to be truly worthy of Your goodness by renewing our faith, and giving us the ability to be charitable. Allow us to be inspired by Your goodness, and to help us be as good in keeping our promises, and acting upon the truth. Guide us in good conduct in other's company, for You are the source of all that is good.

At Tawwaab: My Lord, it is You who is the Acceptor of Repentance, the Oft-Forgiving. It is you who inspires us to repeatedly ask for forgiveness, otherwise we are nothing but misguided individuals. It is You who forgives us when we return to goodness, and it is You who restores us in grace and honor once we repent. You reward good deeds, and You forgive those of us who forgive others. Allow me and my beloved to be more forgiving and accepting of the faults of others. Allow us to make excuses for those who have wronged us, and widen our hearts to be more tolerant. If one of us is harsh, let the other be a means of guidance and softness to help us become less harsh. All forgiveness comes from You, and let our softness and tolerance towards others be a means of Your forgiveness.

Al Muntaqim: You are the Avenger, the Disapprover, and the Inflictor of Retribution. My Lord, You are always watching and You register all our deeds. You aware of everything, for nothing is hidden from You. You disapprove of the wrongdoers, and You remind us when our behavior is not right. It is You who avenges us when we have been wronged, such that we do not need to seek any revenge. It is You who is most just when it comes to vengeance and does not wrong anyone even when inflicting retribution. Allow me and my beloved to be as just, and inspire us to leave our affairs to You without ever seeking any personal vengeance, for You are the disposer of our affairs and Your justice will not wrong us. Make my beloved soft towards me, and make me soft towards my beloved so that we do not hold grudges against one another. Protect us from the wrongdoings of others, and strengthen our bond during times of hardship and when others have conspired against us.

Al Afuww: My Lord, You are the Eliminator of Sins. Not only do You pardon us, but You also eliminate our sins and faults at Your will, as if such faults had never existed! When we turn to You in repentance, You give us more than what is due. Once You become pleased with us, You bestow blessings upon us willingly without being asked. Such is Your mercy and Your grace. When You choose to forgive, You conceal our sins and faults, and You ensure that we are not punished for them, however they remain in our book of deeds. But when You choose to Pardon us, the sins are completely erased from our book of deeds, so that we are never questioned of them. Inspire us out of Your mercy so that me and my beloved are also not only able to forgive people, but to pardon them completely and to never judge them by their previous faults. Allow us to fight against our egos and leave no trace of resentment in our hearts against others, and purify our relationship to the extent that our hearts hold no trace of resentment towards one another. Pardon us, my Lord, and guide us into being among those whom You love most.

Ar Ra'uf: You are the Most Compassionate, the All-Pitying, and the Most Kind. Your kindness and affection are beyond our understanding. You gently warn us, withhold from us, and instruct us to do good. Once You are pleased with us, You bless us in abundance. You bestow pity and mercy upon us in many different forms, including warnings and withholding, in order for us to be guided and to better understand You. Increase us in mercy, and allow our hearts to be softer. Make me merciful towards my beloved, and my beloved merciful towards me. Inspire us to be feel tender towards Your creation.

Maalik ul-Mulk: You are the Master of the Kingdom, the Onwer of the Dominion. You own and rule over all of creation and all of existence. Your power is supreme, and Your command is the highest. You are the King of all kings, the Owner of all owners, and the Ruler of all rulers. Your Kingdom consists of all that was, all that is, and all that will be created. You give sovereignty to whom You will, and You take sovereignty from whom You will. You honor whom You will, and you humble whom You will. In Your hand is all good. Despite Your authority and sovereignty, You are most just and most kind. Inspire me and my beloved to be as kind, and humble us to not misuse our authority over others. Allow us to remain within the boundaries set for us, and make us among those whom You give sovereignty to, and among those whom You honor in this world and the next. Allow us to be kind and just towards our own dominions. Allow my beloved to remind me that I will be asked about my leadership and will be accountable for my actions towards my dominion, and allow me to remind my beloved of the same.

Dhul-Jalaali wal-Ikraam: You are the Possessor of Glory and Honor, and the Lord of Majesty and Generosity. You own all Your attributes, and You are the Most Precious and Most Honored. You are the Source of all generosity, blessings, and bounties. Allow me and my beloved to be inspired by Your generosity. Make us among those who, when we do something for someone else, then may praise and recognition be the last thing on our minds, for our only purpose would be to please You.

Al Muqsit: You are the Most Equitable, The Just. You establish justice, and create harmony and balance. You do not punish more than anyone deserves, despite being the All Mighty upon whose command the world could easily perish. However, You remain kind and just, and You lead mankind to justice and harmony. Allow us to be as equitable as You, and as just as You. Inspire me and my beloved to remain within our boundaries. Guide us to suppress our anger first and foremost, but when it is hard, allow our anger and our retribution to be proportionate to the wrongdoings. Inspire me and my beloved to make us among those who insist on justice from ourselves for others. May our intentions be for nothing more than Your pleasure.

Al Jaami: You are the Gatherer, and The Uniter. You have brought the entire universe together. It is You who reconciles hearts, and connects opposites and that which is similar. You gather all of Your creation and allow it to live side by side in this world, and it is You who will disassemble us and compose us again when You gather us on the Day of Judgement. Allow me and my beloved to always be conscious of the Day of Gathering, when we will all be assembled and held accountable for whatever we have done in our lives. Make us among those who inspire each other to strive for your shade on the Day of Judgement. Allow us to be the kind of people who bring others together, and who try to reconcile other hearts in conflict. Increase love between me and my beloved, unite us again in the hereafter, and never allow our hearts to grow in distance from one another.

Al Ghani: You are the Self Sufficient, The Independent One. You are the One without any needs, and You are always completely satisfied, free from any wants or any dependencies. You flourish without anyone's aid, and yet the entirety of existence is dependent upon You. Allow me and my beloved to be able to fulfill the needs of those who are dependent on us, and bless us in provision and sustenance so that we are motivated to share from our wealth and provision. Allow us to never need any aid from anyone else but You, and increase us in self-sufficiency. If I am ever unable to provide for my beloved, allow my beloved to be strong and wise, and able to provide for us. Protect us from ever needing assistance from Your creation, for You are enough for us.

Al Mughni: You are the Enricher, the Bestower of Wealth, and the Fulfiller of Needs. You create all appearances of independence and self sufficiency, and bestow satisfaction and contentment among us. Allow me and my beloved to always be satisfied and content, no matter how hard our circumstances may be. Allow us to always remember that You are the source of all wealth, and there is always wisdom behind withholding sustenance and provision from us. Allow Your wisdom to guide us into being patient, and allow our patience to earn your reward. Make us a means of patience for each other, so that when one becomes impatient, the other is a reminder of Your benevolence.

Al Mani': My Lord, You are the Preventer of Harm, the Protector, and the Defender. You guard us from harmful situations, including the ones that are apparent, hidden, immediate and subtle. Always keep me, my beloved, and our families under your protection, and give us the means to protect ourselves from those who seek to harm us. Give strength to our sons and our daughters, for them to be strong, assertive, and steadfast in Your faith. Give them the wisdom and power to prevent and restrain from undesirable actions, and to never be among those who inflict wrongdoings onto others. Bless the union of me and my beloved, and make our family among those highest in honor in both worlds.

Ad Dharr: My Lord, You are the one who is the Corrector, the Balancer, the Distresser, and the Afflicter. It is You whose wisdom may choose to use forceful corrections, and who creates adversity or distress in order to discourage or correct wrongful behavior. I ask of You to watch over me and my beloved, and protect us from Your inflictions and punishments. Guide us to be corrected in the most beautiful of ways, and make us obedient and steadfast on Your religion.

An Nafi': My Lord, You are the Creator of Good, the Benefiter, and the Auspicious. It is You who helps and grants all advantages, and creates all that produces a benefit to us or has any usefulness. You are the source of all favorable circumstances, and the One who confers all benefits. You are the continual source of all blessings and goodness, and it is through You that all our needs are fulfilled. Allow me and my beloved to be conscious of your goodness and to be able to reflect on the benefits you have conferred to us through various means and resources which all come from You. Make me a means of goodness for my beloved, and make my beloved a means of goodness for me. Make us remember You, and honor You in circumstances which are favorable to us, and also in circumstances which are trials and tribulations for us; for verily, it is only You who can change our conditions.

An Nur: You are An Nur, the Light, and the Illuminator who has brought us out of darkness, and illuminated our hearts and minds with knowledge, faith and guidance. You are the source of all light in both the heavens and the earth. Without You, there would have been darkness, barbarism, and chaos. You have put the Nur of faith, knowledge and love into our hearts and given us clarity. Make me and my beloved a means of knowledge for one another. Allow us to learn from one another, and allow our marriage to be an example for other couples. Perfect for us our light, and forgive us, for You are over all things competent. Place light in our hearts, on our tongue, in our ears and in our sight, and place light above and below us. Place light in our soul, and magnify light for us. Guide us in following Your religion, so it can be a source of light for us in this life and in the next.

Al Hadi: My Lord, You are the Source of all Guidance. It is You who found us lost, and it is You who guided us with Prophets and Messengers to direct our senses and our hearts to the straight path. You have given the entire creation a sense of general guidance, including plants, minerals, and animals. You have guided the bees to find nectar and build hives. You have guided the birds of migration during the winter; and you have guided the hibernation of bears; and you have guided the tides and the winds to remain humble, for their might could easily subdue us. It is You that has guided Your dominion over all things. You have guided the jinn and mankind by defining paths of good and evil through various Prophets and Messengers sent by You. You guide us through hardships to remain strong, and You have promised us ease. Guide me and my beloved when we begin to go astray, and make us a means of guidance for one another. Allow us to become the best of believers, and keep us far away from misguided company. Allow us to be an inspiration for those in need of guidance, but let not their misguidance impede us from the right path.

Al Badi: You are the Marvelous One who originates, commences, invents and creates all that exists. You don't need a model to follow, or any material, for never do you experience a lack of resources. You are incomparable in your will power, and You bring into existence all unique and amazing creations without any similarities or discrepancies in shapes and sizes. You create out of nothing, which includes both animate and inanimate physical things, as well as intangible things such as feelings, thoughts and ideas. Once You have created feelings of love and affection between me and my beloved, I ask of You to preserve them, and allow such feelings to only become stronger with time. Keep evil thoughts and ideas out of our minds, and inspire us with thoughts of goodness and kindness. When we find ourselves at our lowest, and are faced with thoughts of depression, My Lord, I ask You to rid us of such thoughts, illuminate us with Your religion, and allow us to seek Your mercy. Create nothing but good between us and within us.

Al Baaqi: You are the Everlasting, and the Eternal. You have always existed, and You will never cease to be. You remain forever; unaffected by time. Once You have united me and my beloved in the form of spouses, allow our union to be everlasting and eternal. Strengthen our relationship in this life, so that we spend an eternity together in the life hereafter. Make all aspects of our life everlasting; give us good health, and inspire us to take care of our health so that it will be as if it were ever lasting. Allow us to utilize our wealth for permissible means, and give us the means to donate to the needy, and increase us in provisions as if it were ever lasting. Fill our hearts with faith and love so that we become satisfied and giving, so that we live as if the goodness in our lives is everlasting. Bless our marriage and our lives with Your eternal goodness.

Al Waarith: You are the Supreme Heir, and the Inheritor of All. You are to remain after all of creation has perished. You are the One to whom all things return. You have the everlasting ownership of all that has ever been and of all that will ever be, and You are the One to whom all possessions return when the possessor is gone. Allow me and my beloved to avoid being distracted by worldly possessions, and let not our attraction come in the way of our obedience to You. Allow us to raise our children to not be distracted by the allure of this world, and to not pair success with wealth, status, and luxuries, but to instead think of success as attaining Your pleasure. Allow us to be in a pure and honorable state when we are returned to You. Allow us to submit to You as You have complete ownership of us, and when we forget this, allow me and my beloved to be a means of a reminder for each other. May whatever my beloved and I leave behind in this world, be inherited and used for permissible means, and may our inheritors be guided towards goodness. Make me, my beloved, our children and our families among those who abide by Your laws, and among those who will inherit the highest Paradise.

Ar Rashid: Oh Appointer of the Right Path, it is You who unerringly decrees, appoints and ordains the right way. You are always aware of what is happening, and where we are headed. You alter the way and guide us to where we are supposed to be. You perfectly and righteously direct all matters towards their proper conclusion, and You need no aid in doing so. All of the universe is subject to Your will, and when Your will needs to be carried out, the entire universe conspires towards its fulfillment; for You have sovereignty over everything. Allow me and my beloved to always observe the right path, and when we are led astray, guide us back to each other on the path of righteousness. Strengthen the bonds between our families, and when our hearts begin to distance away from one another; guide our hearts back to each other and bind them together, stronger than they were before. Watch over our children, and aid them when they are amongst the wrong company, allow them to differentiate between right and wrong, and may righteousness prevail over their hearts and minds.

Al Saboor: My Lord, You are the Most Patient, and the Patiently Enduring. You are not moved by haste to carry out any action before its proper time. You patiently endure, and You do everything in its proper time and proper manner, no matter how long it may take. You control time, and know when to attend to our concerns. You delay and You expedite based on what is best for us out of Your wisdom, for You know what is truly best for us. Allow me and my beloved to have patience when we make Du'a, and allow us to understand that the fulfillment of our prayer is subject to its proper timing. In doing so, help us observe a beautiful patience. Teach us to be beyond content with Your timings, for Your plans are far better than our plans. May we submit to You without complaint, and may we be among those You prefer over others under Your shade based on our patience and righteousness.

A review of the attributes of Allah ﷻ allows us to know Him, and to have a stronger perspective of the One we worship. It allows us to love Allah ﷻ in all the ways that we can comprehend, however, Allah ﷻ remains incomprehensible and incomparable as ever. It also teaches us that we can call upon Him for anything, for He has authority over all matters. There is no aspect of our lives in which we cannot ask Allah ﷻ for His help, and there are surely at least 99 ways of asking Him to bless us with love, to strengthen our love, and to aid us in legitimating and preserving our love.

Some of us fall in love, and we are among those who are united with the ones they love. Others are united with someone else that Allah ﷻ may think is better for us out of His wisdom. May you learn to love whoever Allah ﷻ has decreed for you, for your heart is capable of wonders beyond your knowledge. May your beloved be of your choice, if it is best for you. Otherwise, may you accept as your beloved, that which Allah ﷻ has decided.

May Allah ﷻ make it easy for us all. Ameen!

SECTION TWO

2.1
SAAZISH-E-KAINAT
(CONSPIRACIES OF THE UNIVERSE)

The universe and its actions are subject to the will of Allah ﷻ. As illustrated through the attributes and beautiful names of Allah ﷻ. He is Al-Baseer, for He sees everything. Nothing is beyond His perception, and no secret is hidden from Him. Nothing happens without His knowledge, for even the tiniest of creation is visible to Him in the darkest of places, in the deepest ends of the earth, including all that walks on it and all that is both below and above it. He is As-Samee, for He hears everything. No whisper is beyond Him and no language is unknown to Him, for He listens to all of creation simultaneously with undivided attention. He hears even the softest of footsteps of the tiniest of creation in the loudest of places. He is Al-Azeem, the King in whose hand rests the dominion of all things. All is in compliance with His decree, for nothing can happen without His will.

In Surah At-Tawba, Allah ﷻ commands Prophet Muhammad ﷺ to give us the assurance of His protection, and states that nothing happens unless ordained by Him.

> Oh Prophet, tell them: "Nothing will happen to us except what Allah ﷻ has written for us; He is our protector," and in Allah ﷻ let the believers put their trust. [Holy Quran, 9:51]

Allah ﷻ goes on to make this even more explicit in

Surah Hadid, where He says that it is He who decides everything that happens to us in our lives, and that He has a purpose for it all.

> No calamity can ever befall the earth, and neither your own selves, unless it be (laid down or inscribed) in Our Book of Decree before We bring it into being: verily, all this, is easy for Allah ﷻ. [Holy Quran, 57:22]

It is important to keep our trust in Allah ﷻ, because it is He who has divine wisdom and knows all that which we do not know. As discussed earlier, He is Al-Lateef, who knows what is best for us and guides us towards it in the subtlest of ways.

> (Know this,) so that you may not despair over whatever (good) has escaped you nor exult (unduly) over whatever (good) has come to you: for, Allah ﷻ does not love any of those who, out of self-conceit, act in a boastful manner. [Holy Quran, 57:23]

Therefore, it is Allah ﷻ who decides whatever happens on earth and in our lives. The administration of the entire universe rests in the Hands of the All-Mighty, for we have neither the permission to be unduly boastful over the good we gain, nor the permission to be upset over the good we lose - our success and our failures are all subject to the decree of Allah ﷻ as nothing is truly in our control.

In "The 40 Hadith Compiled by Imam Nawawi," Abu al-'Abbas 'Abdullah bin 'Abbas (may Allah ﷻ be pleased with them) reports:

> Know that if all the people get together in order to benefit you with something, they will not be able to benefit you in anything except what Allah ﷻ has decreed for you. And if they all get together in order to harm you with something, they will not be able to harm you in anything except what Allah ﷻ has decreed for you. The pens have stopped writing [Divine (Allah's) Pre-ordainments]. And (the ink over) the papers (Book of Decrees) has dried.)

> [This Hadith is also quoted in Sahih At-Tirmidhi, and is Hadith 19 from the Collection of Imam Nawawi.]

If something is destined for us, we wouldn't miss it, for there is no power on earth that could escape or cause us to escape whatever good or hardship which has been pre-ordained by Allah ﷻ.

Often we feel irrelevant and small when we come to terms with the vastness and supremacy of Allah ﷻ. Indeed we are small and irrelevant, for there is no comparison between the creation and its Supreme Creator. However, the beauty of our existence is that Allah ﷻ has created us knowing exactly what we need, for there is no quality or shortcoming of ours that He is not aware of. Even in our irrelevance, to Allah ﷻ we are all equally relevant.

Allah ﷻ says in Surah Qaf, "We are closer to him

than [his] jugular vein." [Holy Quran, 50:16] This means much more than we give it credit for, as it implies that even at our most vulnerable point of our body, Allah ﷻ is there to protect us. It affirms our relevance to Allah ﷻ, and how close He is to us. We are individually the most relevant things on the face of the earth, for He is always watching us, and listening to us; He is always guiding, always saving, and always protecting us.

The One who made the universe with all its infinite galaxies, the sun, the stars, and the moon has also finely crafted us into the people that we are. You are a masterpiece, and individually the most loved, for the Master of Existence, the Most High, the King of Kings is closer to you than your jugular vein, and to Him you are everything. If that is not significant enough for you, consider the fact that you are the creation for which the Creator has created another creation, just to ensure that you are never alone in your journey to become as close to Him as He is to you.

> And of everything We have created in pairs, so that you might bear in mind (God alone is one). [Holy Quran, 51:49]

Subhan'Allah (Glory be to Allah ﷻ), how beautiful is that? Somewhere out there is a set of eyes that has been created only to look into yours and find the home you both have been searching for. Somewhere out there is a voice that has been finely tuned to call out your name and erase away all your worries. Somewhere out there is a smile that is ever so beautiful, and it is meant to become even more of a wonder when it smiles at you. Somewhere out there is a heartbeat that is meant to synchronize with yours. Somewhere out there is a pair of hands that is meant to hold onto yours, and when they do, their grip is equivalent to the world holding on to you.

The idea of such a partner is often compliant with the understanding of what a soul mate is. In *Soulmate*, by Richard Bach, he outlines the positive aspects of soul mates.

> A soulmate is someone who has locks that fit our keys, and keys to fit our locks. When we feel safe enough to open the locks, our truest selves step out and we can be completely and honestly who we are; we can be loved for who we are and not for who we're pretending to be. Each unveils the best part of the other. No matter what else goes wrong around us, with that one person we're safe in our own paradise. Our soulmate is someone who shares our deepest longings, our sense of direction. When we're two balloons, and together our direction is up, chances are we've found the right person. Our soulmate is the one who makes life come to life. [Soulmate, Richard Bach]

Similarly, Thomas Moore, in his book *Soul Mates: Honoring the Mysteries of Love and Relationship*, describes a soul mate as someone we feel profoundly connected to.

> "… as though the communication and communing that take place between us were not the product of intentional efforts, but rather a divine grace. This kind of relationship is so important to the soul that many have said there is

nothing more precious in life." [Soul Mates: Honoring the Mysteries of Love and Relationship, Thomas Moore]

Like everything that is decreed, one's soulmate is also a provision that has been decreed for him/her.

> And there is no living creature on earth but depends for its sustenance on Allah ﷻ; and He knows its time-limit (on earth) and its resting-place (after death): all (this) is laid down in (His) clear decree. [Holy Quran, 11:6]

It is important to acknowledge at this point that a soulmate does not guarantee a happy worldly life, because like all aspects of life, love and marriage too are a test of patience irrespective of how loving one's spouse is. The only guarantee of everlasting bliss is in Paradise. Moreover, marriage in this world does not guarantee that your spouse is in fact your soulmate, for surely soulmates are prescribed to you, but the world in which you two would be united was not made clear. This world is meant to be a trial for the believer, and the best of believers are put through the hardest of trials. It is best to always pray that Allah ﷻ makes the one you marry more of a blessing as opposed to a trial whether or not they are your soul mate.

Depending on the decree of Allah ﷻ, some of us are united with our beloved or soul mate in this world, whereas others are united with their other half in the world hereafter. Regardless, marriage in this world is one of the provisions that has been decreed, and it requires patience and commitment towards one another. Even being united with the one you love, or one who feels like your soul mate does not mean you will not face trials and tribulations. Everyone faces their own trials in different ways, some through love, some through other provisions such as status, wealth, rizq (i.e. sustenance), children, patience, etc.

The universe is always conspiring at the will of Allah ﷻ, either in fulfilling the decree, or at the fulfillment of one's prayers. With regards to the decree of Allah ﷻ, there is no power that can stop two souls from uniting once Allah ﷻ has decided for them to be together. As discussed earlier, the union through marriage, a union in which love naturally grows, is inevitably blessed by Allah ﷻ.

> And among His wonders is this: He creates for you mates out of your own kind, so that you might incline towards them and dwell in tranquility with them, and He engenders love and tenderness between you: in this, behold, there are messages indeed for people who think. [Holy Quran, 30:21]

Allah ﷻ plants love and kindness in the hearts of two spouses, for them to love for the sake of Allah ﷻ, and that is the biggest trial of marriage; to learn to love for the sake of Allah ﷻ. This is made easier as one opens his heart towards his wife, and willingly fulfills his obligations towards her, and similarly as she opens her heart towards him and fulfills her obligations within the marriage. Abu Hurairah (May Allah ﷻ be pleased with him) has stated that Prophet Muhammad ﷺ said,

"The most perfect man in his faith among the believers is the one whose behavior is most excellent; and the best of you are those who are the best to their wives." [At-Tirmidhi, Book 1, Hadith 628]

Therefore it is understood that the best of men are the ones that accept themselves to be the overseers of their wives, and the ones who honor their wives and fulfill their responsibilities and religious obligations towards them as righteous spouses for the sake of Allah ﷻ. In doing so they attain the blessings of Allah ﷻ in their marriage.

Men are the overseers over women because Allah ﷻ has given the one more strength than other, and because men are required to spend their wealth for the maintenance of women. Honorable women are, therefore, devoutly obedient and guard in the husband's absence what Allah ﷻ requires them to guard which is their husband's property and their own honor. As to those women from whom you fear disobedience, first admonish them, then refuse to share your bed with them, and then, if necessary, discipline them. Then if they obey you, take no further actions against them and do not make excuses to punish them. Allah ﷻ is Supremely Great and is aware of your actions. [Holy Quran, 4:34]

Ibn Kathir in "Tafsir of Ibn Kathir," warns that the

words of Allah ﷻ in the above verse of the Holy Quran [4:34] are a threat to men, "that if they transgress against women without justification, then Allah ﷻ, the Exalted and Grand, is their Protector, and he will exact revenge on those who wronged them and transgressed against them." Therefore, it is important to be just towards one's spouse, and to learn to accept the decree of Allah ﷻ. There is no escaping, for the universe is actively conspiring to fulfill the decree. What is written to be yours will reach you.

You might have heard people often claiming to meet the right person at the wrong time; this usually happens when someone feels right but due to certain circumstances it feels as if the timing isn't right. Maybe they met too late, and if they had met earlier, it could have been another way. Maybe they met too soon, and if they met a little later they might have been ready for each other. It is common to think that perhaps if it had been in another time or in another place that things could have been different. Many people begin to develop ideas about time being against them, but they are oblivious to the fact that everything is in the hands of Allah ﷻ, and He makes no mistakes! Everything happens the way it is supposed to, so there is no such thing as the wrong time for anything, as everything happens in its own 'good time'. On the authority of Abu Hurairah (may Allah ﷻ be pleased with him), the Prophet Muhammad ﷺ said:

> "Allah ﷻ said: 'Sons of Adam inveigh against (the vicissitudes of) Time, and I am Time, in My hands is the night and the day.' As the Almighty is the Ordainer of all things, to inbeigh against misfortunes that are a part of Time is tantamount to inveighing

against Him." [Hadith Qudsi, Hadith 4] It was related by al-Bukhari (also by Muslim).

It is important to remember that there is no such thing as the wrong time, for if everything is in the hand of the Lord of the Worlds, the All-Mighty, then everything that happens, every interaction, every red light you stop at, every puddle you walk into, every friend that you lose contact with, every gain and every loss was meant to happen as it happened.

You are never alone, for Allah ﷻ, Exalted and Grand, is always with you, and the universe steers you into the direction of where He wants you to be. In Surah Al-Hadid, Allah ﷻ reminds us:

> "It is He Who created the heavens and the earth in six aeons, then firmly established Himself on the throne of authority. He knows all that enters the earth, and all that comes out of it, as well as all that descends from the skies, and all that ascends to them. And He is with you wherever you may be; and Allah ﷻ sees all that you do." [Holy Quran, 57:4]

Therefore, it is clear that you are never alone and Allah ﷻ is aware of all that happens around you. Perhaps the red light that you stopped at which frustrated you because you could have made it through was Al-Latif subtly protecting you from what could have been a severe collision at the next intersection. Perhaps the three job interviews that rejected you were the doings of Al-Qabid who was withholding the provision of rizq from you in order for Al-Basit to extend a fourth job interview towards you which was meant to bestow upon you an even higher position than you were initially applying for. Perhaps you being wronged and humiliated at your previous job by your supervisor are ways for Al-Qahaar to teach you what it feels to be subdued and oppressed, so Al-Mutakabbir can humble you, and teach you not to be oppressive, and to fulfill your rights and obligations towards people below you in status when Al-Azeem finally grants you honor and bestows upon you responsibilities in a position of leadership. Perhaps a failed relationship with someone you loved dearly was Al-Aleem teaching you that if you can learn to love the wrong person so much, imagine how deeply your heart is capable of loving the person that is decreed for you when Al-Fattah opens the door of marriage for you. Everything that happens is by the will of Allah ﷻ, and the universe conspires for the will of Allah ﷻ to guide you and take you where you need to be at the right place, at the right time - it is the divine workings of the universe that ensure there is no such thing as the wrong time, nor a thing as coincidence.

Allah ﷻ is the Master of the Universe, and all the forces of the universe are subject to Allah ﷻ. There is nothing He does not control, nor fails to oversee. What harms you will not be able to harm you any more than what Allah ﷻ has decreed for you. Similarly what benefits you will not be able to benefit you in anything more than what Allah ﷻ has decreed for you. Every friend that you have gained, every enemy that you have made, every acquaintance you have met with, and every stranger you have crossed paths with has been steered into your direction according to the decree. Similarly, every friend you have lost, every enemy you have overcome, every acquaintance you could not meet, and every stranger diverted from you was all at the hands of the universe, working to uphold the decree. Indeed, you may think that a single day could have altered your life significantly if you had decided to stay home for an hour longer before you left for work, or if you had taken a different route back home other than your usual, or if you had chosen not to interact with a specific stranger. However, it could not have been any other way, for the universe would have conspired for you to be where you needed to be, and for you to have met who you needed to meet all at the right time and right place.

> For, with Him are the keys to the things that are beyond the reach of a created being's perception: none knows them but He. And He knows all that is on land and in the sea; and not a leaf falls but He knows it; and neither is there a grain in the earth's deep darkness, nor anything living or dead, but is recorded in (His) clear decree. [Holy Quran, 6:59]

This verse highlights the Greatness of Allah ﷻ, for He is aware of every movement, every creature, every sound, every affair. In fact, not even a leaf falls by chance anywhere in the world without the awareness of Allah ﷻ. Of course, one would lose their mind counting the number of leaves on the tree in their backyard; now imagine the number of trees in the whole world. Surely the number of leaves on each tree is incalculable, but Allah ﷻ is aware of each and every leaf; such is his Magnificence.

> Consider, a single, solitary, lone leaf separating from its branch, from its tree - one of millions upon millions

on this Earth - perhaps in the
darkness of the night, perhaps in the
isolation of the most remote of
locations found upon this Earth, areas
where mankind has barely tread upon.
It floats and flutters in the air
momentarily in silence and finally
comes to rest upon the ground. An
incident that occurs whilst we are
oblivious to it, having no knowledge
of it. Yet Allah ﷻ states, "not a leaf
falls, but He knows it." [Abu Muadh
Taqweem Aslam, The Salafi Center of
Manchester Online, April 28, 2014]

Imam Ibn Kathir (may Allah ﷻ have mercy on him) also
commented on this in his Tafsir saying, Allah ﷻ knows
of all movements. He is even aware of the movements
of inanimate objects. So what therefore do you think is
Allah ﷻ's knowledge of the animals and especially those
whom responsibility is upon and are legally obligated and
bound by the Shariah from amongst the humans and
Jinn? [Volume 6, page 53] With everything in His
knowledge, and under His control, it is foolish to believe
in coincidences.

The thunder extols His limitless glory
and praises Him, and (so do) the
angels, in awe of Him; and He (it is
who) lets loose the thunderbolts and
strikes with them whom He wills. And
yet, they stubbornly argue about Allah
ﷻ, notwithstanding (all evidence) that
He alone has the power to contrive
whatever His unfathomable wisdom
wills! [Holy Quran, 13:13]

In the above verse from Surah Ar-Ra'd, Allah ﷻ makes clear that it is He who commands lightning to fall, and lightning strikes whom Allah ﷻ wills. Allah ﷻ goes on to further warn that the movement of clouds and the falling of rain and hail are also subject to His will, in Surah An-Nur:

> Art thou not aware that it is Allah ﷻ who causes the clouds to move onward, then joins them together, then piles them up in masses, until thou canst see rain come forth from their midst? And He it is who sends down from the skies, by degrees, mountainous masses (of clouds) charged with hail, striking therewith whomever He wills and averting it from whomever He wills, (the while) the flash of His lightning well-nigh deprives (men of their) sight! [Holy Quran, 24:43]

Therefore, if the leaves cannot move without permission, and lightning cannot strike without being given its direction, how then can our hearts be moved towards one another without the will of Allah ﷻ? How can love between two souls be coincidental if the signs are absolutely clear that there can be no coincidence? Indeed it is Allah ﷻ who alone has the power to contrive whatever His unfathomable wisdom wills. Has Allah ﷻ not said in Surah At-Takwir, that you cannot will anything unless Allah ﷻ, the Sustainer of all the worlds, wills to show you that way? Your wishes are nonexistent and of no avail unless Allah ﷻ, the Rabb of the worlds, pleases so.

"Where then are you going? This (message) is no less than a reminder to all the worlds. To everyone one of you who wills to walk a straight way, but you cannot will it unless Allah ﷻ, the Sustainer of all the worlds, wills (to show you that way)." [Holy Quran, 81:26-29]

The relationship between the will of Allah ﷻ and the decree of Allah ﷻ is a beautiful concept. As absolute as it seems - the beauty of it is that Allah ﷻ is always actively watching, listening, deciding, and answering prayers. Thus, the absolute nature of the decree too becomes ever-changing and adjusting to the will of Allah ﷻ according to His mercy.

Du'a (prayer) is most commonly described as the weapon of the believer, and it is said to be the only thing which can change destiny and what Allah ﷻ has decreed. In fact, Du'a is the most important act of worship and has great power to change many things. Allah ﷻ says in Surah Al-Mu'min:

"And your Lord said: 'Invoke me (i.e. believe in My Oneness and ask Me for anything) I will respond to your (invocation). Verily, those who scorn My worship (i.e. do not invoke Me, and do not believe in My Oneness) they will surely enter Hell in humiliation!" [Holy Quran, 40:60]

The verse implies that the invocation to Allah ﷻ requires utmost humility through the recognition and acknowledgment of the dependence on Allah ﷻ alone with full faith that He is in fact the All-Mighty, the Most High, and the only One who has the power to do whatever He wills. Moreover, in Surah Al-Baqara, Allah ﷻ says to Prophet Muhammad ﷺ:

> "When my servants question you about Me, tell them that I am very close to them. I respond to the call of him who calls, whenever he calls unto Me: let them, then, respond unto Me, and believe in Me, so that they may be rightly guided." [Holy Quran, 2:186]

Allah ﷻ promotes Du'a; in fact, He indirectly commands one to acknowledge their dependence on Him and make Du'a when He declares that He is near and He responds when called upon. Du'a is a way of acknowledging not only the Oneness of Allah ﷻ, but the acknowledgement of His existence wherever one is, and an affirmation of one's consciousness of Him. It is the declaration of utmost faith when one acknowledges that He is listening, and He will respond when called upon, which leads one to believe that surely nothing is impossible for Him. Du'a is a direct conversation between the creation and his/her Creator; it is the relationship between the slave and his/her Master, and a testimony of the love between the believer and his/her Lord. It is an intimate conversation full of secrets between a soul; and its Khaliq (One who brings to life). It is the appreciation of all that it is, between what could easily have been inanimate and Al-Baari. There is absolutely nothing more beautiful or more personal than Du'a.

Prophet Muhammad ﷺ said: "Nothing can change the Divine decree except Du'a." [Narrated by Ahmad, 5/677; Ibn Maajah, 90; al-Tirmidhi, 139. Classed as Hasan by al-Albaani in Saheeh al-Jaami', 76687. See also al-Saheehah, 145] Engaging in the act of Du'a is so valuable and precious to Allah ﷻ that it can change both what has been, and also what has not yet been decreed.

It was narrated from Ibn 'Umar (may Allah ﷻ be pleased with both of them) that Prophet Muhammad ﷺ said:

> "Whomsoever of you the door of supplication is opened for, the doors of mercy have been opened for him. And Allah ﷻ is not asked for anything - meaning: more beloved to Him, than being asked for Al-Afiyah. The supplication benefits against that which strikes and that which does not strike, so hold fast, Oh worshippers of Allah ﷻ, to supplication."
> [Al-Tirmidhi, Book 45, Hadith 3548]

When one makes Du'a, it is not solely at his own discretion, but rather he has been guided by Allah ﷻ himself to engage in the act because Allah ﷻ wants to give. Nothing is more beloved to Allah ﷻ than being asked, and acknowledging ones dependence on Him. Du'a is not only a weapon against what could potentially harm you, but also a remedy for what has already been inflicted upon you. In fact, it is the best of all remedies. Prophet Muhammad (Peace and Blessings be upon him) said:

> "No precaution can protect against the decree of Allah ﷻ... The Du'a meets the calamity that has been decreed and wrestles with it, until the Day of Resurrection." [Narrated by al-

Tabaraani, 2/800 (33). Al-Albaani said
in Saheeh al-Jaami', 7739, (it is) Hasan]

Perhaps one of the most beautiful aspects of Du'a is that Allah ﷻ is already aware of what you seek before your prayer is even whispered to Him. He is aware of your need before you even feel it, and He knows the selection of the words to your Du'a before the thought even comes to your mind. How remarkable is it that He knows the thought before you've even thought of it, and the formation of words before you've even arranged it in your mind, and He has heard it before you've even spoken it? Irrespective of already being aware, He still listens as attentively. Allah ﷻ wants to give, and He commands you to simply ask for it.

Allah ﷻ asks us thirty-one times in Surah Ar-Rahman, "Which of the favours of your Lord will you - men and jinn - then deny?" [Ar-Rahman, Surah 55] The verse simply demands us to be continuously aware of, and thankful for all that which has been provided to us without even asking, including provisions such as wealth, food, health, the safe environment in which we live in, the beauty both below and above the earth that we walk upon, and everything else that we may sometimes take for granted. The entire Surah is a reminder of our existence, and the favours bestowed upon us by the benevolence of His Grace, Ar-Rahman. Everything that has been created, even the most delicate of creations, is part of an intricate ecological system. Everything is connected to one another, for each being and each entity has a purpose that it serves. It makes one wonder, if Allah ﷻ can give us so much beyond our wildest imagination without us even asking for it, but purely out of His kindness and mercy, then there must be absolutely nothing that He is incapable of giving when we sincerely ask.

74

Out of all that He has given us, arguably the most special gift is the ability to love, and to dwell within each other's heart as soulmates. This is often taken for granted, because at first glance it seems so natural, ordinary, and so intrinsic to life, that we forget how chaotic it could have been if it hadn't been for the natural order of things set in the way that they are. In Surah Al-A'raf, Allah ﷻ reminds us:

> It is He who has created you (all) from a single soul, and out of it brought into being its mate, so that man might incline (with love) towards woman. [Holy Quran, 7:189]

This verse refers to the creation of all of mankind out of Prophet Adam (Peace and Blessings be upon him) including the First Woman, Hawwa' (Eve) (Peace and Blessings be upon her) who was created from the short rib on Prophet Adam's left (Peace and Blessings be upon him). Another look at a previously quoted Ayah from Surah Ar-Rum makes this even clearer:

> And among His wonders is this: He creates for you mates out of your own kind, so that you might incline towards them and dwell in tranquility with them, and He engenders love and tenderness between you: in this, behold, there are messages indeed for people who think. [Holy Quran, 30:21]

The Ayah explicitly says that Allah ﷻ has created for us mates out of our own kind. This in itself is a huge favour from Allah ﷻ. Imagine how easy it could have been for Allah ﷻ to do so otherwise. If He had chosen to make the entire male progeny of Prophet Adam (Peace and Blessings be upon him) out of humankind, and created the females from another kind, such as Jinns or animals, then surely there would not have been harmony between them as spouses. Out of Allah ﷻ's mercy and wisdom, He made our spouse out of our own kind, and created love and kindness between the two partners. A man and woman stay together because of the love between them, or because they feel compassion towards each other, and these emotions are strengthened further if they have a child together. Therefore, if Allah ﷻ can take care of the smallest details without being asked, and give us immense blessings out the what we easily take for granted, and what could otherwise have been catastrophic, then He can surely give us what we ask for.

Du'a changes the decree very beautifully, for Allah ﷻ is always aware and waits for you to ask. There are many provisions which are conditional on being asked for; that Allah ﷻ has decreed for us to attain by means of Du'a or repentance through His forgiveness and mercy. That is why we should always ask of our Lord, for He is always willing to give. Since Allah ﷻ is the All-Knowing, he knows you better than yourself. He knows of the duration of your breath to the intervals in between each inhale and exhale. He hears the rhythm of your heartbeat as though it has a voice of its own. He's aware of your thoughts and habits, from your impulses to sudden reflexes, your desires and your secrets, without any coincidences and with no vice or virtue unknown to Himself. He knows why you do the things you do, your likes and dislikes, what you love and what makes you hate. He knows it all, for He created you. Similarly, each Du'a of yours is also decreed and already known to Him and with time He guides you to make them.

Many of us make Du'a consistently, and eventually abandon it because it goes unanswered. How often do we give up? Think of something that, at one point in your life, you prayed for very frequently. Perhaps its fulfillment was delayed, and whatever you prayed for was not granted to you, so you gave up on praying for it. Can you think of anything? Surely as time has progressed there is something else that you make Du'a for, and in that time you make Du'a for it very consistently. How many times have you felt that it is something which will not be yours, and how many times have you wanted to give up on it? Have you ever felt that something inside of you fights the urge to give up, and makes you ask for it again and again? That urge is your Emaan, it is your faith in Allah ﷻ's benevolence, and knowing that anything is possible for Allah ﷻ. On the other hand, the whispers in the back of your head which continually encourage you to give up, is an experience of Waswaas (whispers of Shaytan). Such whispers are to be regarded as a sickness which needs medicine; that medicine is simply a reminder of who your Lord is, and what He's capable of. Strengthen your belief with reminders that if He can bring you and rest of the universe into existence, the fulfillment of absolutely no Du'a is impossible for him, unless He refuses; if it is Haram and/or forbidden to begin with. Surely, for all of which is permissible, Allah ﷻ has impeccable timing.

He promises, "Call upon Me, and I will respond to you," [Holy Quran, 60:40] and a delay in His response is a test. Perhaps He waits for you to acknowledge that no matter what it is, regardless of being good or bad for you, it is still in His power and He can make good for you that which is bad, as he can make better for you that which is good. Ibn al-Jawzi (may Allah ﷻ have mercy on him) in one of his books comments:

> "I think part of the test is when a
> believer supplicates and receives no
> response, and he repeats the Du'a for
> a long time and sees no sign of a
> response. He should realize that this is
> a test and needs patience." Sayd al-
> Khaatir [59-60] (This publication is in
> three volumes containing aphorisms
> and wise counsels)

In the same excerpt, Ibn al-Jawzi (may Allah ﷻ have
mercy on him) further explains that there is sometimes
an interest to be served by delay, and haste may be
harmful. He explains, another reason that the response
may be withheld is because of a fault in you. Perhaps
there was something questionable in what you ate, or the
way you behaved before, or even at the time of making
your Du'a, or perhaps your heart was heedless. Allah ﷻ's
wisdom works in mysterious ways, and it is always most
beneficial for you. Perhaps the delay in response to your
Du'a is simply a means of decreasing your punishment
for a sin which you have not yet repented sincerely over,
and through observing patience during this trial the
torment of the grave shall be lessened for you, and
perhaps even protection from hellfire. Allah ﷻ knows
best.

One verse which I often deeply contemplate over is
Surah An-Nur:

> (In the nature of things,) vile women
> are for vile men, and vile men for vile
> women - just as good women are for
> good men, and good men, for good
> women. (Since Allah ﷻ is aware that)

these are innocent of all that evil
tongues may impute to them,
forgiveness of sins shall be theirs, and
honorable provision from Allah 🕌.
[Holy Quran, 24:26]

The more time I spend in contemplation of this verse,
the more it reminds me of all the faults that I have within
myself. This makes me think that perhaps the fulfillment
of my Du'a is a sincere repentance away from a certain
sin that I may have previously committed. It is important
to remember that we all have faults, and we are all
vulnerable to certain sins and vices, for no individual is
perfect. But Allah 🕌 has given us all the ability to repent
and ask for forgiveness, to appeal to His mercy and to
beg to be pardoned of whatever stands in the way of His
provisions, His benevolence, and between us and
Paradise.

When you make Du'a to be united with your
beloved, take a moment to reflect on the idea that
perhaps you are not yet worthy. Perhaps your beloved is
such an immense blessing for you in this world and in the
next, that he/she will only be granted to you upon
becoming worthy of such a blessing. Perhaps you have
engaged yourself in a sinful habit that Allah 🕌 despises,
one which you must rid yourself of before having your
Du'a answered. Perhaps there is a certain sin that you
have committed and not yet realized, and the fulfillment
of your Du'a is dependent upon the realization and
atonement of it. This could also be equally true for ones
beloved.

Perhaps the one you are making Du'a for is also
being tried by Allah 🕌. Your love may be a trial for them
so that they become closer to Allah 🕌 first, and increase
themselves in piety, until they can truly deserve you as a

partner in this world and the hereafter.

One may lose hope at the thought of this all, but it is important to realize that no one is perfect. Allah ﷻ knows this, and verily it is He who is Most Merciful. A vile man is always a sincere moment of repentance away from becoming a good man, and similarly a good woman is always a sincere moment of repentance away from becoming a better woman. One of the most common errors in judgement is that people give up on themselves, and in doing so, they give up on Allah ﷻ's mercy. This is an enormous error on their part, for Allah ﷻ says in Surah Al-Furqan:

> "Excepted, however, shall be they who repent and attain to faith and do righteous deeds: for it is they whose (erstwhile) bad deeds Allah ﷻ will transform into good ones - seeing that Allah ﷻ is indeed Most Forgiving, Most Merciful." [Holy Quran, 25:70]

This verse clearly states that as long as one repents over their sin and tries to maintain their faith, Allah ﷻ will indeed forgive. Therefore, when one sins and finds his sin to be enormous, Allah ﷻ has asked not to be in despair of His mercy. In Surah Az-Zumar, Allah ﷻ continues to say:

> "Oh you servants of Mine who have transgressed against your own selves! Despair not of Allah ﷻ's mercy: behold, Allah ﷻ forgives all sins - for, verily, He alone is much-forgiving, a dispenser of grace!" [Holy Quran,

Therefore it is clear that any sin, no matter how major or minute, is expiated by sincere and proper repentance, and no sin is too big in comparison to His forgiveness. There is a narration of a Hadith in *Al-Bukhari and Muslim* which talks about a prostitute who is forgiven by Allah ﷻ, and subsequently admitted into Jannah, due to a good deed that she has performed.

> "Once a dog was going round the well and was about to die out of thirst. A prostitute of Banu Israel happened to see it. So she took off her leather sock and lowered it into the well. She drew out some water and gave the dog to drink. She was forgiven on account of her action." [Riyad as-Salihin: Book 1, Hadith 126, Sahih Bukhari: Book 54, Number 538.]

This is an example of Allah ﷻ's mercy. Truly all that it could take for any of us to be pardoned is a single good deed that is within our power as Allah ﷻ does not expect the impossible from us. The act of quenching the thirst of a dog was very simple, but she could have easily ignored it and let the dog perish. This demonstrates that to Allah ﷻ, no good deed is too little, and no sin is too big. On the authority of Abu Hurairah (may Allah ﷻ be pleased with him), Prophet Muhammad ﷺ said:

> "When Allah ﷻ decreed the Creation He pledged Himself by writing in His book which is laid down with Him: My mercy prevails over my

wrath." (Related by Muslim, al-Bukhari, an-Nasa'i and Ibn Majah) [40 Hadith Qudsi, Hadith 1]

No matter what you do, constantly fight the urge to give up on your yaqeen (unfaltering faith) in His mercy, and continue to find ways to call to Him. He responds. If it is not granted to you in this temporary life, then you will surely be rewarded with it in the eternity that is promised in the hereafter. One of our biggest fears is time, and we fall into deep despair for not being granted what we want, when we want it. We are so used to measuring life and our existence through the lens of worldly timing, that we forget this is only a temporary transition.

Sometimes we pray for something for years and yet it has not been granted to. So we begin to wonder, is it even worth it? We may start to think, "I've spent years praying for this, and if I haven't been granted it yet, so it'll never be mine, and it's not worth wasting my time." One needs to remember that it is always worth the time. For the Muslim, this world is only the beginning, not an end. An integral part of being a believer is to believe in the hereafter, and to understand this world to be a mere transition between now and our final destination. We have always known that this life is temporary, for there has never been a promise of waking up from our sleep. We do not know how much time we have in this world among one another. However, we must be certain of the fact that it does not end with death - the Hereafter is eternal, and time will be the least of our worries in Paradise. Why would you give up on praying for something, and fall into despair if it is not granted to you in this temporary world where you might not even be here tomorrow? Perhaps you pray for someone who might seem perfect to you, but Allah ﷻ has knowledge of an incompatibility that would destroy your lives in this world and upon being asked He secured you for each other in the Hereafter where the incompatibles have been rendered void. Why compromise an eternity with your beloved by losing faith, when you can continue asking for it and have yaqeen that perhaps Allah ﷻ's withdrawal of it in this world is only so you can have it eternally, without withstanding the hardships and the worries of the world with your beloved. Perhaps your hearts, and souls are compatible with one another but the circumstances and trials decreed to each of you may prove to be otherwise. Allah ﷻ knows best.

One of the most important factors regarding Du'a is the quality of Du'a. There is no one way to call to Allah ﷻ, for He listens indiscriminately, understands all languages and hears each individually and simultaneously. However, when making Du'a and offering supplication, it is always necessary to remain humble and remember that you are worth nothing compared to His glory, and it is the honor of being his slave that esteems you. As previously explained, Du'a is a direct conversation between the creation and his/her Creator; it is the relationship between the slave and his/her Master; and a testimony of the love between the believer and his/her Lord. It is an intimate conversation full of secrets between a soul, and its Khaliq (Creator). It is the appreciation for all that is exists, between what could easily have been inanimate and Al-Baari.

The best place to make Du'a is in the state of being in Sujood (prostration). The beauty of Sujood is that in Sujood you are closest to Him, and it displays an acceptance of weakness and dependence. Moreover, it is an affirmation of His infinite power, and a proclamation of your love and submission towards He whom you worship. Abu Huraira (may Allah ﷻ be pleased with him) reported that Prophet Muhammad ﷺ said:

"The nearest a servant comes to his Lord is when he is prostrating himself, so make supplication (in this state)." [Sahih Muslim, 482]

Therefore, the soul of the people is brought closer to Allah ﷻ when in the state of Sujood. Allah ﷻ is surely aware of what He has created, and He knows it is of utmost disgrace and humility for a man or woman to kneel before another. Thus the act of Sujood by Muslims is to be done exclusively to Allah ﷻ, and to nothing else. Nothing could be more submissive than the highest part of your body placed on the ground before Him, and for that He rewards you. He elevates you in status, and increases you in provisions. It was narrated from 'Ubadah bin Samit (may Allah ﷻ be pleased with him) that he heard the Messenger of Allah ﷺ say:

"No one prostrates to Allah ﷻ but Allah ﷻ will record one Hashanah (good reward) for him, and will erase thereby one bad deed and raise him in status one degree. So prostrate a great deal." [Sunan Ibn Majah, Vol. 1, Book 5, Hadith 1424]

May Allah ﷻ forbid that anyone ever has to kneel before His creation; but if one kneels to a tyrant then it would surely be out of fear, for no one is to even kneel before a beloved in such a way. But when one prostrates and kneels before Allah ﷻ, it is beautiful because it is not just out of fear but rather a combination of several underlying factors and emotions including love, commitment, loyalty, dedication, submission, attachment, and for the search of spiritual and soulful peace and tranquility. Therefore it is the quality of Sujood and not the quantity that matters to Allah ﷻ. Your entire life's hasty and absentminded Sujood combined could be equivalent to the one Sujood that you prolonged as you were caught in a vulnerable moment where your heart was heavy, and your eyes were filled with tears as you asked for His mercy in utmost humility and absolute dependence in Him. In Surah Al-Hajj, Allah ﷻ has said that whatever is in the heavens and the earth prostrates to Him.

> "Do you not see how all who dwell in the heavens and the earth bow down in worship to Allah ﷻ, including the sun, the moon, the stars, the mountains, the trees, the animals, and a large number of people, even a large number of those deserving punishment. He who is humbled (he whom Allah ﷻ shall scorn on Resurrection Day) by Allah ﷻ will have no one who can raise him to honor; surely Allah ﷻ does what He pleases." [Holy Quran, 22:18]

This does not necessarily mean that these creations of Allah ﷻ put their foreheads on the ground, but they prostrate to Allah ﷻ in a manner which suits them. Similarly, we as humans prostrate in a manner that suits us. An example of this was narrated by Abu Dharr (may Allah ﷻ be pleased with him) who said:

> "The Prophet ﷺ said when the sun had set, it goes (i.e. travels) till it prostrates itself underneath the

Throne and takes the permission to rise again, and it is permitted. But one day a time will come when it will be about to prostrate itself but its prostration will not be accepted, and it will ask for the permission to go on its course but it will not be permitted, but it will be ordered to return whence it has come and so it will rise in the west. And that is the interpretation of the Statement of Allah ﷻ:

'And the sun runs its fixed course for a term (decreed). That is the Decree of Allah ﷻ, The Exalted in Might, The All-knowing' [Holy Quran, 36:38]" [Sahih al-Bukhari: 3199, or Book 59, Hadith 10]

Therefore, all of creation is created according to its own means of worship and prostration to Allah ﷻ. Unlike the other creations of Allah ﷻ which are created with a limited will, humankind is given the ability to feel humility in order for us to take advantage of it and seek out its treasures, as humility in front of Allah ﷻ is rewarded in the most beautiful of ways. Another key element to Du'a is Yaqeen (faith) and determination; there should be absolutely no doubt in your heart and mind that your Du'a will be accepted. Prophet Muhammad ﷺ said:

"When anyone of you appeal to Allah ﷻ for something, he should ask with determination and should not say, 'O Allah ﷻ, if You wish, give me.', for nobody can force Allah ﷻ to do something against His will." [Sahih al-Bukhari: 6338, Similarly in Sahih Muslim: 2678]

Most often we make a Du'a and incorrectly follow it with the words "In Sha Allah" which means "if Allah 🕋 wills." These are the words that Prophet Muhammad 🕋 told us to specifically refrain from when making Du'a because it is akin to giving Allah 🕋 a choice. Neither of us are in a position to ever give Allah 🕋 a choice, for that would imply being in a position of power or authority, and surely all authority belongs to Allah 🕋 alone. We can only ask and have faith in His mercy. In another narration, Prophet Muhammad 🕋 said:

> "The invocation of anyone of you is granted (by Allah 🕋) if he does not show impatience (by saying, 'I invoked Allah 🕋 but my request has not been granted by Him.')" [Sahih al-Bukhari: 6340, Similarly in Sahih Muslim: 2735(a)(b)]

Moreover, it was narrated in *Sahih Muslim* by Abu Huraira (may Allah 🕋 be pleased with him) that Prophet Muhammad 🕋 said:

> "The supplication of the servant is granted in case he does not supplicate for sin or for severing the ties of blood, or he does not become impatient... He should not say I supplicated and I supplicated but I did not find it being responded, and then he becomes frustrated and abandons

supplication." [Sahih Muslim, 2735(c)]

Upon making Du'a one must be convinced that nothing is impossible for Allah ﷻ and that even if there is a delay in the fulfillment of one's Du'a, it will come true. Indeed it is hard to make the same Du'a over and over again, and the continued repetition of it eventually makes one think of abandoning it. The key is to try and to plead with as much expectation from Allah ﷻ as you had the first time you prayed for it. On the authority of Abu Hurairah (may Allah ﷻ be pleased with him), Prophet Muhammad ﷺ said:

> "I am as my servant expects Me to be." (It was related by al-Bukhari, Muslim, at-Tirmidhi, and Ibn-Majah) [40 Hadith Qudsi, Hadith 15]

This means that the forgiveness and the acceptance of repentance as well as the fulfillment of Du'a by the Almighty is subject to His servant truly believing that He is forgiving, and merciful.

One of the most important things to keep in mind when making Du'a is to be attentive to Allah ﷻ and to be conscious of His presence. Imagine having a conversation with a friend, in which you are seeking advice or you are having an emotional heart-to-heart conversation, but your friend seems to be inattentive; surely that would upset you, would it not? But Allah ﷻ is always attentive to you, and never does He withdraw His attention from you. So when asking from Allah ﷻ, you must be equally as conscious of His presence and be as attentive to Him. In one account, Prophet Muhammad ﷺ said:

"Call upon Allah ﷻ while being certain of being answered, and know that Allah ﷻ does not respond to a supplication from the heart of one heedless and occupied by play."[Jami' at-Tirmidhi, 3479]

Similarly, in another narration by Abu Huraira (may Allah ﷻ be pleased with him), Prophet Muhammad ﷺ advised a man about attaining a level of perfection in his worship by "Worshiping Allah ﷻ as if you see Him, and if you do not achieve this state of devotion, then (take it for granted that) Allah ﷻ sees you." [Sahih al-Bukhari, Prophetic Commentary on the Qur'an (Tafseer of the Prophet (pbuh)), Book 65, Hadith 4777]

As previously mentioned, there is no one way of making Du'a, but according to a Hadith narrated by 'Amr bin Malik Al-Janbi:

"The Prophet ﷺ heard a man supplicating in his Salat (prayer) but he did not send blessings upon the Prophet ﷺ, so the Prophet ﷺ said: 'This one has rushed.' Then he called him and said to him, or to someone other than him: 'When one of you performs Salat (prayer), then let him begin by expressing gratitude to Allah ﷻ and praising Him. Then, let him send blessings upon the Prophet ﷺ, then let him supplicate after that, whatever he wishes.'" [Jami' at-Tirmidhi, 3477]

It is beneficial to begin our Du'a with acknowledging Allah ﷻ's might and benevolence, expressing our gratitude, and to praise Him using His attributes and names. Verily, depending on your need there is a name of your Lord to call Him by. Moreover, it is equally important in Du'a to send blessings to Prophet Muhammad ﷺ. Umar bin Al-Khattab (may Allah ﷻ be pleased with him) narrated:

> "Indeed the supplication stops between the heavens and the earth. Nothing of it is raised up until you send Salat upon your Prophet." [Jami' at-Tirmidhi, 486]

Therefore it is of utmost beneficence to remember to give salutations to Prophet Muhammad ﷺ. After making Du'a, one must remember that no Du'a goes unheard, for Allah ﷻ knows what you speak before you speak it. However, there are various responses to Du'a. Jubair bin Nufair (may Allah ﷻ be pleased with him) narrated that 'Ubadah bin As-Samit (may Allah ﷻ be pleased with him) narrated to them that, the Prophet Muhammad ﷺ said:

> "There is not a Muslim upon the earth who calls upon Allah ﷻ with any supplication, except that Allah ﷻ grants it to him, or he turns away from him the like of it in evil; as long as he does not supplicate for something sinful, or the severing of the ties of kinship." So a man from the people said: "What if we should increase (in it)" He ﷺ said: "(With)

Allah ﷻ is more." [Jami' at-Tirmidhi, Vol. 6, Book 46, Hadith 3573]

This is contrary to the belief that the response from Allah ﷻ can only be of one kind, which means to be blessed with what you asked for in Du'a. This Hadith explains that the response from Allah ﷻ can take various forms. One of the responses is that you are granted what you asked for. The second response is that He delays it and grants your Du'a when you are ready for it, or when it is ready for you. Lastly, instead of granting the Du'a, Allah ﷻ removes an obstacle or misfortune from your worldly life that was equal or greater than the fulfillment of your Du'a, and grants that Du'a in the Hereafter. Perhaps you asked for some wealth, and some calamity such as an accident was decreed to you in your future. Allah ﷻ uses that Du'a instead to save you from such an obstacle and grants the Du'a to you in Paradise, where your happiness will not be subject to the end of time.

When the actual time for the fulfillment of your Du'a comes, the entire universe becomes subject to the will of Allah ﷻ in order to carry that fulfillment out. It is in this moment you truly realize that all of existence is in the hands of Allah ﷻ, and He uses His powers to guide everything to carry out His will. So when you are finally ready for the fulfillment of your Du'a, or perhaps what you ask for is finally ready for you, in that moment Allah ﷻ uses all of His powers to steer you into the right direction. Time, space, gravity, the stars, the moon, the winds, the weather, the laws of nature, everything in the universe begins to work in favor of you. Essentially, Allah ﷻ coerces all of existence to cater to your needs.

Imagine praying for something your entire life, and

one day the time for fulfillment comes. For this scenario, let's imagine you've prayed for true love and faithful companionship and the doors of marriage have finally opened for you. Consider being on a road trip from point A to point B, and on the way to your destination you undergo the frustration of having to stop at every single red light possible. At this point you're absolutely frustrated and it seems as if nothing is going your way. Eventually your car runs out of petrol, and you take the exit off of the highway and stop at a gas station. While leaving the gas station your car breaks down, and it needs a battery boost. What else could possibly go wrong? You shouldn't have asked. At this point it starts to rain, and when it rains it pours! You wait there for a half an hour because no one seems to have a booster cable to give your battery a jump start.

Somewhere not too far away is a beautiful woman caught in the rain, who happens to be a novice driver too afraid to drive in the rain. Her father who happens to be in the passenger seat urges that she takes the next exit, and from there he will continue driving. She decides to take the exit off of the highway and pulls up into the gas station at the pump across from you. As they are switching seats, you approach them to ask if they have a booster cable, and lo and behold, they do! Perhaps everything that day, the red lights, the traffic, the running out of petrol, the car breaking down, and the rain, was all a set up. It was Allah ﷻ using His powers to coerce the universe to steer you into the right direction to be at the right place in the right moment for you to meet someone, and your life from that moment on would never be the same. Perhaps you strike an engaging conversation with the father of that woman, and it leads to exchanging numbers. Perhaps it leads to a family friendship, and you eventually ask for her hand in marriage. Such is the beauty of fulfillment and the miracles of Allah ﷻ. The red lights, the forces of nature, essentially everything in this scenario slowed you down to meet with these strangers at the right timing, while you naively thought nothing was going in your favor that afternoon. In fact, the entire universe was catering to the fulfillment of your Du'a. Subhan'Allah, how glorious is Allah ﷻ?

In another instance, imagine if Allah ﷻ for whatever reason known to Him, has withheld the fulfillment of your Du'a and has granted to you its fulfillment in the hereafter. This in itself is beautiful because we spend so much time and effort in proving our love to the people we love, and especially the beloved. We make poetic gestures, and buy gifts, and yet sometimes our actions fail to speak louder than words, and even our words may have no effect on them. However, one day, we will not have to prove anything, but everything will speak for us. To establish this, I am going to make a few references. First, it was narrated that the Prophet used to say:

> "On the Day of Resurrection, that portion of the earth on which prostration was made will testify to the devotion of the man." [Jami' al-Ahadith, vol. 5, pg. 189]

It is also relevant to quote that in Surah Ya-Sin, Allah ﷻ says:

> "On that Day, We shall set a seal on their mouths - but their hands will speak unto Us, and their feet will bear witness to whatever they have earned (in life)." [Holy Quran, 36:65]

Moreover, Allah ﷻ reminds us again in Surah Ha-Mim:

"Hence, (warn all men of) the Day when the enemies of Allah ﷻ shall be gathered together before the fire, and then shall be driven onward till, when they come close to it, their hearing and their sight and their (very) skins will bear witness against them, speaking of what they were doing (on earth). And they will ask their skins, 'Why did you bear witness against us?' - (and) these will reply: 'Allah ﷻ, who gives speech to all things, has given speech to us (as well): for He (it is who) has created you in the first instance - and unto Him you are (now) brought back." [Holy Quran, 41:19-21]

With these references, we've established that the earth will be witness to where we prayed, and of our devotion and our entire bodies shall be witnesses to our deeds as well. Moreover, in Surah Qaf, Allah ﷻ says:

"NOW, VERILY, it is We who have created man, and We know what his innermost self whispers within him (the prompting of his soul): for We are closer to him than his jugular vein. (And so,) whenever the two demands (of his nature) come face to face, We have assigned to everyone two scribes (guardian angels), the one seated on his right and the other on his left, not a single word does he utter but there is a vigilant guardian ready to note it down." [Holy Quran, 50:16-18]

Allah ﷻ reminds us of this again in Surah Al-Infitar:

"You should know that guardian
angels have indeed been appointed
over you, who are noble writers,
generous and recording (they are the
Kiraman Katibeen) and they are aware
of whatever you do!" [Holy Quran,
82:10-12]

Therefore you can spend hours writing love letters to
your beloved, and spend your entire wealth on buying
gifts to prove how much you care for them, how much
you love them, and how much you pray for them.
Despite all your efforts, it may all go in vain. But imagine
if Allah ﷻ has decided for you to be united with your
beloved in the Hereafter, how beautiful would it be for
every spot on the earth in which you prayed for them, to
testify to your love? Imagine every single time you were
at home and you prayed for your beloved, and surely you
will have prayed in different spots depending on where
you were at the time of a specific prayer. Imagine all of
the times you went to the mosque and all the specific
spots you may have prayed on, and perhaps you may have
done so in various parts of the world and even on a
flight! Essentially what this means is that all those places
on the earth; and surely even the skies will testify of your
love. Imagine how beautiful it would be for the earth to
testify the number of times you thought of your beloved
and you delayed your Sujood. If that isn't enough, Allah
ﷻ has said that your limbs will testify of all that you have
earned and done on earth. Your eyes will testify the tears
that you shed while asking Allah ﷻ to fulfill your Du'a,
and your hands and every single finger will testify of all
the number of times you raised them in order to ask
Allah ﷻ. Your tongue will testify of all the times you

evoked Allah ﷻ, and the various ways in which you made your Du'a. Your legs and your feet and your toes will testify of every time you thought to walk or travel to a mosque in order to pray in congregation to attain even more blessings towards the fulfillment of your Du'a. Allah ﷻ has specifically appointed guardian angels, the Kiraman Katibeen (the Honorable Scribes) to write down each and every word you have spoken to testify one day, and they will bear witness to every Du'a you may have made for your beloved for every single word either spoken or whispered will have been written down. Imagine a lifetime in paradise with your beloved with so much testimony of your love and of each and every Du'a you may have made for them. Subhan'Allah, all Praise and Glory is due to Allah ﷻ, the Lord of the Worlds, the Heavens and the Earth.

It then becomes of utmost significance that when making Du'a, you must give yourself reasons to reinforce your belief in His wisdom, for surely there is divine wisdom behind any delay that you may experience before the fulfillment of your prayers. Perhaps the fulfillment of that Du'a was conditional on you praying for it in a certain way, a specific number of times, by remembering Him with a specific name. Perhaps it is to be yours when you beg for it in a certain state of mind. Perhaps it will be granted to you in the life to come. Make Du'a by praising Allah ﷻ and sending blessings upon His Prophet ﷺ, and wait for the universe to conspire in bringing you what is best for you. Allah ﷻ has heard you.

2.2
WHAT IS LOVE?

Allah ﷻ knows everything, and in whatever areas He has given us freedom to act, we act freely. Thus we are responsible for the things in which we have the freedom to act, and we are judged according to the choices we make within those areas that Allah ﷻ has given us. One of those areas is love.

How does one define love? I believe that love is something that is so sacred, it becomes undefinable. It is everything from a feeling that makes you euphoric and feel complete, to an overwhelming emotion that makes you cry unexpectedly in the middle of a lecture hall, to an act of worship that makes you appreciate the number of blessings Allah ﷻ has moulded into another being in order to complete and compliment your own existence, to a tear that falls out of your eyes in appreciation of a blessing bestowed upon you by your Creator. In order to absorb my understanding of love, I would beg the reader to forego any and all preconceived notions or definitions of love. To love is to breathe to your fullest potential, and to breathe without restrictions is to live; love is the essence of being alive.

Hazrat (the honorable) Inayat Khan who was the founder of The Sufi Order in the West in 1914 (London) and teacher of Universal Sufism defines love as intelligence, and seeks to explain that in love abides all knowledge. He explains that no one can truly know another except for the lover, because anyone in the absence of love is blind from the inner eyes, and can only see from the outer eyes which are merely the spectacles of the inner eyes. Therefore, if the inner eyes are blind, what use are the spectacles?

"It is for this reason that we admire all those whom we love, and are blind to the good qualities of those whom we do not love. It is not always that these deserve our neglect, but our eyes, without love, cannot see their goodness. Those whom we love may have bad points too, but as love sees beauty, so we see that alone in them. Intelligence itself in its next step towards manifestation is love. When the light of love has been lit, the heart becomes transparent, so that the intelligence of the soul can see through it. But until the heart is kindled by the flame of love, the intelligence, which is constantly yearning to experience life on the surface, is groping in the dark." [Hazrat Inayat Khan, Volume V: Spiritual Liberty, Part IV, Chapter 1]

He further elaborates that the whole of creation is made for love, but man is most capable of it. Inanimate objects such as stones will not be aware of our love because such objects lack intelligence, but a plant will be conscious of it, and it will respond to our care and flourish. Similarly, animals feel affection and through affection and love an animal begins to become tamed and grows to become an affectionate family member. But since man has the largest share of intelligence, he has the most love in his nature.

"The Sufis say that the reason of the whole creation is that the perfect Being wished to know Himself, and did so by awakening the love of His nature and creating out of it His object of love, which is beauty. Dervishes, with this meaning, salute each other by saying, 'Ishq Allah Mabud Allah - God is love and God is the beloved.'" [Hazrat Inayat Khan, Volume V: Spiritual Liberty, Part IV, Chapter 1]

Islamic Mystics also make the comparison of love with intellect, similar to the Mystics of Universalism. Shaykh Zulfiqar Ahmed in "Ishq-e-Ilahi" says that Allah ﷻ bestowed humanity with two gifts in Alam al-Arwah (the land of souls). He states that when Allah ﷻ created Prophet Adam (Peace and Blessings be upon him), He struck His right hand (His might) on the back of Prophet Adam (Peace and Blessings be upon him), causing offspring to emerge from his body. The bodies of these humans were short, and their faces were glowing with Noor (radiance). Allah ﷻ struck the back of Prophet Adam (Peace and Blessings be upon him) another time, and more offspring emerged, but this time the faces lacked the Noor that was evident on the faces of the previous set of offspring. When Prophet Adam (Peace and Blessings be upon him) was told that these were his children, he asked, "Why are they not all alike, my Lord?"

Allah ﷻ replied, "The ones with Noor are the inhabitants of Heaven, and those devoid of Noor are the inhabitants of Hell." At this point there was no veil between Allah ﷻ and the children of Prophet Adam (Peace and Blessings be upon him). A conversation followed, and Allah ﷻ addressed the progeny by saying:

"Am I not your lord?"
[Holy Quran, 7:172]

All replied,

> "Veriliy, You are (our Lord)."
> [Holy Quran, 7:172]

It was this conversation which resulted in the two gifts which Allah ﷻ bestowed upon humanity. Shaykh Zulfiqar Ahmed explains that by displaying His Jamal (beauty), Ishq (love) for Allah ﷻ was instilled in humanity. And by asking the question, "Am I not your Lord," humanity was endowed with Ilm (faculty of knowledge).

> "For the inculcation of His love, Allah ﷻ granted humanity a beating heart; and for the acquisition of knowledge, Allah ﷻ gave human beings acute minds. Thus, the sustenance of the heart is Ishq (love), and the sustenance of the mind is Ilm (sacred knowledge). Love alone leads to Bid'at (deviant innovations), and it is knowledge that restores a balanced equilibrium. Knowledge alone leads to Takabbur (arrogant pride) and it is love that restores Tawadu' (modesty and humility). Love and sacred knowledge are inseparable; a complete person requires both blessings. If someone is deficient in either, then there is a danger of leaning towards extremes." [Shaykh Zulfiqar Ahmed, Ishq-e-Ilahi translated by Faqir Publications, page 55]

My understanding of love has always been that love in

itself, and how you love is a reflection of both heaven and hell on earth. When you give love the honor and respect that it deserves, and treat it as the blessing that it is, and when you legitimate it through the union of marriage by making it Halal (Permissible), it not only elevates in itself, but it also blesses you both emotionally and spiritually. Therefore when in love, its ultimate goal should be marriage, and when that love is reciprocated through a marriage, when the duties, rights and responsibilities towards the beloved are fulfilled, it is no less than a reflection of paradise. Hazrat Inayat Khan proposed that there are three kinds of love:

> The first love is for the self. If illuminated, man sees his true benefit and he becomes a saint. In the absence of illumination man becomes so selfish that he becomes a devil. The second love is for the opposite sex. If it is for love's sake it is heavenly. If it is for passion's sake it is earthly. This, if it is quite pure, can certainly take away the idea of the self, but the benefit is slight and the danger is great. The third love is for the children, and this is the first service to God's creatures. To reserve it for one's children only is like appropriating to oneself what is given to us as a trust by the Creator, but if this love expands to embrace the whole creation of the Heavenly Father, it raises man to be among the chosen ones of God. [Hazrat Inayat Khan, Volume V: Spiritual Liberty, Part IV, Chapter 1]

The differentiation between the love for the sake of love,

and love for the sake of passion is a powerful concept, and is one that I personally agree with. Love for the sake of love, is heavenly, whereas, love for the sake of passion is earthly but has devastating consequences. People often end up in marriages and find that it was not what they expected, and such marriages fall apart. It is important to realize that the marriage itself is no magic spell nor does it guarantee an effortless sense of happiness or bliss. It is important to approach it with the right mindset and remember what the purpose of marriage is, and only then should one get married. It is human nature to desire intimacy, for it is a craving that is natural to both you and me. In fact, it is recognized to be such a strong desire that it is prescribed upon both man and woman to lower their gaze in order to help control such desires. People often transgress their limits when in love and it ultimately it leads to the burning of an intense desire for the beloved and warrants intimacy. Marriage is a great option at this point to avoid engaging in Haram (Islamically forbidden and impermissible) and extra marital physical relationships, but making that the sole purpose to look forward to getting married is ultimately flawed. What do you do after you are done exploring your carnal desires and after your needs are satisfied? Do you not communicate with one another? Do you schedule another intimate spousal session for the next day and move on with life for the time being? It doesn't take long to realize that going into marriage with such an idea of love is not exactly what you thought it would be like.

We are too consumed with the false representation of love that we see through media, and unfortunately we understand it through the limited few pages of fairytales. There is more to love than kissing a beautiful damsel out of her sleep and living happily ever after, and it is far deeper and more complicated than kissing a frog that turns into a prince who changes your life around. Happily ever after requires a lot of work and mutual commitment.

Islam promotes the idea of love which completes two people as being two halves of a single whole. Islam promotes a kind of love that involves a spiritual, physical and emotional journey together; a relationship that involves learning and building together. When you are ready to get married, or are contemplating marriage, it is important to ask yourself what is it exactly that you are ready for? What is it that you seek? Do you wish to only engage in exploring your carnal desires and carry to on an intimate relationship with your spouse that is validated through your Nikkah (Islamic Marriage Contract)? Or are you ready to build a lifelong relationship with another soul to find Allah ﷻ through the worship and remembrance of Him? Are you ready for the ups and downs? Are you ready for the fights and arguments that are only natural when two people live together and are exposed to their truest sides? Are you ready to put aside your differences and focus on inspiring, motivating and bettering each other? Marriage will not be the romanticized version that you've always read about, it won't be racing to the prayer mat, it won't always be waking each other for Fajr (morning) prayer, it won't always be using each other's fingers as prayer beads, or competing to complete the Holy Quran, but all of that is indeed the end goal. We all must wish to have someone to motivate us, inspire us, and someone to teach and to learn from. Equally importantly, we must all equally strive to be that kind of a person in someone else's life.

The Holy Quran and Hadith, both offer insights on the potential and purpose of marriage. In Surah Al-Israa, Allah ﷻ commanded Prophet Muhammad ﷺ to let it be known that we are to not approach unlawful sexual intercourse including adultery and fornication. "For, behold, it is an abomination and an evil way (of fulfilling sexual urge)." [Holy Quran, 17:32] Therefore, sexual relations   both outside the marriage and before marriage are immoral acts against the rights of Allah ﷻ and one's own sexual organs. This is further clarified in Surah Al-Muminun:

> The believers are... those who protect their sexual organs (not giving way their desires) with any but their spouses - that is, those whom they rightfully possess (through wedlock) ... Therefore, whosoever seeks more beyond that limit (in sexual gratification), then they are the transgressors. [Holy Quran, 23:5-7]

The last sentence makes it clear that any means of sexual gratification outside marriage is considered a transgression of the Law of Allah ﷻ, for those who stay within the prescribed limits are the believers. In Surah Al-A'raf it says:

> It is He who has created you (all) from a single soul, and out of it brought into being its mate, so that man might incline (with love) towards woman. And so, when he has embraced her, she conceives (what at first is) a light burden, and continues to bear it. Then, when she grows heavy (with child), they both call unto Allah ﷻ, their Sustainer, "If Thou indeed grant us a sound (child), we shall most certainly be among the grateful!" [Holy Quran, 7:189]

This is a very important verse which highlights that it is Allah ﷻ who created all of us from a single soul; the soul of Prophet Adam (Peace and Blessings be upon him), but before the creation of his progeny, Allah ﷻ created from Adam his mate so that he could find tranquility in her. True tranquility is only attained through a lawful marriage, and any love outside of such a union will eventually lead to the opposite of a sense of tranquility.

Al Imam ibn Katheer (may Allah ﷻ have mercy upon him) in "The Stories of the Prophets" explains that upon being created, Prophet Adam (Peace and Blessings be upon him) tried to speak with the Angels, but they were a creation based solely on the worshipping of Allah ﷻ. The angels had no knowledge or freedom of will, and they existed for sole the purpose of worshipping and praising Allah ﷻ. On the other hand, Prophet Adam (Peace and Blessings be upon him) was given the ability to identify and designate names to everything. He was taught language, speech and the ability to communicate with an insatiable need for the love of knowledge, but he eventually began to feel very lonely in Heaven because he was the only one of his kind. One day he opened his eyes and looked into the beautiful face of a woman staring at him. In complete awe, he asked the woman what the purpose of her creation was, upon which she revealed that she was to ease his loneliness and bring tranquility to him.

The Angels were aware that Allah ﷻ had given Prophet Adam (Peace and Blessings be upon him) the knowledge of things they did not know about, so they asked what her name was. He replied, "This is Eve." Eve is Hawwa in Arabic; which comes from the root word Hay, meaning living. Prophet Adam (Peace and Blessings be upon him) informed the Angels the reason for her name was because she was made from a part of him and he was a living being. Allah ﷻ reminds us again in Surah

An-Nisaa:

> "Oh mankind! Have fear of your Sustainer, who has created you from a single soul, and out of it created its mate, and out of the two spread abroad a multitude of men and women. Be careful of your duty toward Allah ﷻ in Whom you claim (your rights) of one another, and toward the wombs (that bore you). Verily, Allah ﷻ is watching you very closely." [Holy Quran, 4:1]

The traditions of Prophet Muhammad ﷺ relate that Eve was created while Adam was sleeping from his shortest left rib and that, after sometime, she was clothed with flesh. He used the story of Eve's creation from Prophet Adam's (Peace and Blessings be upon him) rib to guide people to be gentle and kind to women. Narrated Abu Huraira (may Allah ﷻ be pleased with him), Prophet Muhammad ﷺ said:

> "Treat women nicely, for a woman is created from a rib, and the most curved portion of the rib is its upper portion, so, if you should try to straighten it, it will break, but if you leave it as it is, it will remain crooked. So treat women nicely." [Sahih al-Bukhari, 3331 or Book 60, Hadith 6]

These verses are significant because they demonstrate that since the first woman was created from the first man, she was meant to complete him. The purpose of her creation was to ease his loneliness. Together in a union, they were to make a single self, and this is how in a marriage both spouses must strive to build their lives together, as if they are one being, one person, one soul, and within their marriage they are to find comfort, and tranquility from one another. That is what love is, the existence of two souls as one. In Surah Al-Baqara, Allah ﷻ says:

> "Your wives are a garment for you, and you are a garment to them. Allah ﷻ is aware that you would have deprived yourselves of this right, and so He has turned unto you in His mercy and removed this hardship from you. Now then, you may lie with them skin to skin, and avail yourselves for that which Allah ﷻ has ordained for you." [Holy Quran, 2:187]

This verse suggests that both men and women have an equal status in sharing the responsibilities of a marriage, and towards fulfilling the obligations owed to each other.

The purpose of a garment is to cover one's body entirely as if there is nothing between the garment and the body. Therefore, the metaphor suggests that spousal relationships should be so close and intimate to one another that there should be no secrets between them. Moreover, a garment also serves the purpose of enhancing ones appearance. People often spend generous amounts of money on themselves to purchase expensive clothes in hopes that the garment would provide elegance and grace to their personality, and similarly, spouses should enhance one another's dignity in the same respect.

Due to cultural influences, we often forget the rights and obligations we have towards our spouses. For example, nowhere does it prescribe a woman to leave home and settle with a man as a full time, child bearing maid and to provide sexual gratification on demand. In some regard, some cultures prescribe such responsibilities according to gender roles that are taken upon each spouse for the marriage to work accordingly. The verse doesn't create any gender inequalities between the spouses, but lays forth a perspective of equality towards one another. The aforementioned verse reminds us that the purpose of a garment is also to shield or protect the body from outside dangers and influences.

> "My pride is as much yours, as your
> honor is mine." [Arslan Zaidi]

This is something that I have always advised family and friends to mutually and wholeheartedly accept as a philosophy within a marriage. This phrase means that a man's pride and dignity should be equally his wife's as her honor and respect is equally his. Like armor, one is to defend the other as if you are two extensions of one another, against any external influence. The internalization of such a philosophy would guarantee a mutual understanding between spouses to regard one another as two halves of a whole, and not a mere accessory, for when you are clothed, your garment becomes a part of you. Therefore, one is obligated to defend the other in both his/her absence and presence, for an insult or an injustice done to one, is equally a reflection of the insult or injustice done to the other. Spouses are each other's protectors from everything external to the marriage, a union which Islam highly promotes. When such responsibilities and duties are fulfilled to their potential, each partner can feel sheltered in one another's care and guardianship.

A further elaboration of a previously quoted verse from Surah An-Nissa is necessary in order to understand the concept of guardianship.

"Men are the overseers over women because Allah ﷻ has given the one more strength than other, and because men are required to spend their wealth for the maintenance of women. Honorable women are, therefore, devoutly obedient and guard in the husband's absence what Allah ﷻ require them to guard their husband's property and their own honor. As to those women from whom you fear disobedience, first admonish them, then refuse to share your bed with them, and then, if necessary, discipline them. Then if they obey you, take no further actions against them and do not make excuses to punish them. Allah ﷻ is Supremely Great and is aware of your actions." [Holy Quran, 4:34]

Men are explicitly announced as the guardians of women, and the verse clearly states that because of their strength and their social status, Allah ﷻ has made men the overseers of women. The verse further elaborates on how to discipline women. This often allows various cultures to enforce a male dominant worldview, wrongfully said to have been legitimated by the Holy Quran. Each verse of the Quran is to be reflected upon, and upon careful reflection, its beauty becomes even more apparent because of the wisdom behind it. At first glance it seems to promote a sense of male domination because men are allowed to discipline their women, but Allah ﷻ has set the limit to go as far as guarding their own honor and the husband's property in his absence, and any transgression beyond this is expressly forbidden.

Men are not owners of women, but instead they are guardians, and their job is to oversee.

Just as when raising children, the guardian oversees the child and guides and instructs him/her towards becoming a better person and reaching his/her full potential under supervision - the male is to be a shadow over the female that protects her, and guides her in becoming a version of herself that she could not have been without him. Surely she should do the same, for the purpose of her creation was to provide peace and tranquility to her spouse, but the responsibilities of the male are far greater, and most often misunderstood. He is to use his strength and his wealth in her favor in order to better her, as opposed to oppressing her and transgressing over the rights and responsibilities owed to her.

As a male, imagine planting a seed into the ground, and your job is to oversee its growth. You tend to it daily to see if it has received water, and with the nourishment of the sun it begins to grow. Eventually it reaches the point where the scorching heat of the sun is harmful to whatever you have planted, so you shade it. One day it rains and the excessive amount of water overflowing has a potential to harm it, you shelter it from the rain. Under your supervision it grows, and if it had been a rose, then one day you'll find it to have grown into a beautiful rose. If it had been an apple tree, one day it'll give you the fruits of your labor. Similarly, the woman was created to provide you peace and tranquility, and thus you are obliged to care for her. You are expected to use your strength to shade her and be her shield against anything that has the potential to harm her, and use your means to shelter her and to provide for her. With your love and supervision, she becomes multiple times the woman she was, and one day she returns the love by bearing the pain and giving you the fruits of your labor: children.

This does not mean that women are weaker than men, or are subordinate in any way. In "Miraaj - The Night Journey of Muhammad (Peace Be Upon Him) to Heaven" published in Waqf Ikhlas, the status of women has been thoroughly explained. The following excerpt is taken from Waqf Ikhlas:

"As Prophet Muhammad ﷺ ascended towards the Fifth Heaven, he asked: "Jibraeel, what is the secret of this paradise?" Jibraeel said: "Allah ﷻ created this paradise to reflect the beauty and perfection of women. The light of this paradise is the source of the angelic lights of all women on earth. Women have been created to carry the secret of creation in themselves. Allah ﷻ has honored them greatly by making their wombs the repository of His word which represents the Spirit. He looks at the most sacred place and there descends His mercy and blessings. He perfected that place and covered it with three protective layers to shelter it from any damage. The first is a layer of light, the second a layer of love, and the third a layer of beauty. There He fashions and creates human beings... He orders the angels of the womb to perfect His creation by giving the baby life, beauty, health, intelligence, and all kinds of perfect attributes that will make each one distinguished among human beings.

Women are not created weaker but more generous than men. They are created more beautiful and less fierce, as beauty hates to hurt and harm others. That is why they seem weak to people, but in reality they are not. Angels are the strongest of created beings, and women are closer to the angelic nature than men, as they are readier than men to carry angelic light. It is the good manners and ethics of spirituality which they carry which makes them less forceful than men. Even physically, however, they are extremely strong. They undergo great upheavals in their body without flinching for the sake of childbirth, and face the direst physical conditions more successfully than men because Allah ﷻ has enabled them to insure that survival of generations."

[Miraaj - The Night Journey of Muhammad (PBUH) to Heaven. From Waqf Ikhlas.

Ihlas Holding A. S.
Cagaloglu - ISTANBUL
Tel: (90212) 513 99 00]

Allah ﷻ has made neither gender equal nor unequal to one another, but has given each gender its own strengths and weaknesses that compliment one another.

Without a doubt, The Holy Quran in its entirety is a beautiful text, but the following few verses are the most memorable verses with regards to love being a movement towards oneness and unity. Although the following verses have previously been quoted, it is important to make reference to them again in order to further elaborate on the concept that love is intrinsic to nature, and it is at the core of creation. In Surah An-Naim it says:

> "And that it is He who created in pairs, the male and the female." [Holy Quran, 53:45]

It is not to be understood as simply a pair of opposites, but in fact, these are pairs that are unique and complimentary to one another. For example, the moon fulfills the absence of the sun, the night time compliments the day time, and its oneness completes a cycle. Allah ﷻ has created a balance and has set the nature of all things and the entirety of creation in the right equilibrium to exist in perfect harmony. Similarly, two unique partners in a marriage are the separate embodiments of a single soul: the male and female. If the two partners work together and balance their lives according to the prescribed regulations in fulfilling their duties and responsibilities towards one another, they fulfill their relation to not only themselves but also to Allah ﷻ.

The word used for pair in the Quran is "Zawj" which literally means one part of a pair, and when the partners in a pair comes together they begin to reach potentials that were impossible to realize while they were apart, and this is true throughout creation. The human marriage in the Holy Quran is considered a reflection of a nature and tendency that exists at all levels of creation.

When something is created as one part of a pair, it is clearly incomplete without the other. This is further expressed in Surah Az-Zariyat:

> And in everything have We created in pairs, so that you might bear in mind (God alone is one). [Holy Quran, 51:49]

The concept of marriage can also figuratively describe the coming together of various aspects of creation. Such as the relationship between the rain and the soil.

> Are they not aware that it is We who lead the rain onto dry land devoid of herbage, and thereby bring forth herbage. [Holy Quran, 32:27]

A commentary of this verse describes it as:

> Don't you see the phenomenon in your daily life that a land previously lying absolutely barren starts swelling with vegetation and plant life everywhere just by a single shower of the rain though before this no one could ever imagine that under the layers of its soil there lay hidden such treasures of greenery and herbage? [Sayyid Abul Ala Maududi, Tafhim al-Qur'an, The Meaning of the Quran, Surah As-Sajda]

Such is also the fruitfulness of a marriage. As the rain comes together with the soil, and its intimacy brings forth flowers and herbage, new creations and new life and the potential for treasures that would not have existed prior, the act of marriage too is the natural inclination for each pair to come together and reach a higher potential through intimacy and friendship which leads to an elevation in love.

Love in itself is a form of worship, and it can only be valid as long as it has not transgressed the balance between two individuals outside of the guidelines of permissibility; marriage. If the creation of everything in pairs is a reminder that Allah ﷻ alone is One, and if marriage alone allows the legitimacy of love between a pair, and if love itself is a movement towards oneness, then surely the closer the heart is to oneness, the closer one is to Allah ﷻ. It takes two souls to be one.

One of the most beautiful and purest examples of a love marriage which remarkably goes against all stereotypes held against Islam is that of Prophet Muhammad ﷺ and Khadijah bint Khuwaylid. It is a story in which both parts of the pair were complimentary to one another and their unique qualities when brought together by Allah ﷻ produced what neither one alone could produce. It is a story in which each individual underwent a change and transformation of the self, the soul, and the individual personality to cater to the other. This is a story in which love thrived even after the death of one partner, defying the mortality of worldly love.

In "The Wives of The Prophet Muhammad" by Muhammad Fathi Mus, Khadijah (may Allah ﷻ be pleased with her) engaged herself in trade, and since Allah ﷻ blessed her with wealth, it increased. She supervised and administered trade herself to the extent that she became well known for her good morals. However, she never practiced trade herself, but hired men to do it for her. She had been informed of Prophet Muhammad ﷺ's truthfulness, trustworthiness, and good morals which made her offer him a job to run her trade in Syria.

Sayyid Ali Ashgar Razwy in "Khadijatul Kubra, A Short Story of Her Life," explains that upon hiring Muhammad ﷺ, Khadijah (may Allah ﷻ be pleased with her) sent him to Syria with her slave boy Maysara who was surprised at his professionalism in the trade. Muhammad ﷺ protected the interests of both his employer and his customers, and yet he made more profit for Khadijah (may Allah ﷻ be pleased with her) than she had ever made since she had taken charge of her father's business after his death. Upon their return from Syria, Maysara told Khadijah (may Allah ﷻ be pleased with her) the story of the journey to and from Syria, which was less of a story of a successful trading mission, but more about the character and personality of Muhammad ﷺ himself. Khadijah (may Allah ﷻ be pleased with her) found the story fascinating, and was impressed about Maysara's accounts of Muhammad ﷺ's fail-safe foresight, infallible judgement, unerring perception, friendliness, approachability, courtesy and his condescension.

> It appears that Muhammad's charm and charisma had worked upon Khadijah also. Like Maysara, she too became his admirer, and how could anyone help but become his admirer. Khadijah had known him to be a gentle, a modest, a quiet and an unobtrusive young man. She also knew that the Makkans called him Sadiq and Amin. And now he had revealed his ability as a businessman also. His proficiency and savvy were

part of his charisma. Her new assessment of Muhammad, therefore, was that he was no mere starry-eyed dreamer but also was a practical man of affairs. This assessment prompted her decision to "draft" Muhammad as the manager of her business in all future expeditions. [Sayyid Ali Ashgar Razwy, Khadijatul Kubra - A Short Story of Her Life, Chapter 4]

Muhammad Fathi Mus continues to explains that Khadijah (may Allah ﷻ be pleased with her) kept reflecting on what she had heard about Muhammad ﷺ. She had gone to the Kabbah and circumambulated it, and sat for a while of thinking about the issue. That night she had a dream, "She saw that the sun descended down upon her house and filled the house with light. The light spread from the house until it filled the whole earth." [Muhammad Fathi Mus, The Wives of the Prophet Muhammad] She woke up wondering what it could have possibly meant and after consulting her cousin Waraqah ibn Nawfal, he advised that if Allah ﷻ renders the vision true, the light of prophethood would enter her house.

Khadijah (may Allah ﷻ be pleased with her) remained looking forward to the fulfillment of her dream and one day went to participate in a festival at the Kabbah. After circumambulating the Kabbah she sat amongst the women and overheard a man speak of a Prophet which was to rise among them, and advised the women that whoever could marry him, should do so.

"The man's words had a great influence on her heart and made her recall her vision. Now, Khadijah became sure that Muhammad is the seal of the Prophets and aspired to be his wife; but how could she attain this? Khadijah informed her cousin, Waraqah ibn Nawfal and then expressed her wish to marry Prophet Muhammad, and Waraqah agreed with her." [Muhammad Fathi Mus, The Wives of Prophet Muhammad]

Yasin T. Al-Jibouri in "Khadijah, Daughter of Khuwaylid, Wife of Prophet Muhammad," states:

Khadijah was by then convinced that she had finally found a man who was worthy of her, so much so that she initiated the marriage proposal herself... She simply fell in love with Muhammad just as the daughter of the Arabian prophet Shu'ayb had fallen in love with the then fugitive prophet Moses as we are told in 28:25-26 of the Holy Quran (in Surat al-Qasas). [Yasin T. Al-Jibouri, Khadijah, Daughter of Khuwaylid, Wife of Prophet Muhammad]

Yasin T. Al-Jibouri continues to explain that Khadijah sought the advice of a friend named Nufaysa, a high-born lady of Makkah. Sayyid Ali Ashgar Razwy also writes that Nufaysa was aware that Khadijah had turned down many proposals of marriage, and often wondered if there was any man in Arabia who would come up to the standards set by her. Khadijah was not impressed by any man's wealth or rank or power, but was instead drawn to a man of sterling character. Nufaysa happened to know that there was such a man in Makka, and his name was Muhammad ﷺ. Nufaysa offered to approach him on Khadijah's behalf and, if possible, arrange a marriage between them. She then met with Muhammad ﷺ and consulted him about the proposal, to which Muhammad ﷺ wished to inform his uncle and guardian, Abu Talib (May Allah ﷻ be pleased with him), to consult him in the matter before giving her an answer. Upon the approval of Abu Talib, who gave his blessings to the proposal of their marriage, Muhammad ﷺ told Nufaysa that her suggestion was acceptable to him, and that she had the authority to negotiate, on his behalf, his marriage with Khadijah.

> The marriage of Muhammad and Khadijah was the first and the last of its kind in the world. It was the only marriage in the whole world which abounded in heavenly blessings as well as material blessings. It was a marriage which was immeasurably and incalculably rich in the blessings of both the heaven and the earth. [Sayyid Ali Ashgar Razwy, Khadijatul Kubra - A Short Story of Her Life, Chapter 4]

At the time of marriage, Prophet Muhammad ﷺ was only 25 years old, and Khadijah was 40 years old. She was much older, much wiser, significantly wealthy, and successful. Khadijah had all the qualities that would bruise the male ego, but Prophet Muhammad ﷺ welcomed her into his life wholeheartedly. It is entirely possible that in Arabia, no woman ever brought so much dowry with her into the house of her husband as Khadijah did. What was even more unprecedented was that this dowry was not a gift to Khadijah from her uncles or from her brothers, but was a product of her own efforts. She also brought with her the riches of heart and mind which immeasurably enriched the life of Prophet Muhammad ﷺ.

> Marriage changed the character of her dedication and commitment. She had found Muhammad Mustafa, the greatest of all treasures in the world. Once she found him, gold, silver, and diamonds lost their value for her. Muhammad Mustafa, the future Messenger of Allah ﷺ and the future Prophet of Islam, became the only object of all her affection, attention and devotion. Of course, she never lost her genius for organization, but now instead of applying it to her business, she applied it to the service of her husband. She reorganized her whole life around the personality of Muhammad Mustafa. [Sayyid Ali Ashgar Razwy, Khadijatul Kubra - A Short Story of Her Life, Chapter 4]

Khadijah proved to be an immeasurable blessing. She did not transgress or overstep her boundaries by compromising her modesty; in fact she tried to immediately legitimate her love towards Prophet Muhammad ﷺ through marriage. It was decreed in Heaven that the Prophet of Islam should marry the most well-born and most understanding woman in all of Arabia, and there did not exist another like Khadijah. She was known to be the embodiment of piety and purity, and a guardian of supreme ideals and values. From all the times she rejected marriage proposals of the wealthiest of men, it could be assumed that if it had not been decreed for the universe to conspire and bring Prophet Muhammad to her, she would have spent her life in a single state. Allah ﷻ is the best of planners, and He indeed had a specific purpose for her to fulfill. It was a fruitful marriage, one in which the love only grew with the blessings of Allah ﷻ, to the point that it is said his love for Khadijah not only outlived her but actually went on to growing even after her death.

> "If Khadijah had shown kindness to someone at any time, and even if she had done it only once, Muhammad Mustafa remembered it, and he made it a point to show the same kindness to that person even after her death, and he did it as often as possible... The recipients of the generosity and the kindness of Khadijah, became, after her death, the recipients of the generosity and the kindness of her husband." [Sayyid Ali Ashgar Razwy, Khadijatul Kubra - A Short Story of Her Life, Chapter 16]

Such is the account of the most beautiful marriage that the Heaven and the earth have ever known. Her only explanation was that she was guided by Allah ﷻ Himself, and could therefore never misjudge.

> When she met Muhammad, the future Prophet, she recognized in him the Ultimate in Sublimity, and she put her destiny in his blessed hands. Those hands elevated her destiny, and made it sublime. [Sayyid Ali Ashgar Razwy, Khadijatul Kubra - A Short Story of Her Life, Chapter 16]

The lesson that one can take from this is that she was a woman who was known to be the embodiment of piety and purity, with unquestionable modesty. She respected the sacredness of her feelings, and when she felt as if she had found her match, she immediately consulted a close friend to negotiate the terms of the marriage for her, as did Prophet Muhammad (Peace and Blessings be upon them). Allah ﷻ had willed it in the heavens, and the universe brought them closer; love entered the heart of one, and the universe created a means for them to enter into a marriage, and the immense blessings of Allah ﷻ allowed them to reciprocate and dwell in each other's love such that their marriage prospered.

When we think of soul mates, or being with someone in a relationship that satisfies our definition of love, we always think of one person to settle down with and to spend the rest of our lives with. One of the reasons Islam and the life of Prophet Muhammad ﷺ faces criticism is because of his polygamous marriages. In his lifetime, Prophet Muhammad had a total of eleven wives; but the maximum number of wives he had at any one time was nine. What is important to note is that there was great wisdom behind the many marriages. Perhaps Prophet Muhammad ﷺ too had such a similar idea about soul mates, or love. When Prophet Muhammad married Khadija (may Allah ﷻ be pleased with her) she alone was his companion and friend. They lived for each other and they shared the bitterness and sweetness of life together. "He was strong, active, and attractive, yet he married no other lady while the Arab youth were all polygamists," claims Abdul Ghany. It was only after her death that the Prophet ﷺ began to marry, and contrary to popular understanding and ideas of marriage, this wasn't because of the fulfillment of his physical needs and desires, but many social and political reasons such as creating alliances with other tribes, or saving certain women from vengeance and torment at the hands of their tribes.

Polygamy was very common in the pre-Islamic period and women had very limited liberties. Islamic law cared very much of the equality between men and women in the rights and duties according to the laws of nature. Abdul Ghany writes that Islam was revealed for all of mankind and nations all over the world irrespective of time and place, and Islam only encouraged polygamy in the following cases:

> "In the case of wide scale conflicts and military invasions, or even civil wars, the number of males decreases largely leaving a large number of women without support and protection. The answer for this problem is multiple marriages. This solution becomes sometimes a national necessity, and it resolves the problem most adequately." (Abdul Ghany Abdul Rahman Mohammad, Wives of Mohammad the Prophet and Wisdom of Polygamy, pg. 35)

Abdul Ghany also explains that it was due to individual cases such as when a husband's first wife had a severe and prolonged disease, and he needed a companion to help him with his duties. Moreover, with the death of many males in warfare, thousands of children would be left to be called "bastards" and thus multiple marriages gave them the legitimate rights such as the right to inherit from those who married their mothers. Therefore polygamy was engaged in at times of necessity.

When love enters your heart, treat it as a gift for if it hadn't been for Allah ﷻ you would not have willed it. Do whatever is in your power not to transgress the limits, and seek towards making it Halal. It is a seed that has been planted in your heart that has been decreed to grow. If one has no intention of marrying a woman, he must refrain from awakening love in her heart, for the only legitimization of love is through marriage. If he continues to awaken love in her heart without the intention of loving her as such, then that itself is a transgression for it brings calamity to the heart of a woman.

In order to prohibit man and woman from transgressing the boundaries outside of marriage, the Sharia has defined the concept of "Mahram" and "Non Mahram". The woman's mahram is anyone whom it is explicitly forbidden for her to marry because of blood ties, breastfeeding or marriage ties. Allah ﷻ explains this in depth in Surah An-Nissa:

> Forbidden to you are your mothers, and your daughters, and your sisters, and your aunts paternal and maternal, and a brother's daughters, and a sister's daughters; and your milk-mothers, and your milk-sisters; and the mothers of your wives; and your step-daughters - who are your foster-children - born of your wives with whom you have consummated your marriage; but if you have not consummated your marriage, you will incur no sin (by marrying their daughters); and (forbidden to you are) the spouses of the sons who have sprung from your loins; and (you are forbidden) to have two sisters (as your

wives) at one and the same time - except what happened prior to this commandment: for, behold, Allah ﷻ is indeed much-forgiving, a dispenser of grace. [Holy Quran, 4:23]

Therefore the verse indicates that a woman's mahrams on the basis of blood ties are: her son, her father, her brother, her brother's son, her sister's son, her paternal uncle and her maternal uncle. It is important to acknowledge that it is permissible to marry cousins, and therefore a cousin is not a woman's mahram under any circumstances.

Another important distinction to note is that it was narrated from 'Uqbah ibn 'Aamir (may Allah ﷻ be pleased with him) that Prophet Muhammad ﷺ advised men including any from the woman's in-laws to "beware of entering upon women," which meant to avoid being with them alone and entering their houses or rooms without the presence of a mahram. [Sahih al-Bukhari: 4934, Sahih Muslim, 2172] This includes the husband's relatives, except for his father, grandfather, sons, grandsons who are mahrams of the wife. Therefore, the husband's brother, nephew, uncle, cousin, and friends are non-mahram. Often in certain family settings, we take things lightly with regards to these relatives being alone with the wife, and therefore Prophet Muhammad (Peace and Blessings be upon them) said it is more important that these relatives should not be permitted to be alone with the wife for there are chances of temptation.

In order to control and prohibit transgression between a man and a woman through temptation, it is not permissible for a man to be alone with a woman who is not his mahram, and this is especially to be avoided when both are in love. Ibn 'Abbas (may Allah ﷻ be pleased with him) reported that he heard Prophet Muhammad ﷺ deliver a sermon saying:

> "No person should be alone with a woman except when there is a mahram with her, and the woman should not undertake journey except with a mahram." A person stood up and said: Allah ﷺ's Messenger, my wife has set out for pilgrimage, whereas I am enlisted to fight in such and such battle, whereupon he (Peace and Blessings upon him) said: "You go and perform Hajj with your wife." [Sahih Muslim, 1341(a)]

This reference makes it clear that there are absolutely no circumstances a woman should be alone in the presence of a man without a mahram, even if it is for the purpose of Hajj which happens to be one of the most important pillars of Islam. The word that is used for being alone is "Khalwah" which refers to when the man and woman are in a place where they can converse, even if they can be seen by other people, but their words cannot be heard.

> Khalwah has been forbidden because it is the harbinger of zinna and the means that lead to it. So everything that could lead to that, even making an arrangement to do that later, comes under the ruling of physical khalwah or being alone in a place where they cannot be seen. [Fataawa al-Lajnah al-Daa'imah, 17/57]

Khalwah leads to temptation and indecent conversation which becomes a slippery slope to indulge deeper and deeper into   until the chances for Zinna become inevitable. This can be avoided with the presence of a mahram or the presence of a righteous woman. It is also Haram (impermissible) for a man to touch a non-mahram woman under any circumstances. Ma'qal ibn Yassaar (may Allah ﷻ be pleased with him) said that Prophet Muhammad ﷺ said:

> "If one of you were to be struck in the head with an iron needle, it would be better for him than if he were to touch a woman he is not allowed to." [Reported by al-Tabaraani; classed as Saheeh by al-Albaani in Saheeh al-Jaami', 5045]

For a man to touch a non-mahram woman, and similarly for a non-mahram woman to touch a man is also a major cause of temptation and the provocation of desire; and especially the arousal of sexual desire when both are in love or are already attracted to one another. Therefore, it is a dangerous territory and strictly forbidden to engage in.

In contemporary times, one of the most dangerous forms of transgression is the ability to communicate easily. It is dangerous because it has become so common and natural to have a social life, that we fail to understand that it can be a problem. Email, cellular communication, social networking, texting, and similar innovations in mobile applications have led us to be able to easily misuse these platforms because of the privacy it guarantees or exposes us to. In Surah Al-Ahzab, Allah ﷻ gives us a guideline to follow in our speech when He commanded the wives of the Prophet ﷺ to be conscious of God in their communication with men:

O wives of the Prophet! You are not

like the other women, provided that you remain (truly) conscious of God. Hence, do not be over-soft in your speech while talking to the men who are not closely related to you, lest any whose heart is diseased should be moved to desire (you): but, withal, speak in a kindly way. [Holy Quran, 33:32]

The depth in this verse is immense, for it explains not to be soft in your speech. This means to communicate in a concise and decisive manner which has a specific purpose and does not involve aimless communication, otherwise it may mislead a man hoping for immoral discussions, or romance. Thus it is suggested to speak in an honorable manner which maintains decency. These days while texting, and giving each other undivided attention we slowly begin to transgress through simple complimentary phrases, and then flirtation, and towards romance. The privacy of the interaction creates Khalwah which is a communication between man and woman without the presence of a mahram and increases the chances of indecencies between the two.

The intention of forbidding Khalwah was to make the heart of the Muslim as pure as possible: hence Allah ﷻ forbade all possible means that may lead to evil, immorality and obscenity. Therefore, the love between man and woman should also be as pure as possible, and the only way to ensure its purity is to make it Halal. When a man and woman begin a relationship outside of a marriage, there is no commitment which leads to indecent consequences with the chances of immorality and fornication. In order to keep the relationship between man and woman free from any transgression and impurity, the Shariah does not allow for the opportunity of things getting out of hand. Even if ones intention might be pure, Khalwah exposes him/her to temptation where something may cross the mind of either of them; even if nothing physical happens between them at first, frequent meetings may lead to transgression.

A disciple of true love's forgotten creed understands love to be a form of worship, for the oneness of two souls brings them closer to their Creator. But how can one be in love without being able to freely communicate, and enjoy the presence of one another without such limitations? It all depends on understanding ones definition of love as being a sacred gift and a form of worship, and then internalizing the utmost importance of ensuring its purity, as opposed to the desire to simply be together and engaging in fulfilling personal desires. Love can either be a seed, or a spark. When one accepts it to be a gift from Allah ﷻ, one that has been planted in his/her heart like a seed, and seeks to nurture it within a marriage, it grows between the two. Conversely, the failure to regard it as such allows it to become nothing more than a spark, and when it is exposed to the air of transgression, it becomes a sinful flame that eventually becomes a fire. Fire is known to be uncontrollable, and it inevitably burns and leads to disappointments. It damages the heart.

When Allah ﷻ plants the seed in your heart, it becomes a test for you. Will you humiliate yourself by transgressing your boundaries, or will you seek towards permissible means of nourishing it in order for the love to grow? It can only grow through the blessings of Allah ﷻ if it is legitimated through marriage in which there are no barriers between man and wife. If He has inclined your heart towards another, engage in the act of making Du'a for Allah ﷻ to make it easier for you. Even if it is nothing more than a test for you, value its sacredness and pray for it to be yours for only Du'a can change the decree. Perhaps it has been decreed to you, upon the condition of being asked for, and is a prayer away from being yours.

Indeed accepting the decision of Allah ﷻ is the duty of a Muslim, as one is to be happy and thankful under all circumstances. However, people often confuse this for accepting things to be the way they are without making an effort. If Allah ﷻ has willed something and shown you a way, then by refusing to make Du'a for it, or making any effort towards it by simply accepting that if it is His decree it will inevitably come to you, then you deprive yourself of certain provisions. One must always remember that if it hadn't been for the will of Allah ﷻ, you would not have willed it. Therefore, if Allah ﷻ has planted the seed of love in your heart - Perhaps Allah ﷻ wants to give it to you and it is conditional upon Du'a and effort while simultaneously protecting your love from any impurity. It is not always the case that what is meant for you will be yours, but what is equally significant to remember is that, what is meant for you is at times conditional upon being asked for. Ibn Taymiyah, may Allah ﷻ bless his soul, states:

> "Allah ﷻ the Almighty has created His creation with some causes. He has commanded His servants to follow those causes in order to receive His forgiveness, His mercy and His reward in this life and in the Hereafter. Whoever thinks that he or she can achieve anything simply by trust and by neglecting the causes that Allah ﷻ the Almighty has commanded him or her to follow; or whoever thinks that

objects (certain provisions) do not depend on the causes, has really mistaken." [Al-Fatawa, 8/350]

Similarly, Imaam Ibn Qayyim Al-Jawziyyah (may Allah 𐤀 have mercy on him) tries to explain that there are people who believe that if something that is being supplicated for is already decreed for the servant, then there is no doubt that it is going to come to pass for him, regardless of whether he supplicates for it or not. And if it has not been decreed for him, then it will not come to pass, regardless of whether he asks Allah 𐤀 for it or not. He explains that in believing that statement, they have abandoned the supplication since there is no benefit in doing it, and in doing so (abandoning supplication) they are in great error.

> "These people, along with their excessive ignorance and misguidance are in clear contradiction, for if we were to follow their opinion, it would require us to reject all the different means for attaining something desired. So it can be said to one of them:
>
> If satisfying your appetite and quenching your thirst were already decreed for you, then there is no doubt that they are going to come to pass, whether you eat and drink or you don't. And if they were not decreed for you, they will not come to pass, whether you eat and drink or you don't.
>
> And likewise, if a child were decreed for you, then you will definitely receive it, whether you have sexual intercourse

with your wife or you don't. And if that was not decreed for you, then it will not come to pass. Thus there is no need for marrying, having sexual relations and so on and so forth." [Imaam Ibn Qayyim Al-Jawziyyah, in The Sickness and the Cure, pg. 22-23]

Imaam Ibn Qayyim Al-Jawziyyah corrects this view by explaining that the decreed result is preordained along with its proper means, which lead to its occurrence. One of these means is the supplication. With this view in mind, falling in love and being married to your beloved is not necessarily preordained just like that, without any means (leading to its occurrence), rather it is preordained along with its proper means (which will ensure its occurrence). So when a person comes across the means, the decreed matter will come to pass. And if he does not come across those means, the decreed matter is denied. In elaborating on this idea, Al-Jawziyyah says:

"So satisfying one's appetite and quenching ones thirst are preordained with (the means of) eating and drinking. Children are preordained with (the means of) sexual intercourse. Harvesting crops is preordained with (the means of) planting and, the withdrawal of the soul from an animal is decreed with slaughter. Likewise, entrance into Paradise is preordained with (good) deeds, while entrance into the Hellfire is preordained with (bad) deeds." [Imaam Ibn Qayyim Al-Jawziyyah, in The Sickness and the Cure, pg. 22-23]

Therefore if it is preordained for you to fall in love and marry of your choice, it could be preordained to you with its proper means which is Du'a. Hence, when you make Du'a, it shall come to pass and you will be married to the person of your choice. Similarly, if you do not engage in trying to obtain it through the preordained means of Du'a, it shall be denied to you. However, it is equally important to remember that some people are only meant to be lessons, and if they do not seem what is best for us, and are toxic to both our world existence and our hereafter, it is best to accept them to be as a lesson and to let go of them. We cannot make a mere stepping stone or an unavoidable crack in the sidewalk the purpose of our life, when perhaps it was only meant to be a minor setback or a distraction along the way.

Contrary to what we've previously discussed with regards to honoring love, when you disrespect love and humiliate it by undermining its sacredness, and when you fail to regard it as a blessing, it only humiliates you in return. When you abuse it and take it for granted and transgress the prescribed limits, it destroys you both emotionally by putting your heart through extreme distress and calamities, and spiritually because it takes you away from Allah ﷻ. To love is not a sin, but what you do in love and how far you transgress literally becomes your highway to Hell. We build imaginative heavens for ourselves as we stray further and further away from the word of Allah ﷻ through which the impurities in our love inevitably allow our reality to become no less than hell on earth.

In Surah Al-Hijr, Allah ﷻ recounts the story of Prophet Adam (Peace and Blessings be upon him) and Iblis, where Allah ﷻ commanded the assembly of Angels to prostrate to the creation of Prophet Adam (Peace and Blessings be upon him), all of whom complied except for Iblis (Satan) who refused due to his pride and ego. Upon his refusal, Allah ﷻ casted Iblis out of the Heavens and would eventually punish him for his disobedience. Iblis appealed to the mercy of Allah ﷻ and asked for respite until the Day of Judgement. Allah ﷻ being the Most Merciful, granted him respite, upon which a conversation between Allah ﷻ and Iblis goes as follows:

> (Whereupon Iblis) said: "O my Sustainer! Since Thou hast thwarted me, I shall indeed make (all that is evil) on earth seem goodly to them, and shall most certainly beguile them into grievous error - (all) except those of them who are truly Thy servants!" [Holy Quran, 15:39-40]

> Allah ﷻ said: "This course of action is all right with Me. Verily, thou shalt have no power over My creatures - unless it be such as are (already) lost in grievous error and follow thee (of their own will) - and for all such, behold, hell is the promised place, with seven gates leading into it, each gate will be assigned to a separate group from among them. Verily, those who are conscious of Allah ﷻ (shall find themselves in the hereafter) amidst the gardens and fountains of Paradise." [Holy Quran, 15:41-45]

In these verses it highlighted that Iblis promised to lead us astray, upon which Allah ﷻ promised that there are seven gates of Hell for those who follow Iblis. There is no authentic Hadith which mentions the names of the gates of Hell, but certain words are used in the Holy Quran to refer to Hellfire.

Hellfire has different names in the Holy Quran and each has a different description. One name for Hellfire is Jahannam which has a literal meaning of fearful, and dark. The word Jahm in particular (which stems from Jahannam) is used for the darkest part of the night, and verily Jahannam is a very dark place; certainly one in which you wouldn't want to be alone. Moreover, it is bottomless. When one transgresses the boundaries of love, instead of elevating you both spiritually and emotionally, it becomes a bottomless pit full of horrors and terrors which your heart incurs. If you have ever made the mistake of having transgressed its boundaries, have you not felt its eternal embrace both night and day, as equally and frivolously as if you'll never find your way out? Have you not lost sleep over an illicit affair, and felt like you're falling deeper and deeper into its dark bottomless pit in the endlessness of the night? Its transgression detaches you from your once cherished peace of mind, and both night and day become equally as dark and restless for you.

Another name used to describe Hellfire is Ladha. In Surah Al-Ma'arij, Allah ﷻ uses the word Ladha in the following verse:

> "There is no way out for them, except the Ladha (Fierce Blaze) which will scorch the inward organs and the outward flesh!" [Holy Quran, 70:15-16]

Its blazing flame is said to eat away at the body parts of transgressors one by one. Similarly when one transgresses the boundaries of love, the pain and turmoil that one brings upon one's self eats away at them internally. Since the love has not been legitimated through marriage, and therefore is free of commitment and only consists of promises that have no weight, there is always the fear that one could lose the beloved. At any moment when the beloved becomes inattentive, or begins to pull away from you, naturally you begin to doubt yourself of being enough for him/her and the feeling of not being enough eats you on the inside. It affects both your heart and your mind, which could eventually result in depressive symptoms and a loss of appetite which together begin to deteriorate your health. All of this which troubles you on the inside eventually begins to show externally as well, for you cannot hide such sadness for long.

Al-Hutamah is possibly one of the most descriptive names of Hellfire which means to crush something to pieces. It is mentioned in Surah Al-Humaza that:

> "Nay, but (in the life to come such as) he shall indeed be abandoned and thrown into the crushing torment of Hutamah. Ah, what will convey unto thee what the crushing torment of Hutamah will be? (It is) the fire of Allah ﷻ, kindled, which leapeth up over the hearts (of men). Verily, it will close in upon them in endless columns!" [Holy Quran, 104:4-9]

In Arabic the term is also used to describe a person who has a large appetite and is not very easy to satisfy. Similarly Hellfire breaks and crushes everything that is thrown into it like a person that chews his/her food to make it easier to digest, and no matter how much you throw into the Hellfire, it is never satisfied. When there is no blessing in love, it is just like this description of the Hell-Fire. Just like Al-Hutamah, it breaks you and chews

136

at you internally and all you feel is the presence of the pain. It destroys you to the point that there is absolutely no desire to do anything, you lose your appetite, you lose your will, you lose your sense to do anything productive. It literally crushes you into pieces, and as Allah ﷻ uses the terms "leapeth up over the hearts," to enslave the heart completely.

Saqar is also another name for the Hellfire. The term is used in Surah Al-Muddaththir where Allah ﷻ says:

> "(Hence) I shall cause him to endure the Saqar (in the life to come)! And what could make thee conceive what the Saqar is? It is a scorching fire, which leaves nothing to live and spares none (to die), it shrivels human flesh making (all truth) visible to mortal man. It is guarded by nineteen guards." [The Holy Quran, 74:26-30]

The Arabic term Saqara means the scorching of the sun and to further elaborate, Asaqrah refers to the very severe heat of the sun combined with hot winds. Allah ﷻ has promised that the Saqar will eat up the flesh of the human. Moreover, Allah ﷻ goes on to explain who will be cast into the Saqar:

> "Those (dwelling) in the Gardens (of Paradise), they will inquire of those who were lost in sin: 'What has brought you into the Saqar?' They will answer: "We were not among those who prayed, and neither did we feed the needy; and we were of the ones who indulged in sinning together with all (the others) who indulged in it; and

we used to deny the Day of
Judgement - until death came upon us
and we saw the reality of all that we
denied." [Holy Quran, 74:40-47]

Similarly, when love becomes infiltrated with impurities it
becomes a scorching fire in your heart which is so intense
it overwhelms you beyond repair. It continues to eat you
from the inside. The Saqar is for those who are guilty of
failing to offer prayers, who fail to feed the needy, who
indulge in sin, and for those who do not fear the Day of
Judgement, and forget that Allah ﷻ is watching.

When your love is impure, the chances of you going
down a path where you develop a disease of the heart
and mind become higher; esentially, depression.
Depression causes one to become detached from Allah
ﷻ, and therefore one does not fulfill the religious
obligations such as prayers. When depressed, one is too
preoccupied with sadness and self-fulfillment, that he or
she fails to tend to the rights and obligations he or she
owes to the Ummah and people around him or herself.
Moreover, transgressing and engaging in sinful acts with
a non-mahram becomes a slippery slope which
desensitizes you to the point that you may cross all
boundaries and even fornicate. In doing so you
completely abandon your religion and become of those
who are not conscious of Allah ﷻ, and thus the Saqar
burns even fiercely in your heart. Such kind of love is not
blessed by Allah ﷻ and is destined to result in
heartbreak, from various factors such as the lack of
commitment, unfaithfulness, the agony of questions that
have failed to be answered, etc. The overwhelming
emotions become just like the Saqar that neither let you
live, nor let you die and you become so beaten up that
there is no hope.

Another one of the names of Hellfire is Al-Jaheem. It describes hell as a blazing fire that is extremely hot, intense and fierce. When one is in love and has transgressed its boundaries without trying to legitimate it through a marriage, there is absolutely no promise of its survival. The literal meaning of Al-Jaheem is to light and stir up a fire where you add fuel and ensure it keeps burning. This is what happens when you disrespect the sacredness of love by giving your entirety to it, by exposing your deepest vulnerabilities to it without having done anything to commit. It's there today, with a strong possibility of being gone tomorrow. There is no blessing in such kind of a love, and the only thing one really has is a sense of longing; in fact an intense longing. In Surah Al-Haqqa, Allah ﷻ says:

> "(Thereupon the command will go forth:) "Lay hold of him, and shackle him by the neck and then cast him into the blazing fire, Jaheem; and then thrust him into a chain (of other sinners like him - a chain) the length whereof is seventy cubits: for, behold, he did not believe in Allah ﷻ, The Tremendous, and did not feel any urge to feed the needy, and so, no friend has he here today, nor any food except the pus from the washing of wounds."
> [Holy Quran, 69:30-36]

In accordance with the description of Al-Jaheem that Allah ﷻ provides, does the transgressor not attach him/herself completely to the beloved and eventually abandon his/her worship and belief in Allah ﷻ? In consequence of this, does his or her heart not blaze in the remembrance of its beloved? Has there been a time when you transgressed and did the fear of losing the beloved not burn as if you'd want to rip your heart right out of your chest? Upon transgressing and upon engaging in every sinful act, every interaction, every meeting, every touch of the beloved only fueled the fire. Did it not burn ever so fiercely inside of you? Did it not detach you from everyone else around you when became so consumed in pleasing your beloved, and in fulfilling your own illicit desires? That is Al-Jaheem; it is the consequence of failing to fulfill your rights and obligations to those who you owe them to. Eventually with the withdrawal of blessings from Allah ﷻ, the love does not increase, and thus fails to survive. Its failure to survive inevitably leads one to be abandoned by the beloved and to be left with nothing but loneliness.

As-Sa'eer is also another name for the Hellfire which appears in Surah Ash-Shura in which Allah ﷻ says:

> "(Thou art but entrusted with Our message:) and so We have revealed unto thee a discourse in the Arabic tongue in order that you may warn the residents of the Mother City (Makkah) and the cities around it, and forewarn them of the Day of the Gathering, (the coming of) which is beyond all doubt: (the Day when) some shall find themselves in paradise, and some in the blazing fire of Sa'eer." [Holy Quran, 42:7]

The Sa'eer is the blazing fire which is constantly kindled and ignited and has never ceased to be kindled from the moment it was created. Therefore the severity of its punishment will be so unimaginable that Allah ﷻ continues on to say in Surah Mulk:

"And they will add: "Had we but listened (to those warnings), or (at least) used our own reason, we would not (now) be among those who are destined for the blazing fire of Sa'eer. Thus will they come to realize their sins: but (by that time,) remote will have become all good from those who are destined for the blazing flame of Sa'eer. (As against this), behold, for those who stand in awe of Allah ﷻ although He is beyond the reach of their perception, there is forgiveness in store and a great reward." (Holy Quran: 67:10-12]

The Sa'eer is known to be the pit of agony, which is incomparable and unparalleled to any other type of punishment in hell. Transgression will lead you down the slippery slope, until you come to a point where the agony is nothing like you've ever been through before. It will include the longing for the beloved, the need for attention, and the eventual heartbreak that'll result from the withdrawal of mercy from Allah ﷻ. You will think about it day and night, and you will wish you hadn't done the things you did, you will admit to yourself and confess your sins similar to the inhabitants of As-Sa'eer and appeal to Allah ﷻ for mercy, but it will be too late. The thoughts will become a repetitive cycle of agony that will torture your mind day and night.

Lastly, the term Al-Haawiyah is also used to describe Hellfire. In some commentaries, this is known to be the last and most severe level of Hell. In Surah Al-Qari'a, Allah ﷻ says:

"Then, as for him whose scales are

heavy (with good deeds), he will live a pleasant life. But as for him whose scales are light, then the Haawiyah will embrace him like a mother embraces a child. Ah, what will convey unto thee what she (the abyss) will be? A raging fire." [Holy Quran, 101:6-11]

The Arabic term Hawaa means to fall from a height into a chasm or abyss. Allah ﷻ is specific with the metaphor He uses to describe this stage, saying that Haawiyah will embrace one like a mother. A mother's embrace is one that is incomparable, and if it was up to a mother, she would never let go. Similarly, when one enters Haawiyah, it embraces him or her eternally, and whoever enters this level of hell never gets out. You are thrown into its abyss from top to bottom, and it never ends. Similarly, depending on how far you transgress, its punishment is equally severe. Not only is the punishment severe in Hell itself, but the emotional and psychological torment is unparalleled. You may have heard of people who become so depressed and emotionally broken that it becomes nearly impossible to get through to them and to give them any hope of happiness. They become so entrapped by their own sorrow that life itself becomes a burden on them. It all starts with taking the first step - one touch, one embrace, one kiss, and depending on how far you go, and how detached you become from Allah ﷻ it becomes an endless torment that refuses to escape you.

Unfortunately all our preconceived definitions of love have led us into believing that love is nothing more than the fulfillment of physical desires through intimate relations. However, it is important to understand that each of these illicit relationships and encounters unfortunately leave us emptier and emptier on the inside as we go from individual to individual who fails to truly complete us.

We live in a time where it is extremely difficult to guard ourselves from one another, and our gaze is always exposed to the best versions of other people, not only through how they personally present themselves but also through their misguiding public representations of who they claim to be on social media. This type of love has become a commodity that can be easily marketed, a demand to which the supply is literally a click away. There are a number of mobile applications available to download which promise you that there are single people in your area readily available for a physical relationship without commitment. In many ways we are so exposed to the abundance of people at our disposal with whom we can talk to, share our vulnerable selves, and transgress beyond our comfort levels. Social networks allow us to poke who we like, message who we want, and we have countless options in our Direct Messages on applications such as Instagram and Facebook. It is almost as if people have lost the willingness to commit because as soon as relationships get difficult, there are many options available to us and replacing the beloved has become easier than ever. We've forgotten what a beautiful struggle love was actually meant to be and have replaced it with a completely different concept of the easily attainable. We've confused attraction for lust, and its fulfillment from love to infatuation. "Love" is literally at your fingertips, and you can choose who to be in love with at the easy swipe of either left or right.

One might begin to think that the Islamic understanding of love is completely different from whatever definition they've come across, and therefore the fulfillment of such love might be just as difficult to honor. In contrast, the fulfillment of such an understanding of love is easy. Within the marriage, love is meant to thrive and its only fulfillment is commitment. Sheikh Yassir Fazaga says:

The word 'love' in the Quran appears over 90 times, but it never goes on to provide a definition of love. It only states the very first consequence of love, which is 'committing.' Islam talks about commitment; if you truly love, then commit, if you do not commit then your claim of love is not real.

This means if you truly love something, and claim to make an open declaration of your love towards someone or something, you will commit. For example, if there is a woman you love; you will claim to love her dearly and hope to one day marry her. Since marriage does not happen overnight, what do you do for the several nights that fall between now and the night of your marriage? Love requires you to commit, and if you truly do love her, you'll commit to even the idea of her as being yours, as if she's always present even when she's not there until and even after she is truly yours.

Contrary to several ideas of being faithful in love, you do not just commit to one another after you are married: instead, true love requires you to commit to the very idea of each other and to be loyal to one another despite the absence, even if it is one-sided, unrequited love. That is what differentiates disciples of true love's forgotten creed from the rest of those who claim to be in love. This means to honor your love, you are obliged to guard your gaze, your modesty, and your heart in the name of the one you love. Once they are yours, the commitment leads the relationship between you and your spouse to being equivalent to a novel world full of passion and fulfillment for you to enjoy and grow in together.

In relationships outside of a marriage, there is no

formal commitment, but a mere promise or expectation of it. Although even in a marriage, there is no guarantee that a person will commit, but as long as you've chosen a person who is of good character, the help of Allah ﷻ descends in helping both the spouses maintain love for each other. On the contrary, outside of the marriage you often give someone the fully committed and faithful version of yourself that you are obligated to give to a spouse, without the promise of equal reciprocation, and without a signature on a Nikkah contract (Islamic prenuptial agreement) that would obligate them to honor their rights and responsibilities towards you. This means you do everything you normally would have done in a blessed relationship such as compromising your modesty, exposing your vulnerabilities, and making space in your heart for a person who has not even legally or contractually agreed to meet you all the way through. This essentially leads your heart to go through the levels of hell and compromises your peace of mind.

Eventually you realize that you've given too much of yourself away, and your own need to feel fulfilled is never attained. You give the deepest parts of your affection to someone, and they are not obliged to return any of it back to you. You put your priorities aside and make them your priority when they need you, but when you're alone they're never there for you. You try to communicate with them, but the gaps in communication only seem to get larger and larger, despite your efforts. You begin to give yourself excuses when they fail to explain themselves, because you are so deeply in love with them that you try your best to ignore the shortcomings and make it work as one-sidedly as possible. You begin to accept apologies they haven't even given you because you are so attached, that you are willing to compromise the love you truly deserve for whatever you're holding on to. The levels of hell your heart experiences eventually make you so desperate to want to feel any bit of happiness again, that you eventually begin to have no expectation in return and yet you are equally willing to give so much of yourself to them for the smallest bit of attention. Here is what the problem is. You committed to them wholeheartedly, without making them work for the most precious parts of yourself, and they've accepted it as something they're entitled to. The pedestal that you've put them on has spoiled them to such an extent that they lose the ability to see how much they're hurting you. Yasmin Mogahed in "Reclaim Your Heart," says:

> "If being 'in love' means our lives are in pieces and we are completely broken, miserable, utterly consumed, hardly able to function, and willing to sacrifice everything, chances are it's not love. Despite what we are taught in popular culture, true love is not supposed to make us like drug addicts." [Yasmin Mogahed, Reclaim Your Heart]

All of this agony is essentially Allah ﷻ giving you signs that you are in an illicit relationship in which one is not willing to commit to you, and there is no other way but to let go of that individual and attach to your Lord instead. Chances are you've abandoned the right path, and if you haven't completely, you've obviously let someone in an illicit relationship have a higher place in your heart than Allah ﷻ. Allah ﷻ then breaks you at the hands of that person to call you to Himself, to have you attach your heart to Him so you have another chance to completely cleanse your heart with His love.

Love is supposed to fulfill you and make you happier. Having a companion is meant to make your life easier, as that is what the purpose of blessing you with love and companionship was to achieve in the first place;

for one partner to give the other partner tranquility, and vice versa. But, if that is not what your love is doing, then chances are it isn't love. If you're constantly fighting for attention, and are more full of pain and frustration as opposed to being at peace; Allah 🕌 is showing you signs.

To save one's self from the agony and torment of such relationships, one needs to be reminded of their self-worth. Begin by asking yourself who you are. Your answer should always be that you are the fulfillment of someone's prayer, the embodiment of the second half to another soul who deserves you whole. Somewhere out there in the world, there is someone who longs to finally meet you, so they go into Sujood and pray for your safety. Use Allah 🕌's signs to remind yourself of your own worth. Therefore you need to guard your Emaan (faith), lower your gaze, preserve your modesty, and hold on to your heart so when the time for the fulfillment of the prayers that someone has made for you finally comes, you'd have been worth the wait. It is an absolute torment for someone to have prayed so hard for you, only to finally look into your eyes and to see that you long for someone else. Avoid committing to anyone outside of a marriage, because it has no guarantee of being honored, and Allah 🕌 withdraws His mercy and blessings from such a relationship.

Commitment within the marriage means work ing together to overcome all obstacles. Your spouse is your partner for life, and your other half. You are each other's priority, and the fulfillment of your rights and obligations towards each other takes precedence over everything else. It is the two of you against the world, working to preserve the marriage at all costs through effective communication, and the patience of listening and bonding. Both of you must constantly work together in de-escalating conflicts and in fostering harmony between each other, striking a balance between your marriage and the demands of the in-laws, and surviving financial difficulties, etc. The passion between spouses is a gift that brings them closer.

Wait, what? Passion? Is that even allowed in Islam? Of course it is! Premarital relations between man and woman are prohibited, but the relationship within the marriage should be as passionate as ever, and Islam promotes playfulness and friendship between the spouses.

In Abdul-Muhsin Al-Qaasim's Khutbah, "The Essentials for a Happy Marriage," he says:

> "Smiling enlivens the heart and wipes away hatred and praising the wife for her appearance, cooking and adornment wins her heart. Islam has allowed husbands to lie to their wives in order to increase the love between them... Exchanging gifts is the key to winning a heart and is a reflection of one's love. Being easy upon ones wife, abandoning ambiguity and bad communication and arrogance are ways to achieve a lasting happy marital life.
>
> Umar ibn al-Khattab, (May Allah ﷺ be pleased with him), said: 'A man should be like a child with his wife, but if she needs him, he should act like a man.'" [Essentials for a Happy Marriage, AlMinbar Khutbah No. 2592]

Therefore, playfulness and acts of friendliness such as

praising and adornment are encouraged between spouses. Islam also emphasizes on romance and foreplay between the spouses; in fact sexual intercourse without foreplay is equated to cruelty. Prophet Muhammad ﷺ said,

> "There are three people who are cruel... one of them is a person who has sexual intercourse with his wife without foreplay." [Wasa'il, Vol. 14, p. 40.]

In another occurrence, Prophet Muhammad ﷺ said:

> "No one among you should have sexual intercourse with his wife like animals; rather there should be a messenger between them." When asked about the messenger, he said, "It means kissing and talking." [Tahzibu'l-Ihya, Vol. 3, p. 110.]

Both sexual desire and the shyness between man and woman have been placed for very specific purpose. It is said that the sexual desire is to be unleashed when a woman is with her husband, but it must be shielded with shyness when she is with other people. Imam Muhammad al-Baqir explains the relationship between sexual desire and shyness very eloquently:

> "The best woman among you is the one who discards the armor of shyness when she undresses for her husband, and puts on the armor of shyness when she dresses up again." [Wasa'il, Vol. 14, p. 14-15]

Sayyid Muhammad Rizvi elaborates on this in "Marriage

and Morals in Islam," by saying that:

> "The husband and wife should feel completely free when they are engaged in mutual stimulation which is known as foreplay. There is nothing wrong, according to Islam, for a woman to be active and responsive during sexual intercourse.
>
> This is diametrically opposed to the sexual morality of the Christian Western world before the sexual revolution. Russell in Sex and Destiny says, 'Western women of a generation or two ago can recall being warned by their mothers that sexual intercourse was an unpleasant duty which they owed to their husbands, and that they were to lie still and think of England.' What else but a sexual revolt could such a morality breed?
>
> As for the Islamic Shari'ah, all the scholars are unanimous in saying that the act of sexual foreplay in itself is recommended. Likewise, it is recommended not to rush into sexual intercourse. The operative word is mutual pleasure and satisfaction." [Sayyid Muhammad Rizvi, Marriage and Morals in Islam]

It then becomes clear that the limitations that Islam places between man and woman before marriage are to protect the heart from any attachments that cause it to undergo undue hardships. However, such attachments are encouraged within the marriage itself as a reward, and a gift through which love itself would thrive between the spouses. Love means to commit to one another and to work together in making a marriage work. As long as both spouses are equally dedicated in doing so - love between them elevates in stages.

SECTION THREE

3.1
THE STAGES OF LOVE

At some point in your life, you may have come across someone trying to explain to you that the concept of love is incompatible with Islam. They may have convincingly quoted certain authentic Hadith which explains love to be a mental disease, and verses of the Quran to prove that love is nothing more than a transgression between man and woman. All of that is true only to the extent that your definition of love is incorrect. Essentially then, it is not love, the emotion that is incompatible with Islam, but the very definition of love is incompatible with Islam.

Whatever you've read thus far was meant to redefine the concept of love in your life to be something of a highly sacred nature. My aim was to rid you of the concept of love that fairy tales and mainstream media have instilled in your mind to be your limited understanding of something that is at the core of existence. Love is the divine inclination of one's heart towards another heart. Hazrat Inayat Khan explained that when love is centered in one object it is called love. When it is for several objects, it is called affection. When it is like a cloud, it is named infatuation. When its trend is moral it is devotion. When it is for God, the omnipresent and the omnipotent, in fact, the whole Being, then it is called divine love in which the lover becomes holy. There is no greater power than love, and when honored as such, it elevates in itself. In fact, the Urdu word "Muhabbat" comes from the Arabic word "Hubb(a)", which literally means seed; a seed that every human being has. Love sprouts like a seed and grows in both your heart, and in the heart of your beloved and the togetherness of two souls allows for you to come close to the oneness of your Creator. In consequence, if you disregard its sacredness, love spreads like a wildfire and in its destruction you feel the wrath of your Creator.

Various religions, schools of thought, and civilizations have tried to define love over time, and in doing so they not only defined it in terms of stages but differentiated between the kinds of love. The Ancient Greeks defined six different kinds of love. Roman Krznaric in "How Should We Live; Great Ideas from the Past for Everyday Life," provides a fascinating account of these six varieties of love. The first kind of love was "Eros", named after the Greek god of fertility, and it represented the idea of sexual passion and desire. However, contrary to the way mainstream media has positively portrayed this kind of love, the Greeks refused to see it as something positive. They saw it as something dangerous, and irrational which could take a hold of you and possess you. This idea of the loss of control frightened the Greeks. In today's popular idea of love this would seem highly unordinary because losing control is what most people look forward to in a relationship as they hope to fall madly in love.

The second variety of love was "philia," which meant deep friendship such as the kind of friendship between soldiers who fought side by side on the battlefield. This kind of love involved developing a sense of trust among friends, and showing loyalty to ones friends and sacrificing for them. The Greeks regarded the love between parents and their children as another kind of philia, sometimes called "storge."

The third kind of love was referred to as "ludus," which was the Greeks' idea of playful love such as the affection between children or young lovers. Ludus refers to the playfulness in a relationship most often in its early stages which involves flirting and teasing and adult frivolity which was almost a playful substitute for sex itself.

Roman Krznaric says that the fourth variety of love was perhaps the most radical. It was named "agape" which meant selfless love, or the love for everyone. This referred to the kind of love that one extended to all of mankind, including family members and strangers, and is similar to the idea of universal love understood by Sufis and in Theravada Buddhism.

"Pragma," was the Greek word for the concept of mature love. This stood for the deep understanding that developed between long-married couples who tried anything in their power to make their marriage last . This was done by making sacrifices and compromises to help the relationship work over time with patience and tolerance. This kind of love is focused more on making the effort of giving love as opposed to receiving love.

Lastly, the sixth variety of love was "philautia," which meant the love of the self. The Greeks realized that there were in fact two types of philautia which included the unhealthy kind associated with narcissism, where one becomes self-obsessed, and the healthier variety which enhanced one's wider capacity to love. This latter kind of love reflected the Buddhist inspired concept of "self-compassion" where the idea was that if one begins to love him or herself and feels secure in oneself, he or she will have plenty of love to give others.

On the other hand, Islamic Mystics such as Shaykh Zulfiqar Ahmed of the Naqshbandi Silsila (Naqshbandi Sufi Order) differentiated between true love and metaphorical love. In his book "Ishq-e-Ilahi," which was originally written in Urdu, he defines true love as Ishq Haqiqi which refers to the love for Allah ﷻ, while metaphorical love is Ishq Majazi which referred to the love for the creation of Allah ﷻ when it exists for the sake of fulfilling one's desires. Contrary to mystics of universalism such as Hazrat Inayat Khan, Islamic Mystics have traditionally frowned upon Ishq Majazi, and for that understanding Shaykh Zulfiqar Ahmed provides twelve principles.

The first principle of metaphorical love, or Ishq Majazi is defined as being driven by passion. The physical and external beauty of a man or woman is known as "husn" which generates passion, especially among youth. Nothing is of a greater influence in the material world than husn and it causes even the most intelligent of people to act irrationally. This is similar to the Greeks' idea of Eros, and they feared it for the same reason that it drives people to lose control of themselves because passion is associated with irrationality and sexual desire.

The second principle is that once the image of physical beauty becomes imprinted in a person's heart, that person essentially becomes helpless. Shaykh Zulfiqar Ahmed explains that Shaytan (Iblis/Satan) presents this image in such an attractive form that the person becomes absorbed with each glance.

The third principle is that being totally consumed by husn leads one to die a spiritual death. This happens when, despite being able to see clearly, one begins to view the faults of his beloved with admiration.

The fourth principle is that husn is ephemeral like the foam on the crest of an ocean wave, and therefore love that is based on its physical form cannot be maintained for too long. Since the nafs (the lower self/ soul) is blinded by desire it does not understand the ephemeral nature of husn and it fearlessly pursues the beloved in its attempt at gratification, regardless of the consequences.

The fifth principle is that when one is unable to approach the beloved, the metaphorical lover or Ashiq Majazi tries to reach a level of contentment with the sight of the beloved from afar. He/she consoles his/her heart thinking that seeing the beloved from afar is enough.

The sixth principle is that once the Ashiq Majazi has the opportunity to become close to his/her beloved, then his/her nafs (the lower self/soul) desires some sort of physical contact. The more passionate its desires are, the more it needs in terms of physical gratification. Therefore, even one who initially claimed to have true love in his/her heart free from all impurities, will eventually reveal his/her deceit in this manner.

The seventh principle is that once love degrades itself and its craving for husn leads to fulfillment of lustful desires and selfishness, it loses its humanity.

> "The truth is that no face is as attractive as it seems from a distance. No voice is as enchanting as it seems from afar. Is then the reality of physical attraction based on distance? If so, it would seem that it is better to keep a distance. Regardless, the metaphorical lover desires proximity to such an extent that he cannot be satisfied without physical consummation." [Shaykh Zulfiqar Ahmed, Ishq-e-Ilahi translated by Faqir Publications, page 61]

This then proves that love based on husn alone is a thirst that can only be quenched by physical consummation. It is therefore no more than lust and infatuation.

The eighth principle, Tazkiyah al-Nafs (purification

of the soul) involves a discussion about the purity and sacredness of love that I've been trying to establish throughout this book. Allah ﷻ, the Lord of the worlds, has created both man and woman with an instinctive mutual attraction. However, for their love to remain pure and Halal, He has also placed some restrictions and conditions for their relationships. As long as men and women live within these prescribed limits, they will be rewarded, and if they exceed these limits then they will be punished.

Purification of the soul is achieved through remaining steadfast on the daily prayers and through the dhikr (constant remembrance) of Allah ﷻ. When Tazkiyah al-Nafs is not achieved, a man's mind is always preoccupied with thoughts of women, and similarly a woman's mind is preoccupied with thoughts of men. Shaykh Zulfiqar Ahmed makes reference to one of the most famous love stories that have been told over time with regards to Ishq Majazi, which is that of "Laila and Majnun."

Majnun's real name was Qais who became extremely fond of Laila and his love eventually made him seem as if he had lost his mind completely, and thus he came to be known as Majnun, the Arabic word for crazy. Had he attained tazkiyah al-nafs, he would have held on to his sanity.

> "Majnun's story falls in the period of Hazrat Hasan (Peace and Blessings be upon him)... He once met Hazrat Hasan (Peace and Blessings be upon him) who said, "Qais, I have made peace with Amir Mu'awiyah. I have handed the reigns of leadership to those suited for it." Qais kept silent for a while. Hazrat Hasan (Peace and Blessings be upon him) asked him,

"What are you thinking about?" He replied, "I was thinking that the governorship actually suits Laila." Upon hearing this Hazrat Hasan (Peace and Blessings be upon him) stated, "You are crazy [Anta Majnun]!" and from then on he became known as Majnun." [Shaykh Zulfiqar Ahmed, Ishq-e-Ilahi translated by Faqir Publications, page 62]

The ninth principle is that if at any point the metaphorical lover is to be executed for his love, then he desires that his beloved be present to witness the scene.

The tenth principle is that the lover thinks that his eyes experience so much pleasure in looking at his beloved, that his heart becomes envious. Whereas, on the other hand, thinking about the beloved, his heart experiences so much pleasure that his eyes become envious.

The eleventh principle is that the metaphorical lover thinks that just by seeing a mere glimpse of his beloved he is imbued with new vitality.

The twelfth principle is that the metaphorical lover finds every movement and action of his beloved attractive and wants the beloved to correspond to his desires.

It then becomes clear that the concept of metaphorical love is very similar to the concept of love for the sake of passion as described by Hazrat Inayat Khan. It is driven by lust and attraction of the beloved's outwardly husn, and its only objective is to gratify and fulfill those desires through a physical and intimate relationship.

Shaykh Zulfiqar Ahmed agrees that an important aspect of the human life is to fulfill the physical needs of the body, for which Allah ﷻ has placed the limitations of Haram and Halal, and such needs can only be legitimately fulfilled through marriage. Another aspect is the need to fulfill one's basic desires, and such desires have absolutely no end and become an addiction of a sort, a disease of the mind that is impossible to cure. Therefore, Allah ﷻ has placed limitations and defined mahrams and non-mahrams for one to be able to control temptation and lustful desires, so one does not expose him/herself to vulnerabilities.

Marriage (Nikkah) has been ordained as an act of worship (Ibadah) and even looking at non-relatives (ghair mahram) of the opposite gender is unlawful. The freedom between a man and woman within the marriage allows for each other to fulfill his/her physical needs and provides them the opportunity to remain satisfied and content.

> "It is related in a hadith that if a man's gaze happens to fall on a woman and her beauty attracts him, then he should go unto his wife. Whatever that woman possesses, his wife possesses as well." [Shaykh Zulfiqar Ahmed, Ishq-e-Ilahi translated by Faqir Publications, page 65]

As far as being attracted to different features, figures and complexion is concerned, the creations of Allah ﷻ are so diverse and rivaling each other in beauty, it is impossible for one to obtain it all. One can be attracted to the physique of one, and the smile of another person. Thus if one submits to his base desire to fulfill his lust, it becomes impossible to actually fulfill for one can never be satisfied because of the diversity of the beautiful creations of Allah ﷻ. Therefore, as long one falls in love with the outwardly beauty of another, and that becomes his or her sole basis of 'being in love,' then it will have negative consequences because it is not love at all; it is a mere fascination, or an extreme infatuation - a sickness that must be cured.

At this point one must reflect on a current or past experience of ever feeling as if they have been in love. After reading the perspective provided by Shaykh Zulfiqar Ahmed, can you still say that it is really love? Are your feelings based solely on the outwardly beauty of a woman, or the beauty of a man? Is the primary reason for you not being able to move on because his or her physical features are something that strongly attract you? Shaykh Zulfiqar Ahmed explains that if a person's gaze is tainted and his heart is full of lust, then even if he continues fulfilling his desires, he will tire but his desires will not end. Desire is a thirst that is never quenched, and there is no other cure for such a sickness except the fear of Allah ﷻ, [Ishq-e-Ilahi, page 67]. This is one of the reasons why many marriages in contemporary times do not last for too long because they've been founded on lust that has been confused for love, and either or both of the individuals needed a legitimate means to fulfill the physical desires.

It is important for both men and women to guard their modesty and protect their hearts from pre-marital attachments, especially attachments which are based on mere attraction. You may at some point in your life be approached by someone claiming to be in love with you, and the unwarranted attention may seem flattering, but it is dangerous to open your heart to it. One needs to keep in mind that Allah ﷻ has naturally made men and women attracted to each other, but it is the inclination of two hearts that Allah ﷻ blesses if they seek legitimate means of marriage to be together for the sake of Allah ﷻ, as opposed to being together for the sake of fulfilling one's passion and desire. Shaykh Zulfiqar Ahmed attests that the ultimate consequence of such metaphorical love is the separation of the lover and the beloved and thus, disgrace in this world and in the Hereafter. Allah ﷻ has explicitly warned the believers not to transgress, and when one ultimately forgets the commands and allows him/herself to be taken by such flattery, he/she allows for the person claiming to be in love with them to make room in their heart. In letting their guard down, they often begin to develop feelings in return. Although these feelings may be genuine, for one is naturally reciprocating to the love someone claimed to have for them, but ultimately he/she has allowed him/herself to transgress and for that there are consequences. Do not be the one to let yourself fulfill the desire of another, and temporarily quench their thirst, for once they've taken what they needed, they will discard you.

When one is simply blinded by the metaphorical love for another, all the flaws are naturally disregarded and one pays no attention to the apparent weaknesses in the level of compatibility between them because of the longing to be together at all costs.

> At the time of death, the true reality of life becomes manifest before everyone. All infatuations end. All illusions fade. This is the final end of metaphorical love. Whoever wishes to lead a successful life must abstain from it. [Shaykh Zulfiqar Ahmed, Ishq-e-Ilahi translated by Faqir Publications, page 67]

It is then clear that metaphorical love ends with death, however what needs to be ascertained is that love for the sake of love itself beyond the desire for physical consummation is one that lasts. The prime example of this is the love between Prophet Muhammad ﷺ and Khadijah (may Allah ﷻ be pleased with her).

> "The death of a loved one shows the vulnerability of mortal love. But the love of Muhammad and Khadijah was not mortal; it was immortal. When Khadijah died, Muhammad's love for her did not die. In fact, his love for Khadijah not only outlived her but actually went on growing even after her death. Not even the presence, in his house, of nine wives, could inhibit the growth of that love, and his love for her was always struggling to find expression." [Sayyid Ali Ashgar Razwy, Khadijatul Kubra - A Short Story of Her Life, Chapter 16]

The fruitfulness of a marriage based on love for the sake of Allah ﷻ, and one that maintains the purity and sacredness of love before the marriage is beyond words. The love between Prophet Muhammad ﷺ and Khadijah (may Allah ﷻ be pleased with her) was of the purest of kinds, and with her love she banished all his anxieties, fears and sorrows. Their marriage was as fresh on the last day as it was on the first, and Khadijah (may Allah ﷻ be pleased with her) remained forever alive in his ﷺ's heart.

While it is true that Prophet Muhammad ﷺ was a man from among us, he was no average man. He was the beloved of Allah ﷻ himself, and he was absolutely perfect. Surely there is no comparison between any man and Prophet Muhammad ﷺ. However, the fact that Allah ﷻ has chosen him from among us, and that he left his example behind (Sunnah) for us to follow, is a reminder that we can strive to be equally as perfect. Had Prophet Muhammad ﷺ been from another creation all together, it would surely have been an unreasonable expectation for anyone to follow him, but he was from among us, born into a society equally as corrupt as our own, vulnerable to the same sins, but Allah ﷻ guided him. In Surah Al-Kahf Allah ﷻ explicitly told Prophet Muhammad ﷺ to remind us that he is just as much of a human being as any of us.

> O Muhammad, tell them: "I am but a human being like you; the revelation is sent to me to declare that your God is the One and Only God; therefore, whoever hopes to meet his Rabb, let him do good deeds and join no other deity in the worship of his Rabb." [Holy Quran, 18:110]

Similarly, Khadijah, the wife of the beloved of Allah ﷺ, was from among our own kind as well, which makes their love and marriage an example for all of mankind. She was not specially created like Hawwa (Eve) (may Allah ﷻ be pleased with her) who was created out of the rib of Prophet Adam (Peace and Blessings be upon him), instead she was decreed to Prophet Muhammad ﷺ in this world as spouses are decreed to all of us. If we reject the metaphorical notions of love based on lust and desires, and if we allow ourselves to be subject to the commandments of Allah ﷻ, we too can allow ourselves

164

to be guided to our decreed partners. We too can strive to love as beautifully and as equally as the love between Prophet Muhammad ﷺ and Khadijah (may Allah ﷻ be pleased with her).

Dr. Javad Nurbakhsh of the Nimatullahi Sufi Order in "Discourses on The Sufi Path" discusses that human love can be classified under three categories according to the intensity, quality and limitations. He explains that the first form of love is friendship based on social conventions where two individuals act in accordance with the principle: "I for myself, you for yourself; we love each other, but we have no expectations of each other." Dr. Nurbakhsh defines this as the love of ordinary people.

The second form of love is based on a more solid foundation and is developed among those who live together based on the principle: "I for you, you for me; we love each other, having mutual expectations of each other." Dr. Nurbakhsh explains how this is the form of love that includes profound love as well as familial love which involves emotional exchanges on a more or less equal footing.

Lastly, the third kind of love is one that transcends all conventions that are based on mutual expectations and is founded on the principle: "I am for you, you are for whoever you choose; I accept whatever you want without any expectations whatsoever."

The Sufi's concept of "Divine Love" whether it is a Mystic of Universalism or Islamic Mystic, involves a devotion to Allah ﷻ that exemplifies this latter form of love. This kind of love is devoid of any constraints or conditions, and one who is on the Path of Divine Love says with contentment and submission to Allah ﷻ: "I am satisfied with whatever You want, without any expectations, and love You without any thought of reward."

In the "Sufi Journal", Dr. Nurbakhsh states that "human love begins with an encounter - our conceptions and descriptions of the person we love come later. Descriptions help us to be connected with the person we have come to love only after that love has been ignited though the encounter." (Issue 81, 2011) Various Sufi traditions have described the encounter to be the beginning of love, including Universalists and Islamic Mystics who differentiate between metaphorical love and true love.

Different Sufi traditions have not only defined the types of love, but also described the various stages through which love undergoes. For example, the well known Sufi Khwaja Nasiruddin of Delhi (Chistiyya Order of Sufis) described ten stages of love, and fifty phases of love. Generally, the Chisti stages of love include: Ulfat (friendship and attraction), Sadaaqat (true friendship and loyalty), Mavaddat (excitation of the heart and passionate desire), Hawaa (passionate desire and longing), Shagaf (violent affection), Mahabbat (exclusive attachment), Ishq (true love), Enslavement, Valah (bewilderment). Certain Sufi Orders have also spoken of the stages of Ibadat, Junoon, and Maut.

Before exploring the stages of love in detail, I wanted to remind the reader that Mystics of Universalism such as Hazrat Inayat Khan have differentiated between love for the sake of love, and love for the sake of passion, and Divine Love. Similarly, Islamic Mystics such as Shaykh Zulfiqar Ahmed have differentiated between Ishq-e-Majazi being metaphorical love based on the desire and lust for husn (beauty), and Ishq-e-Haqiqi which is Divine Love. Some Islamic Mystics have further added the category of Ishq-e-Rasul which is the development of an intense feeling of love for Prophet Muhammad ﷺ who was the most beloved to Allah ﷻ.

Throughout the book I have maintained that Islam promotes the idea of Halal love, of which the prime example was the love between Prophet Muhammad ﷺ and Khadijah (may Allah ﷻ be pleased with her). I believe that Islamic Mystics in their discussions and analysis have completely missed this concept and have tried to either dismiss any sort of human love besides Divine Love as being metaphorical, or have tried to include it within the category of Divine Love by claiming that loving anyone for the sake of Allah ﷻ is equal to loving Allah ﷻ himself, as claimed by Shaykh Zulfiqar Ahmed in Ishq-e-Ilahi.

In my efforts to assert that Halal Love is a category of its own, one that is independent of the meaning of metaphorical love and Divine Love, I'd like to remind you of the following few references. In Surah Al-Maida Allah ﷻ says,

> "Today the unbelievers have given up all their hope of vanquishing your religion. Have no fear of them, fear Me. Today I have perfected your religion for you, completed my favor upon you and approved Al-Islam as a Deen (way of life for you)." [Holy Quran, 5:3]

Moreover, there is a Hadith which was reported through conversation between Husain (may Allah ﷻ be pleased with him) and Zaid (may Allah ﷻ be pleased with him) that is of significance here. Zaid (may Allah ﷻ be pleased with him) narrated that one day Prophet Muhammad ﷺ stood up to deliver a sermon at a watering place known as Khumm between Mecca and Medina, he praised Allah ﷻ, extolled Him and delivered the sermon:

> "O people, I am a human being. I am about to receive a messenger (the angel of death) from my Lord and I, in response to Allah ﷻ's call, (would bid good-bye to you), but I am leaving among you two weighty things: the one being the Book of Allah ﷻ in which there is right guidance and light, so hold fast to the Book of Allah ﷻ and adhere to it. The second are the members of my household, I remind you (of your duties) to the members of my family." [Sahih Muslim 2408a, or Book 31, Hadith 5920]

This Hadith was also transmitted on the authority of Abu Hayyan (may Allah ﷻ be pleased with him) but with this addition:

> "The Book of Allah ﷻ contains right guidance, the light, and whoever adheres to it and holds it fast, he is upon right guidance and whosoever deviates from it goes astray." [Sahih Muslim 2408c, or Book 31, Hadith 5922]

A review of these sources concludes that Allah ﷻ has perfected religion within the Holy Quran, and the example of the Prophet ﷺ and his family is to be a means of guidance to us. Therefore, in the Holy Quran, Allah ﷻ has defined the only legitimate love and relationship between a man and a woman to be within a Nikkah (marriage) as husband and wife. He reminded us that He specifically created the two of them for the purpose of completing one another and for being a means of peace and tranquility for each other. The purpose of the creation of Hawwa (Eve) (May Peace be upon her) was so both could dwell in each other's love and so she could provide Prophet Adam (Peace and Blessings be upon him) peace and tranquility. Allah ﷻ has laid out the foundations of Halal love, and Prophet Muhammad ﷺ explicitly told us to hold on to the Quran as guidance, therefore one cannot dismiss this kind of love, especially if Prophet Muhammad ﷺ had exemplified it within his own marriages. This sort of human love which goes uncategorized is worthy of being recognized and cannot be dismissed or included within the category of Ishq-e-Majazi or Ishq-e-Haqiqi.

The love that Prophet Muhammad ﷺ had for his wives including Khadijah (may Allah ﷻ be pleased with her) is what I believe true and pure Ishq is that one can have for another human. This is what the disciples of true love's forgotten creed should strive for. At this point, it is necessary to point out that I mean absolutely no disrespect towards Islamic Mystics, but I firmly believe that true love for another human being exists, and is entirely different from Ishq-e-Majazi (metaphorical love) which is only based on lust and desire for beauty. The love of Prophet Muhammad and Khadijah was an example of this true love, for their love was the purest of all. Confusing this love for an extension of Ishq-e-Haqiqi (Divine Love) is also inappropriate, for the love that any human can have for the Lord of the Worlds, and the King of Kings, is incomparable, and the love for Allah images simply exceeds all forms of love without question. Therefore, Halal love deserves its own category of love for it is no innovation to Islam, but one of the initial purposes of the creation of man and woman, a love that Allah images has defined through the Holy Quran by prescribing the limitations outside of a marriage, and awarding the liberties within the marriage; and the Sunnah of Prophet Muhammad images being an example of it. Halal Love is the purest form of human love; it is Ishq, the basis of this book.

Shaykh Zulfiqar Ahmed writes:

> To love those among creation that Allah images has commanded to love is in truth a completion of love for Allah images. Therefore, to love the Prophet images is in reality to love Allah images. Similarly, having love for the Sahabah (noble Companions), Ahl al-Bayt (the family of the Prophet), and the Awliya (friends of Allah images) also falls in this category... In essence, to have love for the Prophet images is a condition of one's Iman (faith). While, to love one's Shaykh (Spiritual Guide), parents, children, and spouse is the completion and the perfection of one's love for Allah images. Thus, true love being Ishq Haqiqi is to love both Allah images and those among His creation that he commanded us to love." [Shaykh Zulfiqar Ahmed, Ishq-e-Ilahi, pg. 73]

He explains familial love, and the love for one's spouse to

be equal to and precisely the same as the love for Prophet Muhammad ﷺ and the love for Allah ﷻ. I maintain that the love for Allah ﷻ is the highest and purest form of love, and is incomparable to the love for any human. The only love that could possibly compare is the love for Prophet Muhammad ﷺ, the beloved of Allah ﷻ himself. Ishq, or pure humanly love that we now understand to be Halal love, must be understood as a category of its own because while Nikkah (the legitimation of Halal love, marriage) is a form of worship, the love for Allah ﷻ simply is worship.

The stages of Halal love that will be discussed in the upcoming chapters, will overlap with some of the Chistiyya stages of love. These stages of Halal love include Ulfat (attraction), Unsiyat (attachment), Mavaddat (higher dimension of Unsiyat), Hawaa (affection and longing), Shagaf (violent love), Ishq (true love), Ibadat (worship and enslavement), Junoon (madness and bewilderment), and Maut (death of the self).

3.2
ULFAT
(ATTRACTION)

"Human love begins with an encounter," explains Dr. Alireza Nurbakhsh in the Sufi Journal (Issue 81, 2011). As previously quoted, our conceptions and descriptions of the person we love come later. Nurbakhsh claims descriptions help us to be connected with the person we have come to love, only after the love has been ignited through the encounter. One cannot engage and participate in love for too long through descriptions alone, and an encounter with the object of our love is important. One may hear of a person's beauty, or about a person's strength, and qualities, and a desire then rises in him or her engage in some sort of contact with this person. This is the beginning of Ulfat. It creates an inclination of the heart towards the object of love and the encounter affirms the inclination as one becomes pleasantly convinced the object of their love meets these descriptions.

It is human nature for one to be inclined towards the outwardly beauty of other people, and that is called attraction. The stage of Ulfat is essentially being initially attracted to our object of love, the beloved. According to the Chistiyya Stages of love, it is at this point when one seeks to hide the inclination of his/her heart towards the beloved, because one is unsure of his or her own feelings only until a sense of yearning overcomes the individual. The lover then wants some sort of direct contact with the beloved and seeks to pursue a friendship. Upon initiation of contact, one then is overcome by the desire to be fully aware of the beloved's condition, and yearns for the beloved to be aware of his/her condition. At this point one acknowledges his/her own feelings and begins to make subtle professions of love through exchanges of gifts, flirtation, and flattery.

This is a very early stage for one to be professing love, for it is merely a self acknowledgment of one's attraction and an initial encounter with the beloved. It is this self acknowledgement that makes one begin to yearn for some sort of contact with the object of attraction. The eventual contact overwhelms one with the possible reciprocation of attention, and perhaps this excitement is often confused for love. Similarly, many people believe in love at first sight, but for disciples of true love's forgotten creed (henceforth, Disciples of Ishq), this mocks the very essence of love, for love is far deeper than the initial attraction to superficial beauty.

To be convinced of being in love at this stage is simply falling into infatuation, and it reaffirms the idea of love for the sake of pleasure that Mystics of Universalism such as Hazrat Inayat Khan had defined. It is solely based on the outwardly beauty of a person. It is no wonder then that Islamic Mystics have completely denounced it as being metaphorical because it is an infatuation or desire for husn. It is irrational and unrealistic.

There are many love stories told over the years about different lovers who have come to be known as legendary for the sacrifices they made in love, and the hardships they endured. There are many lessons which could be taken from such stories. One of these stories is known as "Heer Ranjha", which is told throughout the Punjab regios of both India and Pakistan.

Harjeet Singh Gill in "Heer Ranjha; and other legends of the Punjab", writes that it was the great poet Waris Shah who initially wrote of the story of Heer and Ranjha in the form of poetry. Gill claimed that it was God who made love the fundamental principle of this universe, who was the first Ashiq (first lover), and the Prophet ﷺ was His Mashuq (first beloved). He claimed that God blesses those who live and die in love.

Harjeet Singh Gill tells the story of "Heer Ranjha" as one that sheds light on many cultural and societal problems that existed during the seventeenth century, some of which are still prominent. The story goes: Dhido Ranjha (henceforth Ranjha) lived in the land of Takht Hazara on the bank of river Chanab. He was the youngest son of the Chief of the village, and was the most loved and spoiled out of all his elder brothers. He was envied by his brothers and their wives, and when the father died, the village was divided and Ranjha got the worst of it. Since he had been spoiled throughout his life, he was unable to manage the affairs of his land, and was insulted and ridiculed by his family members. He eventually decides to leave Takht Hazara one day. On that evening he arrives at a mosque where a Mullah (priest) let him stay the night. In the morning he was on his way to the country of the Sials across the river.

Across the river resided Heer, the beautiful daughter of Chuchak, the Chief of the Sials. On the bank of the Chanab river, when he finally arrives Ranjha is completely oblivious of where he is about to rest, and he falls asleep on Heer's bed. When Heer and her friends arrive, they are disgusted by this act of transgression and begin shouting at him. As Heer is about to strike him with her stick, Ranjha wakes up and is "beholden by Heer's celestial beauty and charm," he smiles and he surrenders. [Harjeet Singh Gill, Heer Ranjha, pg 7]

"Their eyes meet and they exchange sentiments of love and faith." [Harjeet Singh Gill, Heer Ranjha, pg 7] As Heer exchanges her sentiments of love, Ranjha is skeptical, because sacred texts at that time had warned that one should beware of the games women play.

174

However, Heer invokes God, the highest principles of divine love, and promises to be faithful under all circumstances and against all odds.

In order to continue his meetings with his beloved, Ranjha devises a plan and becomes the Sials' family cowherd. Every morning, Ranjha would take the buffaloes and cows around the thick forest along the banks of the river Chanab where Heer would join him daily. One day, her uncle, Kaido, finds out about the affair. Kaido gives news to the family and the Chief of the Sials becomes heavily disappointed that his daughter has brought disgrace to the honour of the family. Kaido proposes that the only viable solution now is to marry Heer off to Saida, the son of the Kheras; the Chief across the river, on the other side of the Sial country.

When Heer returns home, she is met with her mother who is disgusted by her for ruining the family name. Heer respectfully replies that she is doing no such thing.

> "Her relation with Ranjha is the purest of human unions. It is sanctified by God, Himself. She has solemnly promised herself to Ranjha. And, as the Holy Quran itself states, there is no more serious crime than backing out from one's word. This promise of hers is the most sacred word. If she betrays Ranjha, she will be pushed into the fires of Hell forever." [Harjeet Singh Gill, Heer Ranjha, pg 9]

The same scenario is repeated when her father, Chuchak, and her brother, Sultan, admonish her. On the one hand, the honor of the family is invoked, and on the other, the sanctity of love blessed by God, Himself. [Harjeet Singh Gill, Heer Ranjha, pg 9]

In explaining herself to her family, Heer invokes the great lovers of the religious and the secular traditions, who died for the sake of their highest principles of faithfulness and fortitude, whose actions were ultimately approved by the authorities of the Church and State. However, her parents are too quick to negotiate a marriage proposal with Saida, the son of the Chief of the Kheras.

During the marriage ceremony, the Muslim priest, the Qazi, reminds Heer of the rules of the Islamic tradition that both sides must willingly agree to the Nikkah, in the presence of two witnesses and a legal negotiator. She makes him aware that she is already married to Ranjha in the presence of the Almighty God and her witnesses are the saints, and the Prophet ﷺ is her legal negotiator. The Qazi calls this a figment of her imagination and advises her to follow the will of the parents. Heer continues to defend her case by reminding the Qazi that according to the sacred texts those who do not fulfill their promises go to hell. The Qazi then claims that the honour of the family is more important and that she cannot make up her own rules. Heer maintains that she is not making her own rules:

> "She has the highest respect for her religion and her tradition, but above all, she has faith in the supreme ethics of divine love and the sanctity of the union approved by God Himself. The Islamic tradition clearly states that she cannot be married against her will, against her solemn promise given to another man." [Harjeet Singh Gill, Heer Ranjha, pg 10]

176

Clearly, it is not she who is transgressing against the tradition, but it is the Qazi who is misinterpreting the sacred texts. The Qazi soon realizes that there is no use of arguing, and calls for the witnesses and marries her off with Saida. Harjeet Singh Gill explains:

> "After all, this so-called condition of mutual assent is only a formality. One never really bothers about whether the girl and the boy are willing or not. Marriage is a union of the two families, it is invariably a social and economic contract held by the feudal virtues of honor and chastity. If every girl is allowed to marry the boy of her choice, what will happen to the social and cultural order without which no religious tradition can survive. The socio-political order depends upon the equality of exchange." [Harjeet Singh Gill, Heer Ranjha, pg 12]

Ranjha is the son of the Chief of Takht Hazara, despite being a cowherd/domestic servant to the Sial family, which means that Heer is not transgressing the laws of the feudal order. However, the people of the society are worried that love is a contagious disease. The daughters of others may not be as lucky, for their lover may not be the son of a Chief of a neighboring feudal class; hence it would upset the whole order of society which has been a tradition passed down through centuries.

Harjeet Singh Gill explains that apart from the Hindu society which had a caste system, the Muslim social structure in Punjab was also based on distinctions such as professional classes.

"There is a class of cobblers, a class of goldsmiths, a class of ironsmiths, a class of washermen, a class of potters, a class of fishermen and so on. These classes have no religious barriers and probably not much economic discrepancies but culturally these thresholds cannot be crossed. One is born into a certain class and stays there forever." [Harjeet Singh Gill, Heer Ranjha, pg 12]

In the context of Heer and Ranjha, the poet Waris Shah explained that the problem with love is that its 'current' is too strong to be confined within these social classes. If the floods of the emotions of love are not controlled, the whole world order which is built upon these classes will be inundated, and obviously, this cannot be allowed.

"If the daughter of a cobbler runs away with the son of a goldsmith, the goldsmith's daughter with the son of a potter, then what will happen to the purity and the excellence of these professions, for according to Waris Shah it takes thirty-one generations to acquire finesse in art and techniques in each domain." [Harjeet Singh Gill, Heer Ranjha, pg 13]

The end of the story has been narrated in several different ways across the region of Punjab. Waris Shah writes that Heer and Ranjha eventually become one and are consumed by the most violent current of love, desire, and passion. Some narratives explain that they eventually find each other and elope after a long night of celebration of their divine love and profane lust. Another narrative writes that these lovers after eloping are caught by Saida, and are brought to the court of the prince of that domain. The just king awards Heer to Ranjha and they return to Takht Hazara to live happily ever after. Whereas, another version states that when Saida threatens to take Heer away, she swallows snake poison and dies. In this account Ranjha is struck by grief and also collapses on the corpse of Heer, and they are buried together in the same tomb, united forever.

The story of "Heer Ranjha" is one that is known to be timeless and is exemplified as a tragic romance. Many young and passionate 'lovers' when faced with hardships view themselves as Heer and Ranjha, and passionately vouch not to become such a tragic love story for centuries to come. What exactly is so exemplary of this love story? What makes it something to idolize? What makes a man want to say that he will love his partner like Ranjha loved Heer? It is important to note that in this particular account of Heer Ranjha, Harjeet Singh Gill writes that Heer proposed the two of them should elope and run so far away that no one would ever be able to find them. Upon hearing this, Ranjha advised her that love was sacred and eloping would bring them humility. It was only after she was married that Ranjha had gone completely mad and devised many plans to attain Heer at any cost. What is exemplary about this love story is that the two of them did not give up, for one never gives up on true love. Physical separation cannot separate two souls from one another when in love. Heer kept her faith in God the entire time, and remained chaste by abstaining from her husband. Both Heer and Ranjha had faced a tremendous amount of hardships, and Ranjha even became a Yogi under the discipleship of a Yoga Guru in order to reach the land of Heer's in-laws. Eventually when he reaches the land of her in-laws, rumors spread that there is a beautiful Yogi in town from Takht Hazara who is blessed by God and can cure all diseases, and Heer gets excited upon hearing this news as she knows it can only be Ranjha. With the help of her sister in-law, she pretends to be poisoned by a snake so she can meet the Yogi Ranjha. This is how these two lovers are finally reunited, and eventually elope.

I personally refuse to idolize such stories since the love of Prophet Muhammad ﷺ and Khadijah (may Allah ﷻ be pleased with her) itself is beyond any worldly love story. But the lesson one can take from stories like that of Heer and Ranjha is that if two souls are meant to be together, they are eventually united under the right circumstances and after the trials that are destined to them have been faced. This is a story that has been told over and over again for decades, but was it really love? Perhaps we are in no positon to decide if the profession of love at first sight, and vows of loyalty and faithfulness at first encounter constitute as real love, but attraction does play a significant role in who we eventually fall in love with.

One of the questions one may ask is whether attraction is allowed in Islam. It is important to note that attraction is permissible, but there is a difference between physical attraction and the attraction to one's character and personality. Even though both are permissible, they are not necessarily prerequisites to marriage. The love between Prophet Muhammad ﷺ and any of his wives was not based on attraction per se but a mutual agreement, for all of the women he married after Khadijah (except for Ayesha) were very old, and his personal desires did not constitute the reasons for the marriages. In fact, even with regards to his first marriage with Khadijah, her proposal was based solely on admiration of his character and his more soulful characteristics such as the integrity and the intelligence which Khadijah became fond of. Moreover, the marriages that followed had been for political and social reasons. Regardless of the lack of physical attraction in the marriages, the Prophet ﷺ treated his wives equally and fairly even though they were of a different color, age, race, tribe and social status. However, Prophet Muhammad ﷺ understood the significance of attraction between a couple, and encouraged it because the lack of attraction may cause individuals to seek it elsewhere, outside of the marriage.

Islam is very specific about one having to lower his or her gaze in order to encourage people to protect their souls and hearts from any impurities. That is one of the reasons marriage was advised as completing half of one's religion because both men and women are permitted to enjoy the company of one another within a marriage and engage in relations which are otherwise prohibited. It was reported by 'Alqama in Sahih Muslim, and Sahih al-Bukhari:

> While I was walking with 'Abdullah at Mina, 'Uthman happened to meet him. He stopped there and began to talk with him. Uthman said to him: Abu 'Abd al-Rahman, should we not marry you to a young girl who may recall to you some of the past of your bygone days; thereupon he said: If you say so, Allah ﷻ's Messenger ﷺ said: O young men, those among you who can support a wife should marry, for it restrains eyes from casting (evil glances), and preserves one from immorality and helps guard his modesty (ie. his private parts from committing illegal sexual intercourse etc.); but those who cannot should devote themselves to fasting for it is a

means of controlling sexual desire. [Sahih Muslim: 1400 a, or Book 8, Hadith 3231. Sahih al-Bukhari: 5066, or Vol. 7, Book 62: Hadith 4]

Moreover, marriage not only helps one avoid immorality but it is a means to lawfully control sexual desire, and it is important for one to be able to have an attraction towards his or her spouse for these desires to be fulfilled. Jabir (may Allah ﷻ be pleased with him) reported that Prophet Muhammad ﷺ told his companions that a woman advances and retires in the shape of a devil, so when one sees a woman, he should come to his wife, for that will repel what he feels in his heart. This is not to say that the patriarchal notions of the Arab world blame the female to be a devil in order to rid blame from men and normalize their sexual desires, as some would be quick to conclude, instead it means that the inclination towards sexual desire between a man and a woman is instinct, and Shaytaan is easily able to take advantage of this by misguiding and provoking the believer to succumb to his/her desire.

> "When a woman fascinates any one of you and she captivates his heart, he should go to his wife and have an intercourse with her, for it would repel what he feels." [Sahih Muslim: 1403 c, Book 8, Hadith 3242]

It is because of these factors and also on the basis that marriage is a very important decision in one's life, that Prophet Muhammad ﷺ encouraged one to look at a non-mahram woman before proposing marriage. It is also necessary for a woman to be consenting to the marriage, and it is discouraged for her guardians to force her into marriage. Abu Huraira (may Allah ﷻ be pleased with him) reported:

> "I was in the company of Allah ﷻ's
> Messenger ﷺ, when there came a
> man and informed him that he had
> contracted to marry a woman of the
> Ansar. Thereupon Allah ﷻ's
> Messenger ﷺ said: Did you cast a
> glance at her? He said: No. He said:
> Go and cast a glance at her, for there
> is something in the eyes of the
> Ansar." [Sahih Muslim 1424 a, or
> Book 8: Hadith 3314]

In another instance Bakr bin Abdullah Al-Muzani
narrated that:

> "Al-Mughirah bin Shu'bah proposed
> to a woman, so the Prophet said: look
> at her, for indeed that is more likely to
> make things better between the two
> of you." [Jami' at-Tirmidhi: 1087, or
> Vol. 2, Book 6: Hadith 1087]

It was also reported in Sunan Ibn Majah that Muhammad
bin Salamah asked a companion if they knew the opinion
of Prophet Muhammad ﷺ with regards to looking at a
woman one seeks to propose to. The companion said:

> "I heard the Messenger of Allah ﷺ
> saying: 'When Allah ﷻ causes a man
> to propose to a woman, there is
> nothing wrong with him looking at
> her." [Sunan Ibn Majah, Vol. 3, Book
> 9, Hadith 1864]

Moreover, Anas bin Malik narrated that:

> Mughirah bin Shubah wanted to marry a woman. The Prophet ﷺ said to him: "Go and look at her, for that is more likely to create love between you." So he did that, and married her, and mentioned how well he got along with her. [Sunan Ibn Majah, Vol. 3, Book 9, Hadith 1865]

Imam al-Nawawi (may Allah ﷻ be pleased with him) also explained that when a man wants to marry a woman, it is preferable for him to look at her so that he will have no regrets. Moreover, if it is not feasible to look at her, he may send a woman to visit her and describe her to him. He expanded on this and said a woman may also look at a man if she wants to marry him, for she will like in him what he likes in her. (Rawdat al-Taalibeen wa 'Umdat al-Mufteen, pg 7, 19-20) The majority of scholars have said that a man is allowed to look at the woman face and hands because the face indicates the beauty, and the hands indicate the slimness or plumpness of the body as he is not allowed to look at any other body part. Therefore, as important as it is for the man to look at the woman he is proposing to marry, it is equally important for the woman to consent to the marriage. Prophet Muhammad made these rules very clear. 'A'isha (may Allah ﷻ be pleased with her) reported:

> I asked Allah ﷻ's Messenger ﷺ about a virgin whose marriage was solemnized by her guardian, whether it was necessary or not to consult her. Allah ﷻ's Messenger ﷺ said: "Yes, she must be consulted." 'A'isha reported: I told him that she feels shy,

whereupon Allah 🕮's Messenger 🕮
said: "Her silence implies her
consent." [Sahih Muslim: 1420, or
Book 8, Hadith 3305]

Ibn 'Abbas (may Allah 🕮 be pleased with him) also
reported that Prophet Muhammad "Peace and Blessings
be upon him) had said that a woman without a husband
has more right to her person than her guardian, and a
virgin's consent must be asked from her, and her silence
implies her consent. [Sahih Muslim 1421 a, or Book 8,
Hadith 3306] Therefore it is important to acknowledge
that a woman needs to consent to her marriage, and
Islam acknowledges her rights to her own self as being
more superior to the rights of her parents and guardians
over her.

The idea of forced marriages seems to be a social
problem in many parts of the world that enforce cultural
rights of the parents to be superior over the rights of the
individual. There is no doubt that role of parents and
guardians in Islam is important, for a man is encouraged
not to approach a woman with his proposal to marry, but
instead to approach her guardian. However, the rights of
the individual are significant because marriage is a
lifelong commitment that both partners must endure, it
imposes rights and obligations on each of them, and they
must willingly oblige to these for the sake of Allah 🕮.
Prophet Muhammad 🕮 recognized forced marriages to
be an injustice and even rectified it during his time.
Khansa bint Khidam Al-Ansariya narrated that her father
gave her in marriage when she was a matron and she
disliked that marriage. So she went to Allah 🕮's
Messenger 🕮 and he declared that marriage invalid.
[Sahih al-Bukhari: 5138, or Vol. 7, Book 62, Hadith: 69]
In another instance, Ibn Buraidah narrated that his father

told him:

> "A girl came to the Prophet (Peace
> and Blessing be upon him) and said:
> 'My father married me to his brother's
> son so that he might raise his status
> thereby.' The Prophet ﷺ gave her a
> choice, and she said: 'I approve of
> what my father did, but wanted
> women to know that their fathers have
> no right to do that.'" [Sunan Ibn
> Majah, Vol. 3, Book 9, Hadith: 1874]

These references are significant because of the fact that
the Prophet ﷺ would simply deem these marriages
invalid because of the lack of consent from the women,
as being forced into marriage was seen unjust. This
creates a very strict precedent that must be adhered to. It
illustrates the significance of the value of consent from
the woman in the marriage, and Prophet Muhammad
ﷺ's acknowledgement of these rights make them
binding upon believers as it is part of the Sunnah. It also
illustrates that silence is understood as consent, for any
women who truly objects to a marriage must make her
opinion or rejection of the proposal communicated
verbally. Therefore, if a woman does not want to marry
she should openly and clearly object to the marriage
proposal and let it be known verbally. The objection
should be communicated to both her parents, since the
Prophet ﷺ understood silence to be an act of modesty
and shyness. Essentially, failure to communicate an open
objection implies an indirect consent.

This has been one of the major issues in the story
of Heer Ranjha, as Heer had explicitly announced her
discontent to her father and her mother, and was still
forcefully married by the Qazi. As stated previously, the

problems that were faced by Heer and Ranjha are as timeless as the story itself. To this day young men and women are forced into marriages they did not consent to, and divorce eventually becomes the outcome as their discontentment with the marriage does not allow them to love each other for the sake of Allah ﷻ.

Another issue was with regards to maintaining the social order. The spread of Islam in the pre-Islamic world had done more than just eradicating idol worship, but it shook the whole social order. Such a drastic change was feared, and thus people openly revolted against it. What did Islam do that was deemed to be significantly challenging to the social order? It affirmed that Allah ﷻ created man fully accountable, and enjoined duties upon him, to which reward and punishment are connected on the basis of man's free will and choice. This acknowledged that no human being has the right to restrict this freedom or take away one's choice unlawfully; whoever would do so is a wrongdoer and an oppressor. Slavery was common in the pre-Islamic world, and Islam changed the way in which slavery was dealt with. It created rights which were owed to slaves by their enslavers and created new ways of liberating slaves. It established guidelines of enslaving through war, in which slavery was imposed on prisoners of war and on their families in order to maintain security. Prophet Muhammad ﷺ set strict guidelines on the treatment of slaves in a just manner which insured them food and clothing similar to their masters and preserving their dignity by treating them kindly. These slaves were encouraged to be freed if they embraced Islam and no longer posed a threat as being enemies of Islam. Once free, equality was encouraged. To promote this, Prophet Muhammad ﷺ married a female prisoner, Juwayriyah bint al-Haarith, from a defeated tribe to raise her status. This encouraged the Muslims who acquired slaves from this defeated tribe to let them be free, and it set a precedent of equality between former slaves and free-folk.

Equality was one of the major problems of the pre-Islamic social order that Islam had restored, since Allah ﷻ had no concern for the differences in race, skin color, wealth and prestige of an individual. To Allah ﷻ the only relevant distinction among His creation is the distinction in piety. In Surah Al-Hujarat, Allah ﷻ affirms this as he says:

> "O men! Behold, We have created you all out of a male and female, and have made you into nations and tribes, so that you might come to know one another. Verily, the noblest of you in the sight of Allah ﷻ is the one who is most deeply conscious of him, and most righteous. Behold, Allah ﷻ is All-Knowing, All-Aware." [Holy Quran, 49:13]

Therefore the differences of race, color, social status and other factors were only incidental and unimportant. Such differences do not affect the true value of anyone in the sight of Allah ﷻ, and thus equality was not simply a right but an article of faith. By accepting Islam one acknowledges that all of creation is created by One and the Same Eternal God, Allah ﷻ, who is the Supreme Lord. Moreover, all of mankind belongs to the same race and share equally in belonging to the progeny of Prophet Adam (Peace and Blessings be upon him) and Hawwa (Eve) (may Allah ﷻ be pleased with her).

It is also important to understand that Allah ﷻ is

just to all of His creation, and is not partial to any specific gender, race, age, color, or social status, as all of creation equally belongs to Him. Moreover, it is important to realize that all of creation is born equally as no one brings any possessions with him, nor takes any worldly possessions with him. Allah ﷻ individually judges everyone on the basis of his or her own deeds. Therefore, in the case of Heer and Ranjha and in any other similar situation today, if Allah ﷻ does not discriminate between His own creation, who is mankind to discriminate between one another?

In terms of social divisions, Harjeet Singh Gill wrote that these classes have no religious barriers and probably not much economic discrepancies but culturally these thresholds cannot be crossed. One is born into a certain class and stays there forever. If Allah ﷻ refuses to judge humanity based on social divisions, then surely the laws of Allah ﷻ should trump the rules of culture. A goldsmith's daughter should be able to marry the son of a cobbler, and the son of a goldsmith should be able to marry the daughter of a fisherman without the need to discriminate. Under the principles of Islam, there are no barriers when it comes to marriage based on social class, or race, etc. However, one of the major limitations placed on who is deemed permissible for one to marry is in Surah Al-Maida:

> "Today all good clean things have been made lawful for you; and the food of the People of the Book is also made lawful for you and your food is made lawful for them. Likewise, marriage with chaste free believing women and also chaste women among the People who were given the Book before you is made

lawful for you, provided that you give them their dowries and desire chastity, neither committing fornication nor taking them as mistresses. Anyone who commits Kufr with Iman (denies faith), all his good deeds will be in vain and in the Hereafter he will be one of the losers." [Holy Quran, 5:5]

What this means is that it is permissible for a Muslim man to marry a non-Muslim woman if she is Christian or Jewish, but it is not permissible for him to marry a non-Muslim woman who follows any religion other than these two. Moreover, Allah ﷻ has said in Surah al-Baqarah that:

"AND DO NOT marry women who ascribe divinity to aught beside Allah ﷻ until they attain to (true) belief: for any believing slave woman (of Allah ﷻ) is certainly better than a free woman who ascribes divinity to aught besides Allah ﷻ, even though she may be more attractive and pleasing to you." [Holy Quran, 2:221]

The significance of this verse is that it further elaborates on not being able to marry a woman from any other religion, and places the condition that it is only permissible when she becomes a true believer of Allah ﷻ for a Muslim slave woman is better than a woman who does not believe. To clarify, if a Hindu woman truly embraces Islam and becomes a firm believer, it is permissible to marry her. She must be a true believer, otherwise the marriage is invalid; that is adultery, and not marriage. (IslamQA - 8015 - Fiqh of the Family; Invalid

Marriages) Therefore it becomes clear that the only distinction that Allah ﷻ makes between people is of piety and consciousness of Himself. These are the conditions that Allah ﷻ has placed on men. In the same verse, Allah ﷻ continues:

> "And do not give your women in marriage to men who ascribe divinity to aught beside Allah ﷻ until they attain to (true) belief: for any believing slave (of Allah ﷻ) is certainly better than a man who ascribes divinity to aught besides Allah ﷻ, even though he may please you greatly. (Such as) these invite unto the fire, whereas Allah ﷻ invites unto paradise, and unto (the achievement of) forgiveness by His leave; and He makes clear His messages unto mankind, so that they might bear them in mind." [Holy Quran, 2:221]

Therefore, it is clear that Allah ﷻ has not made the same distinction for daughters of Islam as He has for the sons. It is not permissible for a Muslim woman to marry a non-Muslim from any other religion, whether from among the Jews or Christians, or any other religion. It is only permissible for a Muslim woman to marry a Muslim man. Perhaps the reason for this is because one of the purposes of the marriage is to reproduce, and since Allah ﷻ has esteemed women to be bearers of children it is forbidden for them to bear children of non-believers. Piety and the consciousness of Allah ﷻ are the only distinctions that Allah ﷻ has made, and He affirmed the equality between social classes by stating that a believing slave is better than a non-believing free man.

One of the major problems that we face in our societies today is the balance between culture and religion. Much of the negative criticism that Islam is faced with today is due to the inability to put religious principles before culture, and in the failure to do so we allow for the problems that Islam was supposed to eradicate to become the very notions that Islam wrongfully becomes known for among those with little knowledge of it. Islam was sent to all of us as a Deen, and not just a religion.

The difference between religion and Deen is that religion is defined as one's belief in, and the worship of, a superhuman controlling power, whereas Deen is richer in meaning as it refers to the system of laws prescribed upon all of creation irrespective of time and place. Essentially then, Islam is the system of laws prescribed upon creation by the One and Only Eternal God from the day of its revelation to the last day; and all of His creation also includes all of mankind equally. Islam as a Deen teaches us to be inclusive of all our differences, whereas, cultures and nations segregate each other. Islam is based on the creation of one Ummah which means the promotion of a united and collective Muslim nation irrespective of their differences under the banner of Islam as believers of Allah ﷻ. For example, nationalism is prohibited in Islam because it creates divisions among Muslims.

Shaykh 'Abd al-'Azeez ibn Baaz (may Allah ﷻ have mercy on him) was asked for his opinion on nationalism, the belief system that belonging to a race or language takes precedence over belonging to a religion. He replied that it is not permissible to join it or encourage those who promote nationalism. Moreover, he explained that it is a well known principle in Islam that no Muslim has any excuse for not knowing, that the call for Arab nationalism or any other kind of nationalism, is a false call, grave error and blatant evil. [This is explained in a book entitled 'Naqd al-Qawmiyyah al-'Arabiyyah 'ala Daw' al-Islam wa'l-Waaqi' or 'Criticism of Arab Nationalism in the Light of Islam and Reality' and is published in its entirety in Fataawa al-Shaykh Ibn Baaz (1/280-318)] Moreover, in Surah Al-i'Imran Allah ﷻ says:

> "All together hold fast the rope of Allah ﷻ (Faith of Islam) and be not divided among yourselves. Remember Allah ﷻ's favors upon you when you were enemies; He united your hearts, so by His favor you became brothers; you were at the brink of the fiery pit and He saved you from it. Thus Allah ﷻ makes His revelations clear to you, so that you may be rightly guided." [Holy Quran, 3:103]

In Surah Ar-Rum, Allah ﷻ says that among his signs are that He created mankind from dust; and various translations of the Quran have translated the second part of the Ayah as:

> "and then behold you men are scattered throughout the earth." [Holy Quran: Malik, 30:20]

> "and behold you human beings, ranging widely!" [Holy Quran: Pickthall, 30:20]

In the Tafsir of the Quran by Ibn Kathir (may Allah ﷻ

have mercy on him), he explains that this Ayah means that Allah ﷻ had created Prophet Adam (Peace and Blessings be upon him) from a handful of clay or dust from throughout the earth. It is for these reasons that his progeny varies as the earth varies, "so they are white and red and black and colors in between, and also evil and good, easy going or difficult - or something in between." [Quran Tafsir Ibn Kathir] Therefore, differences have allowed mankind to divide amongst each other, whereas Islam reminds them of their equality and brings them together as brothers of the same progeny of Prophet Adam (Peace and Blessings be upon him). It is natural then for people of different races to be attracted to one another, and Islam places no restrictions on being unable to marry outside one's own race so long as they are believers. It is various cultures that place such restrictions against inter-racial marriages; a division among themselves which scholars have referred to as being blatant evil and a grave error.

If two people are attracted to one another, and are both believers regardless of race and social status, and if it is permissible for them to marry (if they are non-mahram) then they should marry one another, for there is no better solution to it than that. Ibn Abbas narrated that Prophet Muhammad ﷺ said:

> "There is nothing like marriage, for two who love one another." [Sunan Ibn Majah: Vol. 3, Book 9, Hadith 1847]

This means that in the eyes of Allah ﷻ, there is no objection for a Pakistani Muslim woman to marry an African Muslim man, or an Afghan Muslim man to marry an American woman who has recently embraced Islam. As long as the individual one seeks to marry is a true believer, the union of marriage will be one that is blessed for both spouses should be conscious of Allah ﷻ and wholeheartedly accept the rights and obligations that Allah ﷻ has prescribed towards the two.

Another reason for why many guardians object to certain suitors is because of wealth or beauty. This is a common problem that is not limited to any specific culture, but encompasses humanity as a whole. We value certain things more than others, and what that means is that we often give priority to the wrong qualities or characteristics. For example parents and guardians want to marry their daughters off to a suitor who is wealthy so she lives comfortably. Perhaps they reject someone she is attracted to based on his lack of wealth. It is necessary to acknowledge that a man's wealth is given to him by Allah ﷻ; he has either been blessed in his provisions as a test for him, or has inherited it through lineage as a favor upon him. Wealth is temporary and can be taken away from him. Similarly a man's family could be more inclined towards marrying him to a beautiful woman, and may reject the woman whom he loves based on his own perception of beauty. Here, it is equally important to acknowledge that a woman's beauty is also temporary and it fades with time. What stays with a person forever is his/her love for religion, their manners, their commitment to their family, their love towards the elderly and children, their attitude towards people who are less fortunate than them, their ability to manage their priorities, etc. Such are the qualities which we should be attracted to as opposed to beauty and wealth. Such are the qualities that Khadijah (may Allah ﷻ be pleased with her) became fond of when she was inclined towards marrying Prophet Muhammad ﷺ. In Surah An-Nur, Allah ﷻ has advised:

"Get the singles among you married as well as those who are fit for marriage including those among your male slaves and female slaves. If they [whom you intend to marry] are poor, [let this not deter you;] Allah ﷻ will grant them sufficiency out of His bounty - for Allah ﷻ is infinite [in His mercy], and is All-Knowing." [Holy Quran, 24:32]

Therefore, Allah ﷻ has explicitly asked us to promote marriage, and not to be an obstacle between those who wish to marry and to encourage those who are fit to marry. Moreover, Allah ﷻ has promised that if wealth is an issue, let it not deter you for Allah ﷻ will bless the marriage and increase who you wish to marry in sustenance out of His mercy.

In most worldly love stories such as Heer Ranjha and the likes of it, love is passionate from the initial encounter. Hence Islamic Mystics denounce it for being nothing more than lust, and not based on anything real, as it is only metaphorical. Most of us fall in love the same way, and if we truly reflect on our situations, we can come to a conclusion that our feelings are based on attraction and what we confuse as love may actually be an infatuation. As explained previously, attraction is important and even Prophet Muhammad ﷺ recognized this. However, it is not what love should be solely based on, because love is something that is deeper than the attraction of beauty. One can say love starts with attraction, and it is other qualities and traits of the object of love that influence love to become deeply rooted. Without the love for qualities such as an individual's character, his/her religion, his manners, the love is indeed an infatuation for the individual's beauty, and the initial physical attraction.

Love for the sake of beauty has natural consequences, and these consequences are self-inflicted. Perhaps even the term self-inflicted does not come close enough to describe it, and one can say that these consequences are actually self-created. The very nature of beauty is that it is unconscious of the value of its being. It is the idealization of the lover which makes beauty precious, and it is the attention of the lover which produces indifference in the beautiful, a realization of being superior. Therefore, most often the beloved is completely unaware of his/her beauty but the admiration and the attention from the lover puts them on a pedestal, one on which the beloved easily finds comfort in. It is the admiration of beauty that instills a sense of pride and ego within the beloved. The more one detaches from Allah ﷻ through his/her attachment to the beloved, the more the sense of pride and ego increases in the beloved along with his/her sense of superiority. When even the vanity of a mere earthy beauty is thus satisfied by admiration, just imagine how much more the vanity of the heavens must be satisfied by His glorification, by He who is the real beauty and alone worthy of all praise?

You may have heard the famous saying by Plato, "Beauty lies in the eyes of the beholder". This means that different people find pleasure and beauty in different things. The beauty of the same object or sight may be assessed differently by a different person. Some have tried to explain this as the idea that a thing is beautiful not because of some intrinsic physical feature it possesses, but it is beautiful because of the perception of the person viewing the object. Therefore, beauty is something that exists in the mind of the person, and the eyes simply figuratively represent the mind of the person perceiving the beauty. Put another way, the lover's Ulfat towards the beloved is unexplainable because the perception of beauty is in the eyes of the lover. Hazrat Inayat Khan explains beauty as perfection, and a reflection of God.

"Beauty may be explained as perfection, perfection in every aspect of beauty. Not love alone is God or the essence of God, but beauty also, even in its limited aspects, shows itself as glimpses of the perfect Being. The mineral kingdom develops into gold, silver, diamonds, rubies, and emeralds, showing perfection in it. The fruit and flower, their sweetness and fragrance, show perfection in the vegetable kingdom. Form, figure, and youth show perfection in the animal kingdom. And it is the beauty of personality which is significant of perfection in the human being. There are some people in this world whose life is absorbed in the pursuit of gold and silver, gems and jewels. They would sacrifice anything or anybody to acquire the object of their love. There are others whose life is engaged in the beautiful vision of fruits, flowers, flowerbeds, and gardens. Perhaps they have no other interest besides. There are some who are absorbed in the admiration of the youth and the beauty of the opposite sex, and nothing else seems to them worth more. There are others who are won by the beauty of someone's personality, and have entirely devoted to the one they love both their here and their hereafter. Everyone has his object of love according to his standard of beauty." [Hazrat Inayat Khan, Spiritual Liberty, Volume V, Part IV, Chapter VI]

I have chosen two poems to further explain this idea.

The first poem is by Syed Abdullah Shah Qadri who is also known as Bulleh Shah, the Honorable Sufi, humanist, and philosopher of Punjab. He wrote:

"Laila kita sawal mian Majnun nu,
teri Laila te rang di kali aye.
Dita jawab mian Majnun ne,
Teri ankh na wekhan wali aye.
Quran pak de warq chitay,
Uthay likhi siyahi kali aye.
Chadh we Bulleyah dil de chadeya,
Te ki kali, ki gori aye."
[Laila by Baba Bulleh Shah]

In English:

"Laila indicated to Majnun that,
His beloved has black (dark) skin.
Majnun was quick in retorting back;
Your vision is inept to apprehend!
The paper of the Holy Quran is white,
Yet the words are written in black ink.
(Are the white pages of the Holy Quran
not adorned with black ink?)
Don't think too much into it Bulleyah!
It matters not if the beloved is black or white." [Laila by Baba Bulleh Shah]

Similarly, the famous Sufi Poet, Khwaja Ghulam Farid of the Chisti-Nizami Sufi Order reiterated the poem about Majnun's love for Laila. The poem in Punjabi is as follows:

"Kis-wal akheya ve Majnu nu,
Oh teri Laila disdi kaali ve!
Majnu ne jawab ditta,
Oh teri ankh na wekhan-waali ve!
Je tu wekhe meri ankhaa naal,
Teri surat na jaye sambhali.
Ved bhi chitta, te Quran bhi chitti,
Wich siyahi rakh ditti kaali ve.
Ghulam Farid, jithhe akhiyan lagiyan,
Uthhe kya, gori kya kaali ve…"
[Khwaja Ghulam Farid]

In English:

"Someone remarked to Majnun, your Laila is dark complexioned! Which Majnun did respond to saying, only because her beauty your eye hasn't fathomed. If you could see Laila with my eyes, Over awed, you'd change the way you apprise. Ved (Hindu holy scriptures) and the Holy Quran are nothing but white sheets, which, the blank ink upon them beautifies and does complete. If Ghulam Farid were to fall in love with someone, the distinction between black and white would not matter."
[Khwaja Ghulam Farid]

As with all Sufi poets, both Bulleh Shah and Ghulam Farid use the example of Laila and Majnun as symbols to express a lot of deeper meanings, one of them being the obvious with regards to the perception of beauty of the beloved being solely for the lover to appreciate. Moreover, they also try to convince people that there is no difference between the one who reads the Ved or the one who reads the Holy Quran, because the Beloved is but One God, and only the lover will be able to apprehend that. For the rest of who decide to read the Holy Scriptures, to them it's nothing more than black ink on white paper.

Hazrat Inayat Khan in "Volume V - Spiritual Liberty" describes the story of Laila and Majnun to have been told in the East for thousands of years as a story that has exerted a great fascination for the lessons in love that it provides.

Majnun became fond of Laila during his school years, and in time the spark grew into a flame. Majnun would become anxious if Laila was a little late in coming to school, and his eyes would always be fixed at the entrance. In time Laila's heart also became kindled with Majnun's love and nothing else seemed to matter to them in the entire world except for one another. In class, Majnun did not see anyone else but Laila, and likewise Laila did not see anyone but Majnun.

> "In reading from the book Majnun would read the name of Laila, in writing from dictation Laila would cover her slate with the name of Majnun. All else disappears when the thought of the beloved occupies the mind of the lover." [Hazrat Inayat Khan, Volume V, Part IV, Chapter V]

Their fondness for each other became so disturbing to everyone in the school that the teachers wrote to the parents that their relationship was coming in the way of their progress at school.

"He was drowning in the sea of love
before he even knew what love was.
He had given his heart to the girl
before he had even realized what it
was that he was giving away. Layla, for
her part, fared no better, for she, too
had fallen. A fire had been lit in both
their hearts, one reflecting the other.
And what could they do to ward off
the flames? Nothing. They were
children, and children accept what
comes to them with little
question." [Nizami, Layla and Majnun
- The Classic Love Story of Persian
Literature, Chapter 2]

Because of this, Laila's parents removed her from class.
They took her away from Majnun, but could not remove
Majnun from her heart. Nor could anyone remove Laila
from the heart of Majnun.

Majnun was no longer Majnun without the presence
of Laila and he became extremely disturbed. It was
obvious to everyone in school that his heart was at unrest
and he was going through grief. His parents were
eventually compelled to take him home and called
physicians, spiritual healers, magicians, and tried to do
anything they could for some remedy to divert Majnun
from the thought of Laila. But there was no cure for the
lovesick.

"No one has ever healed a patient of
love. Friends came, relations came,
well-wishers came, wise counselors
came, and all tried their best to efface
from his mind the thought of Laila,

but all was in vain. Someone said to him, 'O Majnun, why do you sorrow at the separation from Laila? She is not beautiful. I can show you a thousand fairer and more charming maidens, and can let you choose your mate from among them.' Majnun answered, 'O, to see the beauty of Laila the eyes of Majnun are needed.'"
[Hazrat Inayat Khan, Volume V, Part IV, Chapter V]

It eventually got to a point where his parents had tried every remedy they could possibly think of, and the only thing left to do was to seek the refuge of the Kabah and plead to Allah ﷻ as their last resort. When they arrived at the Kabah, a large crowd gathered to observe them. The parents each took turns and prayed to Allah ﷻ to rid the heart of Majnun from the pain and the love for Laila, while everyone listened and anxiously waited for what Majnun would say. Finally his parents asked Majnun to go and pray that the love of Laila is taken away from his heart. Ganjavi Nizami in "The Fire of Love: The Love Story of Layla and Majnun", recounts his prayer as follows:

> "They say, 'Crush the desire for Layla in your heart'. But I implore Thee, oh my God, let it grow even stronger. Take what is left of my life and add it to Layla's. Let me never demand from her as much as a single hair, even if my pain reduces me to the width of one.
>
> Let her punish and torment me. Let her wine alone fill my cup, my name never to be spoken without her seal.

My life shall be sacrificed for her beauty, my blood shall be spilled freely for her. Though I burn for her in agony, like a candle, none of my days shall be free from this pain. Let me love, oh my God, love for love's own sake, and make my love a hundred times as great as it was and is." [Ganjavi Nizami, The Fire of Love: The Love Story of Layla and Majnun, pg. 31]

All his parents could do was listen silently as they didn't know what more to say. They had tried everything but could not find a cure, and there was absolutely nothing left to do now but to return home. Upon returning home people asked, "Tell us, has Allah ﷻ helped? Is he cured?" But all his father could say was:

"I have tried. I have told him how to ask God for relief from this curse, this Layla. But he clung to his own ideas. What did he do? He cursed himself and blessed Layla." [Ganjavi Nizami, The Fire of Love: The Love Story of Layla and Majnun, pg. 31]

In another instance written by Shaykh Zulfiqar Ahmad:

Once, the mayor of the city thought that he should actually see with his own eyes the girl whom Majnun's love had made famous. When Layla was brought before him, he was astounded to see that she was just an ordinary girl without any extraordinary features, figure, or complexion. He said to her, "you are no prettier than any other girl." She retorted, "Keep quiet. You are not Majnun." [Shaykh Zulfiqar Ahmad, Ishq-e-Ilahi, Translated by Faqir Publications, pg. 77]

Shaykh Zulfiqar Ahmad explains it is for this reason that the metaphorical lover claims that Layla should be beheld by the eyes of Majnun. Often we think we are in love, but are merely infatuated with a person and we begin to pray for him/her. We exhaust ourselves continually in asking for them in prayer, but we are not granted this person. Is it Allah ﷻ disappointing us? No, for Allah ﷻ does not disappoint. In Surah Al-Baqara, Allah ﷻ reminds us that:

> "… but it may happen that you hate a thing while it is good for you, and it may well be that you love a thing while it is bad for you: and Allah ﷻ knows, whereas you do not know." [Holy Quran, 2:216]

Some of us find ourselves in positions where we are praying for someone who is totally destructive for us. This person may be lacking a religious commitment, this person may be involved in and heavily engaged in sins that Allah ﷻ extremely dislikes, or this person is simply incompatible with us and yet we are adamant in praying for him/her. Why? Because we "love" them, despite failing to describe or even understand why we feel that way. It is significantly important to ask ourselves questions like, what exactly do I love about a man who is engaged in extra marital affairs and moves from relationship to relationship while you spend your time praying for him to be yours? What do I love about a man whose religious commitments are questionable and who does not follow the commandments of Allah ﷻ? Perhaps in the pursuit of your beloved, you are rejecting proposals from far more suitable people who may be more compatible with you, and of better character in the eyes of their Lord. Perhaps it's the complexion that attracts you? Perhaps it's the physique? Or the voice? These are temporary physical attributes of an individual that will fade one day.

Imagine if Allah ﷻ finally grants you this individual out of His mercy and benevolence, and opens the doors of marriage for you. How long do you think your marriage will last with an individual who has forsaken his religion? You are married to an individual who is absolutely stunning, but his character is the total opposite to the physical beauty he has been blessed with. There stands in front of you the man who you prayed for endlessly because of an attraction to his physical appearance. But what good is a man who has no manners towards you, who is not compassionate towards you, and the very eyes that you were attracted to refuse to look at you with love? Perhaps the fulfillment of your Du'a was destructive for you, perhaps it was to bring your heart significantly more suffering than the actual longing that you endured for this individual. Had Allah ﷻ not granted this to you, you would have thought it is Allah ﷻ disappointing you, you would have thought that the power of Du'a is of no force and effect. You would have failed to trust in Allah ﷻ, and you would have refused to believe in His wisdom, and your failure would have led you to blame Allah ﷻ, (May Allah forgive us for such thoughts; and may we seek refuge in Allah ﷻ from the whisperings of Shaytaan).

Eventually you will admit to yourself that the fulfillment of this Du'a was not good for you, and the delay in Allah ﷻ's response would make sense to you. By then you will have added to your suffering, and out of His grace and perfect knowledge, Allah ﷻ does not want you to suffer. Therefore, some people are only a test for us. Shaytaan will convince you that they are made for you, and fill your mind with conclusions such as their hands are meant to hold yours, and everything in your heart tells you they are created for you, etc. But perhaps the attraction to this individual is a test of your emaan. You pray day and night for this individual, you stand before Allah ﷻ, the Lord of the Worlds, in pleading for this individual; but perhaps the purpose of this individual is solely for Allah ﷻ to see if He does not grant you this individual, will you abandon His call? Most often we do; when we take a mere impediment in our path to be the destination itself, we forsake Allah ﷻ. May Allah ﷻ guide us to strengthen our trust in Him. May we begin to understand that the cracks in the sidewalk are meant to be avoided, and if we refuse to do so, we will trip over them.

Similarly, some of us may be attracted to a woman who does not understand modesty and displays herself in the eyes of the world in search for praise and validation of her beauty. Perhaps she is disrespectful of you, ignorant towards you, causes you grief and anxiety, but you are so compelled by her beauty that you pray for her night and day. She isn't religiously committed, her morals are perhaps questionable, and her ideology is completely different from yours. Can you say you love her for her character? Can you say you love her for her modesty, and she makes you proud in front of other people? Can you say you love her for her loving nature, and you feel as if she'll be good for your worldly life and the life hereafter? Perhaps not, and yet you're adamant in praying for her to be yours because it is her eyes that have captivated you, or her smile that makes you feel euphoric. All this will fade with time, and her character is what will remain. Are you then in love with her beauty, or for who she is? In fact, are you really in love at all? Allah 🖋 knows what you do not, and Allah 🖋 knows what is best. In Sahih al-Bukhari it is narrated by Abu Huraira (may Allah 🖋 be pleased with him) that the Prophet 🖋 said:

> "A woman is married for four things, i.e., her wealth, her family status, her beauty, and her religion. So you should marry the religious woman otherwise you will be a loser." [Sahih al-Bukhari 5090, or Vol. 7, Book 62, Hadith 27]

In another instance it was narrated by Abdullah bin Amr (may Allah 🖋 be pleased with him) that the Prophet 🖋 said:

> "Do not marry women for their beauty for it may lead to their doom. Do not marry them for their wealth, for it may lead them to fall into sin. Rather, marry them for their religion. A black slave woman with piercings who is religious is better." [Sunan Ibn Majah, Vol. 3, Book 9, Hadith 1859]

In this Hadith the distinction was made between a black slave woman with piercings, who was seen as unattractive during that time. Essentially the distinction was made between an unattractive slave woman and a beautiful free woman, and the Prophet 🖋 said that the slave who is religious is a far better choice for marriage.

To determine how religious someone is often becomes a difficult task, for one can not measure religiousness by a percentage, and one can not be compared to another by saying "this person is twenty-five percent more religious than that person". Often we confuse outwardly qualities and characteristics to be indicators of religiousness and judge people based on these circumstances. It is at this point I would like to point out that a man should not be judged based on the length of his beard, for a man without a beard could be more steadfast on his religion in comparison. Perhaps Allah ﷻ has not guided him in observing a beard yet, and surely it is Allah ﷻ who guides. Such a man may have better manners, and be more conscious of Allah ﷻ and his only short coming would be that he does not follow the Sunnah of growing a beard. Similarly a woman should not be judged as being more righteous for observing the Hijab as compared a woman who doesn't. It would not be outrageous to conclude that a woman without the hijab may have more modesty in her gaze, and better manners, and be more conscious of Allah ﷻ than a woman who simply observes the Hijab.

This is an extremely controversial topic, and is often heavily debated among Muslims. There is more to religion than just growing a beard and observing the hijab, and one must carefully focus on the person's character and personality as opposed to his or her outwardly appearance. If the love for Allah ﷻ is in one's heart, the hijab or the beard will eventually follow. But the mere observance of the hijab or beard does not guarantee that the love for Allah ﷻ will follow, for that love is meant to precede it. Perhaps someone is forced to wear the hijab, and observes it out of fear of the authority of her father or brother without understanding its true purpose. Perhaps one keeps a beard due to a fashion sense, or another purpose unknown to you. It is important to remember that some of the biggest enemies of Islam and Prophet Muhammad ﷺ such as Abu Jahl had beards as well. Therefore it is naive to judge an individual based on his appearance. Allah ﷻ has put a veil over our sins in order for us to treat each other indiscriminately, and we must do that regardless of appearance. It is important for each of us to individually adopt the examples of Prophet Muhammad ﷺ and his wives (may Allah ﷻ be pleased with them) first, in order to implement the sense of loyalty, honesty, integrity, humility, and steadfastness in religion before imitating his beard or the hijab of his wives.

When your heart is inclined towards someone, and their heart is inclined towards you, we already know that the answer is marriage. For all the impediments in between, there is Salaat-ul-Istikhara. This is a special prayer that was recited by Prophet Muhammad ﷺ when in need of guidance, and is a two raka'ah salah performed to completion followed by the Du'a for Istikhara. It means asking Allah ﷻ to choose the best for you when you need to make the right decision. One should not make Istikhara for compulsory actions such as asking if one should perform Hajj, etc. Istikhara is only to be performed for finding the right spouse or other optional and preferable actions such as choosing between job opportunities, moving to different cities in search for provisions, etc. Contrary to popular belief, it can be done at any time of the day and not just during the night before sleeping. Moreover, anyone can perform Istikhara but it is most beneficial if you perform it for yourself. One of the most important things to keep in mind is that after performing the Istikhara, it is not necessary to have a dream, for the signs of Allah ﷻ are not limited. Most of the times your heart will naturally be inclined towards whatever Allah ﷻ decides for you, and if He wills to show you the way, that is what you should choose to continue with. The instructions for Salaat-ul-Istikhara are simple:

1. Perform two Rak'aah Nafl prayer and avoid markooh times. The best time is to pray it before Fajr or after Isha.

2. After performing the two Rak'aah Nafl prayer, recite "Astag-firul-laah" (I seek forgiveness from Allah ﷻ) three times, and then praise Allah ﷻ by saying "Al-hamdu-lil-laah" (All praise be to Allah ﷻ).

3. Convey Durood upon Prophet Muhammad ﷺ

- Arabic transliteration: Al laa hum ma sali alaa sayidinaa Muhammadi(w)n wa alaa aaali sayidinaa Muhammadi(w)n wa baarik wa salim

- English translation: O Allah ﷻ, shower Your mercy upon Sayidinna Muhammad ﷺ and the followers of Sayidinna Muhammad ﷺ and Peace and Blessings.

4. If performing the Salaah before sleeping, then sleep with Wudhu while facing the Qibla if possible.

5. It is not necessary to have a dream, therefore, carry out the action that your heart is content with, and trust that whatever your heart is most inclined towards is the guidance that you seek.

6. If you are still in doubt, carry out

the Istikhara for up to a maximum of 7 days and if Allah ﷻ wills, a solution will be found.

Istikhara Du'a:

اللَّهُمَّ إِنِّي أَسْتَخِيرُكَ بِعِلْمِكَ وَأَسْتَقْدِرُكَ بِقُدْرَتِكَ وَأَسْأَلُكَ مِنْ فَضْلِكَ الْعَظِيمِ فَإِنَّكَ تَقْدِرُ وَلَا أَقْدِرُ وَتَعْلَمُ وَلَا أَعْلَمُ وَأَنْتَ عَلَّامُ الْغُيُوبِ اللَّهُمَّ إِنْ كُنْتَ تَعْلَمُ أَنَّ هَذَا الْأَمْرَ خَيْرٌ لِي فِي دِينِي وَمَعَاشِي وَعَاقِبَةِ أَمْرِي فَاقْدُرْهُ لِي وَيَسِّرْهُ لِي ثُمَّ بَارِكْ لِي فِيهِ وَإِنْ كُنْتَ تَعْلَمُ أَنَّ هَذَا الْأَمْرَ شَرٌّ فِي دِينِي وَمَعَاشِي وَعَاقِبَةِ أَمْرِي فَاصْرِفْهُ عَنِّي وَاصْرِفْنِي عَنْهُ وَاقْدُرْ لِيَ الْخَيْرَ حَيْثُ كَانَ ثُمَّ ارْضِنِي بِهِ

English transliteration:

Al-laah-hum-ma in-nee as-takheeruka bi-'ilmika, wa-astaqdiruka bi-qudratika, wa-as-aluka min fadh-likal 'Azeem. Fa-in-naka taqdiru wa-laa 'aqdiru, wa-ta'-lamu, wa-laa a'-lamu, wa-Anta 'Al-laamul Ghuyoob. Al-laah-hum-ma in kunta ta'-lamu an-na **haadhal amra** [then think of the thing to be decided] khayrun lee fee deeni wa-ma-'aashi wa-'aaqibati amri - Faqdur-hu lee wa-yas-sir-hu lee thum-ma baarik lee feeh. Wa-in kunta ta'-lamu an-na **haadhal amra** [then think of the thing to be decided] shar-run lee fee deeni wa-ma-'aashi wa-'aaqibati amri - Fas-rif-hu 'an-ni was-rif-ni 'anhu waqdur liyal khayra hay-hay-thu kaana, thum-ma ar-dhini bih.

English Translation:

O Allah ﷻ, I seek guidance from You due to Your knowledge, and I seek help from You due to Your power, and I beseech You for Your Magnificent Grace. Surely, You are capable and I am not, and You know, and I know not, and You are the Knower of the unseen. O Allah ﷻ,

if in Your knowledge this matter [then mention the thing to be decided] is good for me in my religion (Deen) and in my life and for my welfare in the life to come - then ordain it for me and make it easy for me then bless me in it. And if You know that this matter [then mention the thing to be decided] is bad for me in my religion (Deen) and in my life and for my welfare in the life to come - then distance it from me and distance me from it and ordain for me what is good whatever it may be, then help me to be content with it.

After performing Istikhara your heart will either be inclined towards whatever Allah ﷻ wills, or you may see a dream in which darker colors represent a negative response and a brighter colors are taken as a positive response, or you may see a dream which you wake up from and it leaves a certain feeling of either happiness and satisfaction in your heart, or it may trouble you. Sometimes Allah ﷻ shows you signs, and reveals secrets about a person which are supposed to have an impact on your decision. It is important to reflect on the meaning of the Istikhara Du'a. One is essentially asking Allah ﷻ that if a particular person is good for me and my religion in this life and the hereafter, then to make things easy for me and bless me with it. Therefore if you are confused about the response, trust in Allah ﷻ. If it is good for you, indeed He will make it easy for you. Moreover, in this Du'a one also asks Allah ﷻ that if a particular person is bad for me and my religion in this life and in the hereafter, then distance me from that person and distance that person from me and make it easy for me to be content with whatever You have planned for me. After this procedure, if you notice things are getting difficult for you, or you realize changes in between you and whomever, and both of you begin to drift apart, then trust in Allah ﷻ. Let it go, for if it is meant for you then

He will bring it to you regardless of how far it goes. If it is not meant for you, then this is Allah ﷻ distancing you away from it, and you must put your trust in Him. What is meant for you shall soon be ordained to you. In Surah Al-Anfal, Allah ﷻ promises:

> "...If Allah ﷻ finds goodness in your hearts, He will give you even better than what has been taken from you, as well as forgive you. Allah ﷻ is Most-Forgiving, and Most-Merciful." [Holy Quran, 8:70]

After making Du'a one must put his entire trust in Allah ﷻ, and one must remember what Allah ﷻ has told His believers in Surah Al-Baqara about themselves:

> "We belong to Allah ﷻ and to Him we shall return." [Holy Quran, 2:156]

This helps put everything into perspective, for we do not belong to even ourselves. Allah ﷻ asks us to tell ourselves that we belong to Allah ﷻ, and to Him we shall return. Therefore, when putting our trust in Allah ﷻ, we've already asked Him for what we want, and He is already aware of our need. In the end, we belong to Him and it is for Him to do as He chooses, for He knows what we do not, and what He does is best according to His Divine Wisdom. Surely, we believe if Allah ﷻ can make best what is good for us, He can make good what is bad for us as well, but Allah ﷻ knows best and indeed there is Supreme Wisdom behind His doings.

May our hearts become inclined towards what is best for us in our religion, our present life and in the life hereafter. May we be pleased not just by the beauty of Allah ﷻ's creation, but may we be inclined towards the best of His people in their consciousness of Allah ﷻ and for their manners, good character, and humility towards His people.

3.3
UNSIYAT
(ATTACHMENT)

The Chistiyya have described this stage of love as true friendship; the strong attachment between two people as the lover and the beloved. They've analyzed this to be a stage of love in which one is sincere, and loyal in his/her own love, and completely disregards or remains unaffected by the beloved's fidelity or infidelity. It does not matter to the lover if the beloved disregards his/her love or is in denial of it, and the lover simply continues to love wholeheartedly. According to this description it seems as if it leans towards an obvious imbalance in which the lover is willing to give the relationship his/her all without the need for any reciprocation since he/she is completely unaffected by the beloved's denials and infidelity.

One of the ways to recognize this stage is described as the point where carnal desires are regarded as disrespect towards the beloved, and the lover forsakes the idea of any sexual pleasure in order to maintain a purity in his/her attachment towards the beloved. With utmost respect and admiration in one's heart towards the beloved which is driven by absolutely no feelings of sexual desire, one is in a state of mind in which anything the beloved does is regarded as being beautiful. The love has placed the beloved so high up on a pedestal that anything and everything the beloved does is to be admired. One of the dangers of this state of mind is that there is a severe imbalance, and through such an imbalanced perception, even harshness by the beloved in terms of speech or conduct, is welcomed as a pleasant gift.

According to the Chistiyya Order, another way to recognize this stage is when one reaches the point of jealousy. This is where the lover becomes jealous and can not tolerate anyone even speak the name of one's beloved, and a stranger's glance towards the beloved infuriates the lover more than anything. It becomes harder and harder for one to tolerate the beloved diverting his/her attention towards other people, and the intolerance of other people to be inclined towards the beloved also increases. Perhaps we have all been in a situation where we simply could not share someone we loved. We seem to forget that before we entered the life of the beloved, he/she had other priorities and other friends, and perhaps some he/she may be extremely close to. During this stage, one forgets or completely disregards these social relations of the beloved. Furthermore, one of the interesting perspectives offered by the Chistiyyas with regards to this phase is that as one progresses through the state of jealousy, he/she even becomes jealous of his/her own self. One begins to protect the beloved from his/her own self and takes precautions such as trying not to come off as too strong to not overwhelm the beloved.

The term for jealousy in languages such as Urdu, Arabic, and Farsi is "ghairat/ghairah," which will be explained in further detail in the upcoming chapters. Ghairat/Ghairah essentially broadens the definition of jealousy from being more than just envy, to a fiercely protective instinct of one's possessions, or whatever one regards to be his/her own. It is important to take note of this now because such a definition of jealousy differs from the conventional definition of jealousy which describes an intolerance or envy of another person coming too close to the beloved. Therefore, to be jealous of one's self actually means something beautiful, because one's ghairat/ghairah, or protective instinct would protect the beloved from one's own faults or any potential acts of injustice towards the beloved. For example, if one regards his/her heart to be a sanctuary in which only the beloved is strictly enshrined in, one's ghairat/ghairah would not allow anyone else to share the same place; therefore, the lover would take precautions not to allow anyone else to make room in his/her own heart since it is strictly reserved for the beloved.

Through this attachment and loyalty, one now begins to develop feelings of yearning. Perhaps it is a yearning for the beloved to finally show affection, or signs of reciprocation. Perhaps it could be a yearning to meet and spend more time with the beloved. The craving or desire to meet the beloved becomes so strong that one begins to involuntarily complain. He/she may complain to himself, to the beloved, to Allah ﷻ in prayer, or to his/her friends. It is a state of mind in which life becomes seemingly incomplete or empty without the beloved. The constant yearning and craving leads to the continual remembrance of the beloved. There is an Arabic saying that goes, "He who loves a thing speaks of it often." When one reaches this stage, he/she will find himself often speaking or mentioning the beloved, and even the most irrelevant conversations will become relevant in having to mention the beloved.

The more one becomes familiar with the description of this stage of love, the more it seems as if it as an imbalanced friendship, or a wholehearted one sided commitment. Such a relationship becomes dangerous, and leads to many hardships to be eventually suffered by the heart because, as explained in earlier chapters, being content with an imbalance leads one to fully commit to another one-sidedly as if he/she would have committed in a mutual relationship such as a marriage. In such a relationship, loyalty is taken for granted, and the beloved begins to feel as if he/she is entitled to that kind of love. When you put someone on such a high pedestal, they begin to feel as if you are obligated to love them that way, without the need for any mutual commitment. This is where it begins to hurt, because eventually after giving so much of oneself to the beloved, it is only natural for one to expect something in return. Depending on the inequality in the relationship, one becomes so deprived of attention, or any sort of love, that he/she begins to make excuses and accepts apologies that are never given to him/her. One begins to justify the lack of commitment on behalf of the beloved to him/herself by creating up scenarios and excuses to explain that perhaps the beloved was tired, or busy, or overwhelmed with work or something so necessary and unavoidable, that it was more important than him/her.

As previously explained, such an imbalance in any relationship is extremely dangerous and causes a lot of agony and hardship. It becomes a disease of the heart where the heart becomes overwhelmed with sorrow and misery. One needs to be reminded that all of this agony is essentially Allah ﷻ giving you signs that you are in an illicit relationship in which one is not willing to commit to you, and there is no other way but to let go and attach to your Lord. Chances are you've abandoned the right path, and if you haven't completely, you've obviously let someone in an illicit relationship have a higher place in your heart than Allah ﷻ. Allah ﷻ then breaks you at the hands of that person to call you to Himself, to have you attach your heart to Him so you have another chance to completely cleanse your heart with His love.

When you transgress, you fail to realize that you are setting yourself up for hardships. When placing someone so high up on a pedestal, you cause yourself to instill a natural sense of pride and ego in them and Allah ﷻ uses that very ego, and the pride of your beloved, against you. One may become so overwhelmed with sadness that he begins to think it is a punishment of some sort, but the beauty of the bestowal of such sadness that is that it is only to remind you that you are not a toy to be played with and to be disposed off once you are of no use. It is Allah ﷻ reminding you of your own worth, and the sadness should speak to you and remind you that you are not a pet that is rewarded for its obedience. Nor are you a form of medicine to be of a temporary healing for someone. You are so much more special than you are prepared to give yourself credit for, and committing to someone without the promise or an act of equal commitment is no less than a severe injustice that you willingly inflict upon yourself. Allah ﷻ simply uses these circumstances to show you reason, and although it may seem to be against you, the hardship is actually being used in your favor.

Such is the case if one engages in putting him/ herself through the unnatural course of love, through transgression which is inevitably faced with hardships. The natural course of love is instead a path which requires one to realize that creation has been created in pairs, and thus the legitimation of ulfat is marriage in which unsiyat is to take its natural course, which is far more beautiful than it has been described thus far.

In the previous chapter, it was established that attraction, or ulfat, could be motivation enough for two individuals to get married. When two individuals have the intent to make their union Halal and go into the marriage with equal expectations and intentions to make it work and by being fully aware of their responsibilities and obligations owed towards each other, they are not only successful on their own, but Allah ﷻ blesses the union, and love between them naturally increases. Unsiyat is the first blessing in a marriage.

The man and woman complete each other - and thus the act of completing one another requires a mutual commitment of give and take. Through this mutual commitment, they bind themselves into becoming a single self and that is how they must strive to make their lives easier together - as if they are two parts to a single soul. That is what Allah ﷻ wants for you, an equal relationship with mutual respect and love. When you transgress, you set yourself up for hardships that you only inflict upon yourself. The more you fight for such relationships, the more pain you inflict upon yourself; for hardship is guaranteed to you in such acts of transgression. Staying in such a relationship only prolongs the hardship, therefore one must strive to make it Halal as early as possible.

The beauty of Halal is that marriage is a contract with rights and obligations that the man and woman owe to one another. In this contract either partner can specify specific terms and conditions of the marriage if they wish to do so. For example, if one wishes to enter a marriage on the grounds that the husband and wife should be equal partners in which both are obligated to help out with chores and duties around the house, it should be mentioned in the contract. If the woman wishes to enter a marriage and ensure that she is allowed to continue progressing through her career for a certain time and expects for the husband to accept this, it should be mentioned in the contract. Therefore, by making the practicalities known upfront and made clear at the start of the union, there can be no misunderstandings at a later time. The concept of nikkah is carefully designed to ensure that the husband and wife do not suffer through the same hardships as relationships that involve transgression. This is not to say that the nikkah guarantees peace and tranquility, but it provides a means for Allah ﷻ to shower His blessings on a man and woman as long as they have sincere intentions towards mutually committing to each other. That is why it is a contract between both individuals, as opposed to the sort of commitment in any other relationship which is non contractual. The words of the actual contract are as follows:

The woman says, "I (here mentions her name) have made myself your wife and have accepted the mahr." Then the man responds, "I (here he mentions his name) have accepted the marriage." It is expected for these words to be recited in Arabic, and if one is unable to recite them in Arabic then a representative recites them on behalf of the individuals, as in: "(mentions the name of the female) makes herself your wife…" and, "(mentions the name of the male) has accepted the marriage." Therefore the act of marriage is in the hands of the woman.

The woman is the one who does the giving and sets the conditions of the marriage, and the man either accepts or negotiates the terms of what she is offering. Essentially, she proposes the terms of what she expects and what she is willing to give, and he accepts and promises to fulfill his obligations in return for whatever she has agreed to. There is no guessing that if one gives himself or herself wholeheartedly to a partner, then how much love they can expect will be reciprocated; as long as both willingly enter the marriage, they can expect for love to thrive between them. Once again, it is through the nikkah, and only through the nikkah, that a man and woman become legally permissible to each other for any type of close and intimate relationship, especially one that is signified by marriage.

The Mahr is a "free gift" that a man offers to a woman as a token of his commitment. It signifies the seriousness of his intention and his love for her. The Mahr is like a sacrifice of something of his substance to her as a gift that is hers to do with as she pleases. It could be something that is of significance to him such as property or money, or even a ring, or it could also be something immaterial such as learning and memorizing a Surah from the Holy Quran for her, or simply teaching a verse of the Holy Quran to her. It is significant here to point out that the Mahr must be agreed upon by the man and woman themselves, and not by their parents. Therefore, the Mahr is given to the bride and not her parents. It is for her to do with as she pleases without the pressure from the husband, her in-laws, or her family. The Mahr is part of the contract, and therefore should be given to the wife at some point in the marriage in order for the obligation to be fulfilled.

Therefore, Halal love begins with ulfat or attraction, and if it is legitimated through marriage, Allah ﷻ blesses it to be naturally followed by the stage of unsiyat; a beautiful friendship between the husband and wife comprised of equality and mutual commitment. When talking about Halal love and examples of marriage, the best example possible is that of Prophet Muhammad ﷺ. He was the best example of the ideal husband. Prophet Muhammad ensured that his marriages were beautiful. To ensure this, he fulfilled his obligations and did his part in comforting his wives, wiping their tears and caring for their complaints, helping towards alleviating their sadness, respecting their feelings, making them feel important in his life by discussing important matters with them and seeking advice, being playful with them and giving them adequate time, he supported them in emergencies, and kept their dignity by keeping their secrets, and he even declared his life to them very often. These are things we all expect within a marriage, and Prophet Muhammad ﷺ bonded with his wives psychologically, physically and spiritually. That is what unsiyat is within a Halal union: loyalty and friendship which fulfill the psychological, physical, and spiritual needs of two people.

They often say that there is telepathy between hearts. What does that mean? It means that two hearts are able to communicate with one another without the need for words, and that is one of the biggest blessings that Allah ﷻ has given us - the ability to understand each other's feelings. Hazrat Inayat Khan explains this beautifully in "Spiritual Liberty".

> "For thought-reading, for sending and receiving telepathic messages, people try physical processes in vain. If they only knew that the secret of all occult and physical phenomena lies in love! The lover knows all: the pleasure, the displeasure, the happiness and unhappiness, the thoughts and imaginations, of the beloved. No time, no space, stands in his way, for a telepathic current is naturally established between the lover and the beloved. The lover's imagination, thought, dream, and vision, everything tells him all about the object of his love." [Hazrat Inayat Khan, Spiritual Liberty, Volume V, Part IV, Chapter 1]

This ability becomes even stronger when two friends know each other for a very long time, but imagine how much potential it has for two people who are in love and are married. Over time, a husband and wife should be aware of each other's feelings. As Hazrat Inayat Khan says, it becomes natural for the lover's imagination, thought, dream, and vision, to tell him/her all about the object of his love. It is essential for the husband to be able to read the wife's body language and understand her emotions, or from her behavior, and likewise the wife should be able to read her husband as well. The mutual awareness of each other's feelings allows for both of them to work towards consoling one another, and there should always be healthy communication between the two in order for them to be comfortable with each other. Love for the sake of love allows this to be a natural growth between the lover and the beloved.

> "People call love blind, but in reality it is the light of the sight. The eye can only see the surface, love can see much deeper. All ignorance is the lack of love." [Hazrat Inayat Khan, Religious Gathekas, Number 59, Sufi Thoughts (3)]

Not being able to communicate is an indication that there are problems that the couple needs to work on in order for them to feel more comfortable. The inability to communicate creates hostilities and can become very frustrating, especially within a marriage where one looks forward to the other's presence in alleviating difficulties and stress.

One of the most beautiful examples of this is narrated by Aisha (may Allah ﷻ be pleased with her) in Sahih al-Bukhari:

> One day Prophet Muhammad ﷺ came to me and said, "I know when you are pleased with me or angry with me." I said, "Whence do you know that?" He said, "When you are pleased with me, you say, 'No, by the Lord of Muhammad,' but when you are angry with me, then you say, 'No, by the Lord of Abraham.'" Thereupon I said, "Yes (you are right), but by Allah ﷻ,

O Allah ﷺ's Messenger (Peace and Blessings be upon you), I leave nothing but your name." [Sahih al-Bukhari: 5228, or Book 67, Hadith 161]

This example makes it clear that Prophet Muhammad ﷺ observed the behavior of his wives closely enough to be able to tell when they were upset with him, and when they were pleased. He was equally as active in making sure to console his wives when they were upset. It was narrated by Al-Qasim in Sahih al-Bukhari:

Aisha said, "We set out with the sole intention of performing Hajj and when we reached Sarif, (a place six miles from Mecca) I got my menses. Allah ﷺ's Messenger ﷺ came to me while I was weeping. He said 'What is the matter with you? Have you got your menses?' I replied, 'Yes.' He said, 'This is a thing which Allah ﷺ has ordained for the daughters of Adam. So do what all the pilgrims do with the exception of the Tawaf (Circumambulation) round the Ka'ba." Aisha added, "Allah ﷺ's Messenger ﷺ sacrificed cows on behalf of his wives." [Sahih al-Bukhari: 294, or Book 6: Hadith 1]

Each partner should be there for each other in good times and bad times. Both should find comfort, warmth and love in each other, and this Hadith was an example of how gentle Prophet Muhammad ﷺ was in consoling his wives. He was very compassionate and understanding.

Ones such instance was reported by his wife Safiyah (may Allah ﷺ be pleased with her). Essentially, while on the way to Hajj with his wives, the man in charge of the caravan was riding it too fast, so the Prophet ﷺ advised him to ride the caravan slower and more carefully because there were women with them. On the way the camel of Safiyah suddenly knelt down, so Safiyah became startled and began crying. The Prophet ﷺ came when he was advised of this and began wiping her tears with his hands, but she kept crying as he told her to stop. To console her, he stopped the entire caravan and told them to camp even though it was not where he initially had planned to camp. [Al-Silsila Al-Sahiha, 7/621] This example demonstrates how the Prophet [Peace and Blessings be upon him] was not shy when it came to showing his compassion and feelings towards his wives.

In the earlier chapters of this book, I explained that sometimes people go into marriages only to be able to legitimately explore and satisfy their carnal desires. Such marriages do not last long because these relationships are solely based on desires without being driven by a sense of compassion or the yearning for peace and tranquility with each other. In such instances it becomes hard for two people to spend time together, perhaps because they aren't aware of how to enjoy each other's company beyond anything of the sexual nature. When two people are friends, and accept each other to be lifelong companions together, they begin to enjoy each other's company and crave each other's presence just to be able to spend quality time together. Such is the beauty of unsiyat; to be at peace in the presence of the other, and perhaps to feel a sense of anxiety when away from one another. An example of this was narrated by Aisha (may Allah ﷺ be pleased with her):

The Prophet ﷺ used to lean on my

lap and recite Qur'an while I was in menses. [Sahih al-Bukhari: 297, or Book 6: Hadith 4]

Can you imagine how beautiful a sight it would have been as the Prophet ﷺ would recline in the lap of Aisha (may Allah ﷻ be pleased with her) while she was menstruating? Can you imagine how happy and fulfilled she could have felt at that moment as he would recite the Holy Quran whilst reclining in her lap? Spending a little time with one's wife or husband, reclining in his/her lap, is perhaps a very small gesture, but its satisfaction is immense. It is small gestures like these which have the ability to bring the hearts closer. The psychological impact of such acts is immense, and maintain a certain passionate intensity between the spouses. It is important to note that this must go both ways. The man also equally has the desire to feel wanted and appreciated as the woman does, but the way love has been commercialized in contemporary society is that the male needs to go out of his way to make the woman feel special. For example, on days such as Valentines day, the man is expected to buy his beloved a bouquet of roses, chocolates, and a gift, etc. In Islam there is no one specific day to show your spouse that you love them, in fact, every day is an opportunity to continue to do so. Moreover, it isn't just one partners responsibility to shower the other with gifts and affection, but a mutual commitment towards making each other feel loved. An example of this was narrated by Urwa:

> "Aisha told me that she used to comb the hair of Allah ﷻ's Messenger ﷺ even if he was in Ithikaf (in the mosque). He would bring his head near her in her room and she would comb his hair, even while she was in

her menses." [Sahih al-Bukhari: 296,
or Book 6: Hadith 3]

These are examples that when the love between spouses
elevates in these stages, and when Allah ﷻ showers His
blessings upon them, they find ways to show their love
for each other, even if it is through yearning to complete
tasks for one another such as simply combing the other's
hair.

Another beautiful example of the love between the
Prophet ﷺ and his wives was narrated from Shuraih
when he asked Aisha (may Allah ﷻ be pleased with her):

> "Can a woman eat with her husband
> while she is menstruating?" She said:

> "Yes. The Messenger of Allah ﷺ
> would call me to eat with him even
> while I was menstruating. He would
> take a piece of bone on which some
> bits of meat were left and insist that I
> take it first, so I would nibble a little
> from it, then put it down. Then he
> would take it and nibble from it, and
> he would put his mouth where mine
> had been on the bone. Then he would
> ask for a drink and insist that I take it
> first before he drank from it. So I
> would take it and drink from it, then
> put it down, then he would take it and
> drink from it, putting his mouth
> where mine had been on the
> cup." [Sunan an-Nasa'i, Vol. 1, Book
> 1, Hadith 280]

These are the simple ways in which the Prophet showed

the love he had for his wives, and there is a lot to learn from these examples. To show his affection, he not only drank from the same cup but he would search for the place where the lips of his beloved wife made contact, and he would put his lips on the very same place so that his lips have touched the place where her lips had touched, and it would add a taste of love to whatever they shared together. It is also important to recall one of the most beautiful pieces of advice from Umar ibn al-Khattab (may Allah ﷺ be pleased with him) that was quoted in one of the previous chapters.

> Umar ibn al-Khattab, (May Allah ﷺ be pleased with him), said: 'A man should be like a child with his wife, but if she needs him, she should act like a man.'" [Essentials for a Happy Marriage, AlMinbar Khutbah No. 2592]

The Prophet ﷺ was a great example of achieving this balance with his wives. He knew exactly when his wives needed him to be soft, and he knew exactly when to be assertive, and he did this beautifully. He would often be playful with his wives and engage in healthy competition to keep the spark alive. It was narrated by Aisha that while she was on a journey along with the Messenger of Allah ﷺ:

> "I had a race with him (the Prophet) and I outstripped him on my feet. When I became fleshy, (again) I had a race with him (the Prophet) and he outstripped me." He said: "This is for that outstripping." [Sunan Abi Dawud, 2578]

It was also reported in another instance where Aisha said:

> "The Prophet ﷺ raced with me and I
> beat him" [Sunan Ibn Majah, Vol. 3,
> Book 9, Hadith 1979]

These were examples of how the Prophet kept his wives engaged with a little healthy competition to share good times together, and this ignited the love between them even more.

In one of the earlier chapters, I established that marriage isn't always about racing to do Wudhu (ablution) or waking each other up for Fajr prayer, etc. But the biography of the Prophet ﷺ and his wives was filled with examples of all of this, which tells you that this is exactly what a marriage consists of. Just because one has not yet been able to maintain such a relationship with their spouse, it is not reasonable to say that it is either difficult or impossible to attain. Every relationship develops over time. A husband and wife are not only partners but friends and team mates that are there to make sure they not only enjoy their life together, but lead a life that pleases Allah ﷻ. Most people find it hard to balance life and Islam together because they think it is extremely difficult to do so, but the Prophet ﷺ and his wives were examples of how easy it was to enjoy their married lives and please Allah ﷻ at the same time; for Allah ﷻ does not require us to do anything impossible. Aisha (may Allah ﷻ be pleased with her) provided another beautiful example of her relationship with the Prophet ﷺ.

> "I used to perform Ghusl (ablution) -
> the Messenger of Allah, ﷺ and I -

from one vessel. He would compete with me and I would with him until he would say: 'Leave me some' and I would say: 'Leave me some.'" [Sunan an-Nasa'i, Vol. 1, Book 1, Hadith 240]

Another important distinction between a marriage and other relationships that transgress the laws of Allah ﷻ is that whatever one does for his wife and children is counted as charity, and is rewarded, whereas,relationships outside of marriage lead one into committing sins. The Prophet Muhammad said:

> "And whatever you spend (for Allah ﷻ's sake) you will be rewarded for it, even for a morsel of food which you may put in the mouth of your wife." [Sahih al-Bukhari: 6733, or Book 85: Hadith 10]

Such is the status of marriage, and the way that Allah ﷻ has blessed it is that He encourages the spouses to care for one another, as there is reward for even feeding one's spouse with your own hands. Moreover, it was narrated from Miqdam bin Ma'dikarib (Ar- Zubaidi) that the Messenger of Allah, ﷺ said:

> "No man earns anything better than that which he earns with his own hands, and what a man spends on himself, his wife, his child and his servant, then it is charity." [Sunan Ibn Majah, Vol. 3, Book 12, Hadith 2138]

Therefore, it becomes obvious that even spending one's income on his/her spouse and children is an act of charity which is rewarded by Allah ﷻ. Why then would

232

one willingly want to transgress and not try to legitimate his/her love through marriage as soon as possible? In a relationship outside of a marriage, one tries to do as much as he/she would do in a marriage by making it work and bestowing favors and gifts on his/her beloved. He puts his heart through a lot of hardship just to please the beloved for which there is absolutely no reward, but exposes himself to the chances of sin depending on how far he goes in transgressing. But in a marriage, everything is rewarded as an act of charity, because Allah ﷻ is pleased with everything you do to please your spouse.

One of the biggest examples of this is with regards to the act of sexual intercourse. Outside of the marriage it is an enormous sin, but within the marriage it is rewarded and it increases unsiyat. Abu Dharr reported that the Prophet ﷺ said to his Companions:

> "In every declaration of the glorification of Allah ﷻ (i.e. saying Subhan Allah) there is a Sadaqa (charity), and every Takbir (i.e. saying Allah Hu'Akbar) is a Sadaqa, and every praise of His (saying Alhamdulillah) is a Sadaqa, and every declaration that He is One (La Ilaha Ill-Allah) is a Sadaqa, and enjoining of good is a Sadaqa, and forbidding of that which is evil is a Sadaqa, and in man's sexual intercourse (with his wife), there is a Sadaqa."

> The Companions then said: "Is there a reward for him who satisfies his sexual passion among us?"

> The Prophet ﷺ said: "Tell me, if he

were to devote it to something forbidden, would it not be a sin on his part? Similarly, if he were to devote it to something lawful, he should have a reward." [Sahih Muslim: 1006, or Book 12: Hadith 66]

It is through these blessings that Allah ﷻ encourages us to avoid engaging in sinful relationships and to legitimate love through marriage, so much so that even the fulfillment of the most natural of our cravings (ie. physical intimacy) becomes a reward. This is phenomenal because Islam changes the whole dynamic of what sexual intercourse is, and it becomes something other than just the fulfillment of a sexual desire created by a naturally insatiable instinct of lust and infatuation. Sexual intercourse then becomes a means of attachment that brings together two souls physically, emotionally, and spiritually. What would otherwise be a sin, now becomes something that is seen as charitable and is rewarded in the Hereafter. Therefore, one would be foolish not to try and reap the rewards of marriage.

There are many other beautiful things that happen between a husband and a wife that increase the unsiyat between them. The Prophet ﷺ would call Aisha (may Allah ﷻ be pleased with her) by the name 'Humaira' out of love. [Sunan Ibn Majah, Vol. 3, Book 16, Hadith 2474] Linguistically 'Humaira' means the rosy cheeked, and the scholars have said that in reality what he meant was to praise Aisha (may Allah ﷻ be pleased with her) for being so fair that due to the sun she would get a reddish tan. This is an example of how one can use nicknames to be playful and show endearment.

Ibn Jawziyyah in the book of "Benefits" also mentions times when the Prophet ﷺ would show love and affection to his wives through compliment and praise. Once the Prophet ﷺ stared deep into the eyes of Aisha, and in praise of her beauty he said, "How white are your eyes!" [Ibn Jawziyyah, The Benefits/Al Fawa'id, 796] It is important to remember that when the marriage is reciprocal, both partners are completely satisfied with one another because both make equal efforts to communicate their contentment and love for one another.

It was narrated in "Dala'el Al-Nabuwwah" for Imam Abu Nu'aim with support from (isnad) Imam Bukhari and Imam Ibn Khuzaina that once the Prophet ﷺ was sitting in a room with Aisha and was fixing his shoes. It was very warm, and Aisha happened to glance at his blessed forehead. In doing so, she noticed that there were beads of sweat on it. She became overwhelmed by the majesty of that sight and was staring at him long enough for him to finally notice.

The Prophet ﷺ said, "Whats the matter?" She replied, "If Abu Bukair Al-Huthali, the poet, saw you, he would know that his poem was written for you." The Prophet ﷺ asked, "What did he say?" She replied "Abu Bukair said that if you looked to the majesty of the moon, it twinkles and lights up the world for everybody to see." So the Prophet ﷺ got up, walked to Aisha, kissed her between the eyes and said, "Wallahi Ya Aisha, you are like that to me and more."

Perhaps another one of the most important things between a husband and wife is the need to prioritize. One of the most beautiful things about the Prophet ﷺ was that he was not afraid to show people what his priorities were. He prioritized the needs of his wives above all. It was narrated by Aisha (may Allah ﷻ be pleased with her) in Sahih al-Bukhari that she had borrowed a necklace from Asma which ended up being lost:

> "The necklace of Asma was lost, so the Prophet ﷺ sent some men to look for it. The time for the prayer became due and they had not performed ablution and could not find water, so they offered a prayer without ablution. Then Allah ﷻ revealed the Verse of Tayammum." [Sahih al-Bukhari, Vol. 6, Book 60, Hadith 107]

This is a very significant example because it truly does show the extent to which the Prophet ﷺ would be willing to go to please his wives. He stopped a whole army in times of extreme hostility in a region of the desert that had no water, to look for his wife's misplaced bead necklace.

In another Hadith, Aisha narrated:

> "A necklace of mine was lost at Al-Baida' and we were on our way to Medina. The Prophet ﷺ made his camel kneel down and dismounted and laid his head on my lap and slept. Abu Bakr (Aisha's own father) came to me and hit me violently on the chest and said, "You have detained the people because of a necklace." I kept as motionless as a dead person because of the position of Allah ﷻ's Apostle; (on my lap) although Abu Bakr had hurt me (with the slap).

Then the Prophet ﷺ woke up and it was the time for the morning (prayer). Water was sought, but in vain; so the following Verse was revealed:

"O you who believe! When you rise up for Salah (prayer), wash your faces and your hands as far as the elbows, wipe your heads with wet hands and wash your feet to the ankles. If you had emission of semen, then take a full bath. However if you are sick or on a journey or you have used the toilet or you had intercourse with your wife and you do not find any water then resort to Tayammum - find clean soil and rub your faces and hands with it. Allah ﷻ does not wish to burden you; He only wishes to purify you and to bestow upon you the full measure of His blessings, so that you may be thankful." [Holy Quran, 5:6]

Usaid bin Hudair said, "Allah ﷻ has blessed the people for your sake, O the family of Abu Bakr. You are but a blessing for them." [Sahih al-Bukhari, Vol. 6, Book 60, Hadith 132]

In another Hadith it was narrated by Urwa's father that on this occasion Usaid bin Hudair said to Aisha:

"May Allah ﷻ reward you. By Allah ﷻ, whenever anything happened which you did not like, Allah ﷻ brought good for you and for the

Muslims in that." [Sahih al-Bukhari, 336]

This is an extremely important incident, and its beauty is that simply because the amount of love that the Prophet (Peace and Blessings) had for Aisha (may Allah ﷺ be pleased with her) was so immense, Allah ﷺ bestowed a mercy upon mankind when He revealed the verse of Tayammum (allowing for the purification for prayer using sand or dust). Allah ﷺ also honored her in the eyes of Abu Bakr (may Allah ﷺ be pleased with him) who took the inconvenience to heart and disciplined Aisha for the trouble that was caused because of her necklace. It was narrated that 'Ammar bin Yasir said:

> "Aisha dropped a necklace and stayed behind to look for it. Abu Bakr went to Aisha and got angry with her for keeping the people waiting. Then Allah ﷺ revealed the concession allowing dry ablution, so we wiped our arms up to the shoulders. Abu Bark went to Aisha and said: 'I did not know that you are blessed.'" [Sunan Ibn Majah, Vol. 1, Book 1, Hadith 565]

This resulted in the joyous celebration of the Companions for the ease that Allah ﷺ had provided for the believers in the form of Tayammum. Had it not been for the lost necklace, perhaps the permissibility and the legislation of Tayammum would not have been revealed.

It then becomes clear that unsiyat can mean two different things and have two different consequences depending on the type of relationship one engages in. When one engages in the kind of relationship that Allah

﷽ has prohibited, he/she sets him/herself up for unnecessary hardships which could easily be avoided by trying to legitimate the relationship through marriage. In relationships outside of marriage, unsiyat begins as a one-sided friendship and attachment. However, in such cases there is no contract between two individuals of equal reciprocation or any commitment whatsoever, and therefore one willingly commits to another while not receiving anything in return; this eventually begins to hurt because it is human nature to want to be loved and appreciated in return for all that one does. The union of marriage is a contractual agreement between two people that ensures both individuals agree to their rights, responsibilities and obligations towards one another and as long as two individuals go into a marriage with a clear conscience of wanting to be together for the sake of Allah ﷻ - the marriage is showered with blessings and every act of love and affection between them is rewarded by Allah ﷻ, which would otherwise have been a sin. Every act of love and affection is encouraged by Allah ﷻ, and was practiced by the Prophet ﷺ as an example to all of mankind.

May Allah ﷻ protect us from transgressing and may He protect us from engaging in the fulfillment of our sinful desires. May Allah ﷻ allow us to enter into marriages where our love increases exponentially with every glance and may Allah ﷻ put so much love between us and our spouses that there is immense comfort and mercy in our homes. May our marriages be an opportunity for us to earn the love of Allah ﷻ, and may we find nothing less than peace and tranquility that leads us and our spouses to Jannah.

3.4
MAVADDAT
(HIGHER DIMENSION OF UNSIYAT)

As one progresses through the stages of love, he/she comes to a point where he/she experiences an excitation of the heart and is overwhelmed with passionate desire for the beloved. As simple or romantic as it may sound, its consequences are quite severe. The Chistiyya describe this stage to begin with some sort of lamentation and perturbation where the lover is now constantly in a state of moaning and expressing great agony in regards to still being so far away from the beloved. This stage involves being occupied by great anxiety, and the thought of the beloved is always on one's mind like an obsession.

Eventually the anxiety is said to cause the lover great sorrow and he/she has no other way to express this other than weeping. The feelings become too strong to cope with at times, because the lover has become so attached to the beloved, and at times it may begin to feel as if the friendship is not enough. Passionate desire begins to fill its place, and the intense craving for the touch of the beloved, or the beloved's embrace now enters the heart. This poses a danger because the fact that the beloved is still not reciprocating at this point, or is too preoccupied in his/her own affairs, which might mean that the love is one-sided, and the beloved only understands the relationship to be friendship and nothing more. This uncertainty begins to cause one a great deal of grief. It is marked by the heaviness of the heart, an unexplainable anxiousness while being away from the beloved, and its only cure becomes his/her presence; a presence in which the heart remains excited.

Perhaps at some point the beloved begins to show

some sort of attachment and this excites the heart of the lover even more. Although these signs from the beloved are not necessary, one's own attachment could also lead him/her to developing feelings of regret. It is important to realize that this isn't the type of regret where an individual blames him/herself to have developed such an attachment, but rather is the kind of regret where he/she looks back at his/her own life and contemplates about the life wasted, and feels sorrowful in the memory of the time spent without the beloved. One begins to think that his/her entire life up to this point has been a waste, and it could have been so much more beautiful with the beloved; even at this point he or she is absent minded of the agony this attachment is causing him/her. The perception of the lover is still focused on the charms of the beloved, and perceives every moment without the lover to be worse than death itself.

Even in this stage of love one is met with nothing more than sorrow and agony because he/she is still not with the beloved. His mind is overwhelmingly occupied with the thought of the beloved and the absence of the beloved is like torture. One has prioritized his/her life around pleasing the beloved and trying to get attention in order to be closer to the beloved, but perhaps the beloved has not responded. In some ways, the feeling is euphoric because one is so preoccupied with the thoughts of the beloved, and any sort of attention feels as if it has been earned. Essentially, one has utmost appreciation of even the slightest bit of acknowledgment on behalf of the beloved.

One of the things that we forget to keep in mind is that when one gives his/her full attention to another, and places him/her so high up on a pedestal then the beloved begins to think he/she is entitled to it, and always expects to be treated that way. The beloved has accepted that there is an imbalance because he/she may not have reciprocated any signs of attachment, but you've actually committed to them and given so much of yourself away that they quickly get used to it and begin taking it for granted. This puts the lover in a vulnerable position, because one has become so heavily attached to another who clearly doesn't feel the same for them.

One of the aspects of human psychology is that we naturally enjoy attention, and from childhood we learn to enjoy feeling special. Everyone likes to be pampered, and to be taken care of, and shown that they mean something to another. In many cases one may not have any genuine feelings for another individual but it's the special attention that they enjoy such as the way someone goes out of the way for them to make sure they've eaten, or even simple things like 'good morning' text messages can become something pleasing. One may not even realize that they've gotten used to being treated this way and may have begun to take it for granted due to a sense of entitlement, but they inevitably string you along because it validates their self esteem. Perhaps they don't even respond to or return, such gestures, and the lover, being so infatuated with the beloved, continues to show his/her affection; it becomes a relationship in which one exceedingly gives, and the other exceedingly takes. This is essentially what we see in many relationships. Perhaps at first there may have been some sort of a give and take which was reciprocated from both ends, but the imbalance in feelings eventually leads one to develop the feelings of entitlement which may cause them to back off since the lover gives his/her attention unconditionally.

Here is where we can engage in a bit of self reflection and think to ourselves, have we ever been in a position where we loved wholeheartedly and perhaps the other individual did nothing in return to deserve that love, but we continued to love hoping that it would eventually win them over? This is one of the reasons why transgression isn't only discouraged, but prohibited, simply because it hurts. The purpose of the marriage is to protect one's heart from these imbalances, and to facilitate a reciprocal system of love based on mutual commitment in which both the husband and wife find peace and tranquility in each other.

In another situation, perhaps at this point the facts are completely different. Imagine if both individuals have now developed similar feelings for each other and have equally fallen into a state of mind where both are preoccupied with the thoughts of the other. Eventually the friendship will not be enough because of the excitement of the heart, and the need for intimacy overwhelms the individuals. This is where the stage of Mavaddat ends and the stage of Hawaa begins, and will be discussed in more detail within the next chapter.

In terms of Halal love, the stage of Mavaddat is completely different. One has not exposed him/herself to the vulnerabilities of any inequalities and imbalances and has progressed into a relationship that has promised a mutual commitment. The significance of this becomes even more obvious when we engage in a discussion of the wealths of an individual. When mentioning wealth, the first idea that comes to mind is anything of monetary value. However, there are three types of wealth that the individual has which include: 1) money and materials, 2) body and self, 3) ego and respect.

Most often when one becomes attracted to an individual as discussed in Ulfat, it is the individual's initial inclination towards the object of the love. Here the individual initiates the first steps into getting to know or become acquainted with the beloved. One has not developed the feelings or the intensity behind the feelings to give up more than himself besides things of little monetary value through the bestowal of favors, and exchanges of gifts. In order for one to show sincerity in wanting to get to know the other, and trying to break through the beloved's 'guard' one may engage in simple acts of offering to pay for dinner, or buying flowers and chocolate, or other gifts to show his or her affection, or simply the sincerity behind it.

During the stage of unsiyat one becomes more attached and a genuine friendship between the two individuals develops which causes for one to be comfortable enough to sacrifice more than just money and materials towards the beloved. Here, he/she begins to sacrifice his/her body and self. This doesn't necessarily mean giving access to one's body through intimacy, but it means devoting more time towards the beloved and reprioritizing them into one's otherwise busy life to make sure they feel wanted. One begins to go out of his/her way for the beloved and begins to regard him/herself as belonging to the beloved.

There is a third wealth that everyone has which often means more to one than his/her money, materials, or time and this is his/her ego and respect. This is what creates the vulnerability because one completely begins to belittle him/herself by constantly giving his/her attention to the beloved without any sort of reciprocation. This often means being okay with being ignored, and one allows him/herself to engage in justifying the absence of the beloved. One has so heavily invested his time, effort, money, materials that he/she is attached to a point where he/she fears to start over with someone else, and this allows for the lover to compromise his/her respect and forego the ego just to make the relationship work with the beloved. This is one of the major differences between the relationship within a marriage, and any relationship outside of the marriage.

Within a marriage, when two individuals have decided to love each other for the sake of Allah ﷻ and fulfill their obligations towards one another at any cost, they learn to sacrifice their egos on both ends, and most of all they learn to respect one another. Of course, simply getting married does not ensure that one will sacrifice his/her ego for the other, and won't always ensure that both respect one another either because we see examples of marriages that fall apart due to the spouse's inability to learn where to compromise in order to save the marriage. But as long as two individuals are committed in making the marriage work, and they make mutual efforts towards it, Allah ﷻ blesses the union. As discussed in Unsiyat, whatever wealth one spends towards his/her spouse and children is charity which is rewarded, and this encourages both spouses to mutually spend out of their wealths towards one another.

> "And whatever you spend (for Allah ﷻ's sake) you will be rewarded for it, even for a morsel of food which you may put in the mouth of your wife." [Sahih al-Bukhari, 6733]

> "No man earns anything better than that which he earns with his own hands, and what a man spends on himself, his wife, his child, and his servant, then it is charity." [Sunan Ibn Majah, Vol. 3, Book 12, Hadith 2138]

An example of how the Prophet ﷺ compromised with his wives was when his wives complained of the scent of honey, he forbid upon himself milk infused with honey. He did not argue, he did not defend how much he liked to drink milk infused with honey, instead he respected their distaste for it and took an oath to not drink it again.

Aisha narrated:

> The Prophet ﷺ used to stay (for a
> period) in the house of Zainab bint
> Jahsh (one of the wives of the
> Prophet) and he used to drink honey
> in her house. Hafsa and I decided that
> when the Prophet ﷺ entered upon
> either of us, she would say, "I smell in
> you the bad smell of Maghafir (a bad
> smelling raisin). Have you eaten
> Maghafir?" When he entered upon
> one of us, she said that to him. He
> replied (to her), "No, but I have drunk
> honey in the house of Zainab bint
> Jahsh, and I will never drink it
> again." [Sahih al-Bukhari, 6691]

Then the following verse was revealed:

> "O Prophet! Why do you ban (for
> you) that which Allah ﷻ has made
> lawful to you in seeking to please your
> wives? Allah ﷻ is Forgiving, Merciful.
> Allah ﷻ has already enjoined upon
> you (O believers) the breaking and
> expiation of such oaths. Allah ﷻ is
> your Master and He is the
> Knowledgable, the Wise. When the
> Prophet confined a secret to one of
> his wives, she disclosed this secret to
> another and Allah ﷻ informed him
> about it, the Prophet made known to
> the said wife a part of it and avoided
> mentioning the rest. So when he told

her about this disclosure, she asked: 'Who told you this?' He replied: 'I was informed by Him Who is All-Knowing, All-Aware.' If you both (Hafsa and Aisha) turn in repentance to Allah ﷻ - for your hearts have sinned - you shall be pardoned; and if you back up each other against him (the Prophet), then you should know that his protectors are Allah ﷻ, Gabriel and all righteous believers, furthermore the angels too are his supporters. It may well be that, if he divorce you all, his Rabb will give him in your place better wives than yourselves, submissive, faithful, obedient, penitent, worshippers and keepers of fasting; be they previously married or virgins." [Holy Quran, 66:1-5]

How is it that the Prophet ﷺ can forbid himself of something that Allah ﷻ had made lawful for him simply as a gesture to please his wives out of respect, and yet many of us find it difficult to even give to our wives what is rightfully theirs? Such is the extent to which the Prophet ﷺ could go to, and therefore it is encouraged that we try and go out of our way in trying to please one another. Perhaps it would have been a gesture that Allah ﷻ may have honored, if it hadn't been a conspiracy between Hafsa and Aisha out of jealousy for Zainab, and the fact that they revealed the Prophet ﷺ's secret when he specifically requested that his oath be kept between them. Therefore another lesson from this verse is the importance of keeping secrets between one another safe from anyone else, even if it is another wife in the case of the Prophet ﷺ.

In terms of sacrificing wealth, Sayyid Ali Asghar Razwy in "Khadijatul Kubra," provides an example of the extent to which Khadijah (may Allah ﷻ be pleased with her) went for the Prophet ﷺ.

> "Most of the Muslims of Makka were poor. They had no source of income, and they had no means of making a living in a city the economic life of which was controlled by a cartel of idolators. The members of the cartel had decreed that no one would pay a muslim any wages for any work done by him, and no one would buy anything from him." [Sayyid Ali Asghar Razwy, Khadijatul Kubra, Chapter 13]

During the initial stages of Prophethood, the idolators waged an economic war against the Muslims for them to reach a point where their resistance would break down and they would abandon the Prophet ﷺ. The aim was to starve the Muslims.

> "Khadijah fed the poor Muslims, day after day, so that no one among them ever went hungry, and she provided shelter to them. For her, charity was nothing new but the size and scope of the commitment were; she spent money prodigiously on the poor and the homeless Muslims of Makka, and thus foiled the aims of the cartel" [Sayyid Ali Asghar Razwy, Khadijatul Kubra, Chapter 13]

Her support was integral, and she not only supported the Prophet ﷺ but his mission as well, and her support to the Muslim community guaranteed its survival when it was in the state of a severe blockade. Her love towards the Prophet inevitably became a type of support that was indispensable for the survival of Islam.

There was an integral difference between Khadijah (may Allah ﷻ be pleased with her) and the other wives of the Prophet ﷺ. All the women the Prophet ﷺ married in Medina, received a fixed allowance from the Public Treasury that was created by him, and they complained that it was insufficient for their needs. Some of them also claimed special prerogatives and demanded special perks, whereas Khadijah never asked for anything.

> "She made her own purse a public treasury for the Muslims. In Makka there was no Bayt-ul-Mal (Public Treasury), and it was the boundless generosity and the unlimited wealth of Khadijah that saved the Community of the Faithful from starving. She was so solicitous of the welfare of the followers of her husband that she didn't even withhold even the last coin that was in her possession, and spent it on them." [Sayyid Ali Asghar Razwy, Khadijatul Kubra, Chapter 13]

Eventually a time came where her great fortune was passed from her hands into the hands of Islam. From being rich, she became poor in the material sense, and she exchanged a lifestyle of luxury for a lifestyle of austerity. What is remarkable to acknowledge is that nothing changed in her temperament as she remained as cheerful and idealistic as before and spent even more time than ever in her devotions to Allah ﷻ and in the service to Prophet Muhammad ﷺ.

> "Khadijah told her husband that all her vast wealth was his, and he could spend it just as he wished... but material wealth was not the only investment that Khadijah made in Islam. She also invested her time, talent, energy, spirit and heart in Islam - an investment otherwise known as commitment. She knew her spouse's dreams and hopes, and she shared them all with him." [Sayyid Ali Asghar Razwy, Khadijatul Kubra, Chapter 15]

Such is the purpose of marriage, for two souls to reside as if they are two equal parts of a single soul, where one's dreams and aspirations are the aspirations of the other. The example of Khadijah (may Allah ﷻ be pleased with her) and Prophet Muhammad ﷺ is significant because she not only sacrificed her wealth, but she also accepted him to be of the greatest treasures in the world.

> "Once Khadijah was married, she appeared to have lost interest in her mercantile ventures and in her commercial empire. Marriage changed the character of her dedication and commitment. She had found Muhammad Mustafa, the greatest of all treasures in the world." [Sayyid Ali Asghar Razwy, Khadijatul Kubra, Chapter 4]

Perhaps that is the most beautiful distinction

between the type of Mavaddat that progresses within a relationship outside of a marriage, and one that progresses within a marriage. In a relationship outside the marriage, one sacrifices his/her wealth and faces great anxiety and agony as he receives nothing in return, whereas in a marriage one is easily able to sacrifice all of his/her wealth and accept the other spouse to be their most valuable treasure in the world.

There should be absolutely no need to say that any other example could come close to that of the relationship between Prophet Muhammad ﷺ and Khadijah (may Allah ﷻ be pleased with her). Perfection within the marriage, and in the relationship between a husband and a wife, a man and a woman, begins and ends at their example. However, it is important to illustrate a worldly example. Harjeet Singh Gill in "Heer Ranjha, and other legends of the Punjab", explains how Heer and Ranjha devise a plan in order to continue their romantic meetings.

> "Ranjha is engaged as a cowherd, by the parents of Heer. Every morning, Ranjha takes the buffaloes and cows of the Heer household and wanders around in the thick forest along the banks of the river Chanab. Heer joins him with his mid-day meal prepared with love and affection and all the s w e e t n e s s o f s u g a r a n d honey." [Harjeet Singh Gill, Heer Ranjha, pg. 8]

It is important to remember that Ranjha has not given up his wealth and status specifically for Heer. He willingly abandons all his property, his status as the son of the Chief of Takht Hazara, and his entire family without trying to face his problems. Ranjha doesn't do this for

Heer, but instead does it in search of a new life away from the lack of respect at home; falling in love with Heer was unexpected. Therefore, becoming a cowherd isn't much of a sacrifice but rather a plan devised by the lovers in order to help them transgress and meet each other in private.

> "When Heer proposes a disguise of a cowherd, Ranjha accepts willingly, for this is the most ambitious existence. To be a cowherd of a feudal household is a normal occupation. So naturally, nobody has any suspicion." [Harjeet Singh Gill, Heer Ranjha, pg. 29]

Upon getting caught by the family, the happy romantic days were over. Since he was the son of the Chief of Takht Hazara, he figured there was no reason why he could not marry Heer, but it becomes obvious that transgression has consequences which could either be worldly consequences or in the Hereafter.

> "He did not realize that while a regularly arranged marriage between these two feudal households was perfectly in order, it could not be so, once he and Heer, both had transgressed the prevalent social order and the scheme of things ordained by the elders." [Harjeet Singh Gill, Heer Ranjha, pg. 19]

Harjeet Singh Gill tries to present the argument that in order for Ranjha to become a cowherd, even anthropologically it is not in natural correspondence of the grand scheme of things since Ranjha is the Chief's son. Therefore, due to his status, he cannot be engaged as a cowherd in another equally important feudal household.

> "Moreover, it is not even because Ranjha has been thrown out of his village and it is the economic compulsion that forces such a solution. As such, Ranjha is both is and not a cowherd." [Harjeet Singh Gill, Heer Ranjha, pg. 29]

If one is to entertain the argument that it is economic compulsion which forced such a solution, it would be wrong either way because had they not transgressed in the first place, the outcome would have been different. The fact that they willingly chose to transgress and meet in secret, the only option left was to take advantage of the disguise as a cowherd. Therefore, it wasn't economic compulsion but a choice made willingly to facilitate the desires to transgress.

After Heer gets married, one could say that Ranjha's social status as the son of the Chief is restored since he no longer works as a cowherd. Therefore, when he turns into a Yogi with torn ears, shaved head, and a body smeared with ashes, one could say he eventually sacrificed all of his wealths.

> "The most important requirement is the avoidance of sex. For a Yogi, all women are sisters or mothers. A yogi has not only to take the vows of poverty but also of chastity of mind and body... He has left the pleasures of a feudal household. He has already renounced all wealth and vanity. There is nothing left for him in this world except to follow the path of

God." [Harjeet Singh Gill, Heer Ranjha, pg. 19]

Even though he has left all of his wealths, he had ulterior motives. It is still a plan to transgress as he discloses his real purpose.

> "He had come to the great Guru for the gift of Heer. He could avoid all lust, all the worldly goods, all pleasures of this mundane world, even all women, but Heer was another question." [Harjeet Singh Gill, Heer Ranjha, pg. 20]

It becomes obvious that a relationship which avoids the question of marriage is driven by desires, because it becomes extremely difficult to avoid acts of transgression. Any sacrifice one makes outside of a marriage is solely to become closer to the beloved and to aid him/her in his desire to transgress.

The progression through the stage of Mavaddat has opposite consequences within a marriage as compared to any relationship outside of a marriage. May Allah ﷻ protect us from relationships that have the potential to cause any anxiety and sorrow to our hearts, and if any one of us is involved in such a situation, may Allah ﷻ set our hearts free of such impure captivities and forgive us, for verily He is most Merciful. May Allah ﷻ help us all protect our love from transgression and humility in the eyes of our Lord. May the doors of marriage open for all of us, and may our love bring us nothing less than immense blessings being showered upon us by Allah ﷻ.

3.5

HAWAA
(AFFECTION AND LONGING)

In *The Radicality of Love*, Srecko Horvat explains that a "zero risk" love is not love, and falling in love consists precisely in this contingency, in the fall itself. He makes a reference to an influential yet controversial Sufi, Ibn Arabi, who understood that it is the fall that matters in 'falling in love', and he called this Hawaa. Ibn Arabi explains,

> "Hawaa literally means to fall, i.e. the falling of love or any kind of passion into the heart. A man falls in love for three reasons: 1, seeing; 2, hearing; and 3, bounties received from the Beloved. The strongest cause of Hawaa is seeing, since this does not change upon meeting the Beloved. On the other hand, the second and third causes of the Hawaa are not perfect, because love caused by hearing changes by seeing, and love caused by beneficence can cease or weaken with the ceasing of the bounties." [Srecko Horvat, The Radicality of Love, Publication by John Wiley & Sons]

He further explained that in the Holy Quran, Allah ﷻ commands the believers not to follow Hawaa because the object of Hawaa might be many things and not necessarily Allah ﷻ. Therefore, Hawaa is a kind of love that is polluted with associating partners with the love of God. Moreover, Ibn Arabi admits that although Allah ﷻ has commanded His servants to purify Hawaa and direct it to Him alone, it is impossible to eradicate it completely from the heart since it is a natural sentiment.

> "All human beings have Hawaa for a different beloved. Allah ﷻ commands His servants to direct this Hawaa to Him. But in spite of God's prohibition on following Hawaa, it is impossible to eradicate its existence." [Srecko Horvat, The Radicality of Love, Publication by John Wiley & Sons]

For the Chistiyya this stage is a progression from the overwhelming desire described in the previous stage. The lover is overwhelmingly inclined towards the beloved and longs for him/her. The lover would do anything for the beloved at this stage, and wants to spend his/her entire life in obedient devotion to the beloved by dedicating all that he/she has to him/her. There are two ways in which one could progress through the stage of Hawaa in a relationship outside of a marriage, and it depends if it is either-one sided or if the relationship is mutual. With regards to the love being one-sided, this stage is also a means to experience great agony because it is centrally focused on the concept of patience, one in which the lover has come to terms with the idea that if the beloved is not reciprocating, the only way to the heart of the beloved is to endure patiently as the beloved puts the lover through severe trials. The lover feels that as the beloved continues to test him/her, and as he endures the pain steadfastly, eventually the beloved will be convinced that the love is true. At this stage, the lover is so infatuated with the beloved that he/she cannot seem to understand that the beloved may never feel the same, and the continual denial leads to him/her coming up with justifications, and pushing him/herself to endure a little more because even a mere glance from the beloved ignites hope as the lover is reminded of exactly what he has to lose if he/she gives up hope.

Eventually Hawaa reaches a point where one becomes helpless, and is conflicted with two opposing ideas. On one side he/she thinks that if he/she gives up on the beloved, it would be giving up on love itself. Every fiber of his being will try to convince the lover not to give up on love, because even though he/she may wish to transgress, and even though he/she may be driven by lust and desire, subconsciously he/she understands love to be sacred and worthy of honor. Knowing that it would require enduring more anxiety and more agony, the lover still wishes to uphold the love's integrity. On the opposing side he/she is equally overwhelmed with hopelessness and helplessness. The lover is humiliated to the point where he/she slowly begins to come to terms with the fact that nothing is in his/her power and at this point the lover breaks down. As the lover further progresses in this stage, the anxiety and sorrow give rise to defense mechanisms, and all hope is still not lost. One now turns to whatever idea of God he believes in, and he/she begins to humble him/herself and prays.

One restlessly evokes Allah 襁 night and day, and his hopes of attaining the beloved almost become immortalized as he/she attaches these hopes in the Mercy of the All Mighty. The lover reaches an actively fluctuating state of mind which depends on his/her level of frustration and longing for the beloved. The state of mind consists mainly of a fluctuation in satisfaction and trust in Allah 襁. Moreover, one's satisfaction not only fluctuates in his trust in Allah 襁, but in his/her contentment with the decisions of fate as well. One day the individual may pray for the decision of Allah 襁 to be in his/her favor, and the next day the individual may pray for what is best for the beloved. One day the individual may be content with the separation and will have full faith that if it is destined then nothing could keep the two apart, whereas other times, the lover will be restless and frustrated because his/her desire to be with the beloved will overwhelm him again. On some occasions the lover may even wake up and feel an intense longing, and will weep and complain why his prayers have not been fulfilled, but then a sense of contentment will overcome him and he/she will begin to observe patience again.

As previously explained, much of life has been decreed, but indeed prayer has the power to change the decree of Allah ﷻ. However, when evoking Allah ﷻ one needs to remember that perhaps the beloved is nothing more than a trial and Allah ﷻ has better plans which are perhaps inevitable despite the amount of prayers one engages in. Sometimes the individual we pray for is toxic for us, and no matter how much we are convinced that they are good for us, Allah ﷻ knows what we do not. In the previous chapters it was also discussed that Shaytaan will convince you that the beloved is made for you, and fill your mind with baseless romantic notions such as their hands are meant to hold yours, their eyes are meant to look into yours, and everything in your heart will tell you that they have been created for you. But perhaps the attraction to this individual is a test of your emaan.

You pray day and night for this individual, you stand before Allah ﷻ, the Lord of the Worlds, in pleading for this individual; but perhaps the purpose of this individual is solely for Allah ﷻ to see if He does not grant you this individual will you abandon His call? Most often we do, especially when it was for this specific individual that we became close to Allah ﷻ, and when the prayers are not granted, we abandon the prayer and our attachment to Allah ﷻ, being completely unaware of the beautiful plan that Allah ﷻ has for us. It happens far too often that when we take a mere impediment in our path to be the destination itself, we tend to then forsake Allah ﷻ. May Allah ﷻ guide us to strengthen our trust in Him. May we begin to understand that the cracks in the sidewalk are meant to be avoided, and if we refuse to do so, we will trip over them. The purpose of reiterating this piece of advice is to remind you that Allah ﷻ has a plan in motion, and He wants to protect you and bestow upon you what is best for you. If these prayers are not fulfilled, one must continue to have faith and be content with the divine reasoning in Allah ﷻ's response. This marks the end of the stage of Hawaa with regards to being a one-sided attachment.

In the previous chapter we concluded that when two individuals are mutually inclined towards one another, and are mutually attached, the stage of Mavaddat ends with an uncontrollable desire for one another until the lovers no longer have the capacity to ignore it. This is where Hawaa begins. Ibn Arabi defines Hawaa to be the Arabic term which signifies the falling of desires into one's heart for something. The urdu equivalent of the term is 'Havas/Hawis' which does not simply signify the falling of desire in one's heart, but stands for desire and lust itself. Hawaa begins when one decides to initiate the first step towards the beloved, and engages in subtle transgressions such as holding hands which may initially seem harmless. However, as long as love is driven by lust and passion, it will always begin as a spark and the first act of transgression will become the fuel to the fire. Holding hands may, for some time, be as far as one goes, but eventually it will not be enough and one may desire more, like a kiss. This first kiss will lead to occasional kisses, and for some time that may be as far as the two will go but, just as before, eventually it will no longer be enough. The fire only burns more passionately until it is put out. At some point in the relationship transgressions will no longer feel like transgressions because the hearts will have become so impure that there will no longer be a sense of remorse or guilt, and it may even lead to fornication.

As explained in the earlier chapters, Sufis call the love for anything else other than Allah ﷻ to be metaphorical, and they don't consider it real love because the inclination of the heart is driven by desire. Hence the heart is afflicted with a disease of desire, and once Hawaa enters the heart, and the object of desire submits and acts of transgression take place, the desire and the pursuit of the beloved only increases because the fire in the heart becomes strengthened.

In situations where the object of desire does not submit, and the attachment or inclination remains one sided, the sickness of the heart and mind is also as severe. However, in some situations when the beloved shows no signs of reciprocation, the feelings of desire fail to be satiated and at times the desire weakens. This is why some people are temporarily attracted towards someone, and feel as if they progressed through he stages of love, but easily fall out of it. This is because the love was driven by lust in the first place, and the individual intended for there to be acts of transgression to accompany his/her desire. When the desire is not satiated, the Hawaa extinguishes and the lover simply falls out of love and claims to have 'moved on.'

Some lovers are more passionate than others and progress through the stages of love, but they hold back on their desires and are patient. They resist Hawaa because of their fear of Allah ﷻ and they are rewarded for this. It was reported that Prophet Muhammad ﷺ said:

> "The one who passionately loves someone yet holds back, conceals this and is patient, then dies upon this, will be a martyr." [Al-Jawab al-Kafi, Rawdha al-Muhibbin of Ibn Al-Qayyim and Silsilah ad-Da'ifah of Al-Albani]

It is important to note that this Hadith is known to be the report of Yahya al-Qatat from Mujahid from Ibn Abbas from the Prophet ﷺ and the chain of narration makes it problematic, so such Hadith is not to be depended upon entirely. The reason for including it in this book is that there are evidences from the Quran that if one were to hold back from engaging in unlawful acts (looking, speaking, and acting a certain way) and remains obedient to Allah ﷻ, the pain and inconvenience that he incurs as he observes patience is always rewarded. Allah ﷻ says in Surah Yusuf:

> "Allah ﷻ has indeed been gracious to us. In fact as for the righteous and patient; Allah ﷻ really does not let the reward of the righteous be wasted." [Holy Quran, 12:90]

Allah ﷻ reminds us of this again in Surah An-Nazi'at when He says:

> "But as for him who had feared standing before his Rabb and restrained his soul from lust and evil desires shall have his home in

paradise!" [Holy Quran, 79:40-41]

Allah ﷻ knows that when the soul loves something, it will do everything possible to attain it.

> The nature of life is such that every little pleasure costs incomparably greater pain. The lover, therefore, has collected all pain that is the current coin, and his path will be smoother through life's journey from earth to heaven. There he will be rich when all others will be found poor. [Hazrat Inayat Khan, Spiritual Liberty, Volume V, Part IV, Chapter IV]

Therefore when one restrains his/her soul from fulfilling his desires and engages in being patient, especially when it hurts him to do so, Allah ﷻ rewards the believer for the patience.

One of the very important distinctions made by Harjeet Singh Gill in "Heer Ranjha" is that when the two characters fall in love with each other, it is Heer who takes all the initiatives and Ranjha simply follows her until her marriage. Even when Heer realized that she will be forced to marry Saida, she suggests that they should elope, but Ranjha is not very enthusiastic. This changes when he is separated from her.

> "The prolonged separation transforms a lazy and spoiled Ranjha into an assertive, active lover who must plan and execute his schemes with absolute accuracy and maximum risk... When Heer was active and assertive, Ranjha showed no sign of an active lover. When Heer was helpless and confined

to the house of her in-laws, his existential condition changes and he is then transformed into a resolute man." [Harjeet Singh Gill, Heer Ranjha, pg. 33]

This is an example of how transgression works; perhaps his laziness and inability to show signs of being an active lover to do anything either within the bounds of religion or even outside of religion to secure Heer meant that he wasn't actually in love. He only realized his love for her after the separation where he decided to pursue her actively and assertively. Transgression allows for two people who are mutually inclined towards one another to let their guard down, but one of the primary dangers of this is that there may exist an imbalance of feelings between the two, and one lets his/her guard down whereas the other takes advantage of the opportunity without being completely sure of his/her feelings.

Similarly, in today's world we see two individuals who claim to be in love, and it could be a situation similar to Heer and Ranjha where both show signs of reciprocation. Both mutually transgress under the label of being in love, but one of them is active and assertive, while the other is still unsure. But being unsure of these feelings did not stop Ranjha from meeting in private. Was he not aware that he was transgressing against the laws of Islam by meeting a non-mahram woman in private? It was transgressing, regardless of how much they asserted that their love was a sentiment and a union which was sanctified by the Panj Pirs, the five divine sages. In fact, Gill states that it was not a worldly affair of sex and lust, theirs was the purest relation, a relation approve even by God [Harjeet Singh Gill, Heer Ranjha, pg. 20]; but the reality was simply that they were both transgressing. They were not married, nor did they take the initiative to legitimate their love through marriage, until it was made impossible due to the consequences of transgression.

We see this happening quite often in our society, and perhaps we are guilty of this to a certain degree. Even if our goal is marriage, the moments that we spend together with the beloved, the conversations, the flirtation, the awakening of desires, and any type of physical contact are still acts of transgression. However, we continually engage in such acts because we've justified to ourselves that we are trying our best to legitimate the love and make it Halal. We need to remember that the ends do not justify the means, nor do the means justify the end. Consider a situation in which Hawaa has led two individuals to transgress because in their minds they've convinced themselves that they are going to get married when the time comes. Perhaps in a moment of weakness they have held hands, kissed, and eventually let their guard down to such an extent that it eventually resulted in fornication. Now let's imagine that for some reason marriage is made impossible for the two individuals due to family not approving of the partner due to cultural circumstances. Essentially, these two individuals have become so attached to one another, and have transgressed so far that their sins are enormous in the eyes of Allah ﷻ, yet it is impossible for them to get married with the blessings of the family. Eventually one of them may back out and does not marry the other because he/she is not ready to face the familial consequences. Can you imagine the pain and agony that would result from such an attachment? You loved them more than anything in the world, and you even committed a sin to please them, but that same individual that you trusted could not stand up for you. Would it all have been worth it?

Consider another situation in which both individuals willingly transgressed and met in private, and Hawaa similarly led them into fornicating. However, in this situation it is similar to the case of Heer Ranjha where one of them had been active and assertive in his/her love for the other, whereas the other was still confused and unsure of his/her feelings. Imagine if you were in a similar situation (May Allah ﷻ forbid and protect you from such situations). You may have let your guard down, let someone into the deepest and most precious depths of your heart, become so attached that you're ready to fight for them no matter what obstacle faces you, and have even transgressed to the point where you've had sexual intercourse with them. Imagine if at this point they back off, and realize it was all a mistake and it shouldn't have happened. Imagine if they didn't 'love' you in the first place. Can you imagine the agony that you'd put your heart through if you allowed yourself to be a victim of such a situation? The laws of Islam are there to protect you from all of this. The laws of Islam, and particularly marriage as an institution, are designed to protect your heart from agony and from impurity. If someone truly loves you, they'll actively seek your hand in marriage and fight against all odds for you. If the feelings are mutual and if the individual really wants to marry you, they will do what is in their power to secure you as a spouse because of the fear of losing you. If someone truly loves you, they'll respect you enough to protect you from even the smallest acts of transgression that would humiliate you in the eyes of Allah ﷻ.

As previously explained Hawaa in a marriage is not regarded as a sin; in fact sexual desire for one's spouse doesn't even come under the definition of Hawaa because, as Ibn Arabi explained, Hawaa is something that Allah ﷻ has prohibited. The marriage, being a union that Allah ﷻ has encouraged, promotes sexual relationships; in fact anything within the marriage that promotes unity and love is an act of charity. The concept of Halal and

Haram are worlds apart, but out of His Ultimate Grace and Generosity, Allah ﷻ has ordained all that which would otherwise have been Haram to be totally permissible within a Halal union. If men and women love one another within a marriage for the sake of Allah ﷻ, this love becomes a blessing, while those who love each other only out of natural lusts are ignorant of the blessings in Halal Love. As Srecko Horvat explains in "The Radicality of Love",

> "Take sex: if it is being done between two people who are not only attracted to one another but have fallen in love, isn't this sex the most wonderful merging of divine and profane? All those bodily fluids that are normally considered disgusting suddenly become divine." [Srecko Horvat, The Radicality of Love, Publication by John Wiley & Sons]

Why then would anyone willingly want to expose him/herself to becoming so vulnerable under Hawaa and instead not take every possible measure to legitimate his/her love? Why would one expose him/herself to the chances of anxiety and agony to the point where he/she becomes so helpless that the only thing left to do is to weep out of such helplessness? May Allah ﷻ protect us from falling into Hawaa for anything other than Him, and if such a trial is destined to us, may Allah ﷻ give us the strength to overcome the uncontrollable urge to transgress. If we find ourselves to have transgressed, may Allah ﷻ ease our trial and have us repent before casual transgressions lead to greater sins. Verily, Allah ﷻ is Most Forgiving and the All- Compelling. May Allah ﷻ compel our hearts into love for the sake of Him, a love that guarantees us His Eternal Paradise.

3.6
SHAGAF
(VIOLENT LOVE)

The state of Shagaf is marked by extreme passionate desire and an overwhelming excitation of the heart. It is distinct from the kind of passionate desire in the earlier stages because the lover now has developed a sense of ownership over the beloved. Moreover, the lover has also lost himself to the beloved in complete submission. This is often referred to as violent love because there are underlying feelings of aggression involved, which may mean different things to different people. For some it may mean choosing death over a life without the beloved because one can no longer imagine living a life in which the beloved does not play a significant part. For others it may mean extreme jealousy which may be caused by insecurities that were not addressed in the earlier stages or even because of valid reasons of suspicion, which may lead to aggressively trying to uphold one's authority or ownership over the beloved.

The word Shagaf has been used in the Holy Quran to describe the love Zulaikha had for Prophet Yusuf (Joseph) (Peace and Blessings be upon him). In Surah Yusuf, Allah ﷻ describes Zulaikha being overwhelmed with the desire for Prophet Yusuf (Peace and Blessings be upon him):

> The women of the city began to talk about this incident (to one another) "The wife of the ruler is trying to induce her slave-boy to yield himself unto her! Truly hath he inspired her with violent love, we see that she is undoubtedly suffering from an

aberration!" [Holy Quran, 12:30]

In this stage, one's feelings have become so strong and aggressive that the lover now sees him/herself as belonging to the beloved. The lover is convinced that no love will be worthy enough to replace the love for the beloved, and the lover begins to guard his/her heart from turning towards anyone else. One can already begin to see why Islamic mystics would have a problem with this kind of love, for one has now completely submitted to the beloved. One has come so far into transgressing that he/she has allowed his/her heart to forsake everyone but the beloved, and this means he/she has become detached from religion.

The purpose of life is now the beloved, whatever the lover does is for the beloved, and every act is solely to please the beloved. It sounds very much like an extreme obsession, as one is beginning to lose control of him/ herself. The lover begins to shun everything that is distasteful to the beloved and accepts the likes of the beloved to be his/her own. Moreover, as one progresses through the stage of Shagaf, the lover begins to accept everything that belongs to the beloved as his/her own. The lover also begins to seclude himself away from what once belonged to him/herself. At this point the lover may have distanced himself from his/her friends that he once was very attached to, or from his/her family who may oppose the beloved, and this may also include forsaking religious obligations.

For some, the obsession reaches a point where he/ she is determined that at some point in time the prayer to be with the beloved will be fulfilled. Therefore, the lover clings on to praying for the beloved and absolutely refuses to acknowledge how toxic this attachment is. For others, the obsession means complete submission to the beloved and forsaking one's religious commitments including prayers.

This is a stage which also signifies a type of symbolic death of the self, where everything about the lover is now in accordance with the likes and dislikes of the beloved. This is extremely unhealthy and dangerous because the beloved still may not have responded to the love, and the attachment the lover has to the beloved could still be one-sided.

Although marriage does not singlehandedly guarantee peace of mind with respect to having a loyal relationship, if both partners have willingly bound themselves to one another for the sake of Allah ﷻ, and have taken it upon themselves to fulfill the obligations and duties owed to each other another, what results is a sense of satisfaction and contentment. Both individuals are then at peace in knowing that they belong to one another; and this provides a sense of ownership of each other which is contractually binding. In relationships outside of a marriage, no matter how committed one can be, this sense of satisfaction or peace of mind is considerably much less. This creates a dangerous potential for insecurities to develop within the earlier stages of love, where the lover may feel as if he/she is not enough for the beloved and the lover also feels that he/she could easily lose the beloved to another. These feelings aggressively come to the surface in the stage of Shagaf through jealousy.

Since the lover has committed himself entirely to the beloved and devoted himself in his/her submission, the lover easily gets jealous of the interactions that the beloved cannot seem to forsake or gives any importance to. The lover always feels as if he/she has to compete for the beloved's attention, and this insecurity causes the lover a great amount of agony.

The example of the Prophet ﷺ and his marriage with Khadijah (may Allah ﷻ be pleased with her) shows that within the marriage, Shagaf has the potential to play out beautifully as opposed to surfacing feelings of aggression and agony within the lover. Outside of the marriage, the lover feels as if he/she needs to compete with the beloved's other social connections, however within a marriage the lover begins to have a special place for the friends of the beloved and accepts them to be his/her own. This is exactly how the Prophet ﷺ loved Khadijah (may Allah ﷻ be pleased with her), such that even after her death he continued to love and respect not only her friends, but anyone else she showed even the slightest bit of kindness towards in her lifetime.

In "Khadijatul Kubra, a short story of her life", Sayyid Ali Asghar Razwy explains that even if Khadijah (may Allah ﷻ be pleased with her) had shown someone kindness only once, Prophet Muhammad ﷺ remembered it, and he made it a point to show the same kindness to that person as often as possible.

> "In Medina, once an old woman came to see Muhammad Mustafa with some request. He greeted her cordially, showed much solicitude for her welfare, and complied with her request there and then. When she left, Aisha who was one of his wives, asked him who the old lady was. He said: "When Khadijah and I were in Makka, this woman came from time to time to see her." [Sayyid Ali Asghar Razwy, Khadijatul Kubra, Chapter 16]

Therefore, after the death of Khadijah (may Allah ﷻ be

pleased with her) the recipients of her generosity and kindness became the recipients of the generosity and kindness of her husband. It was reported by Aisha:

> Whenever a goat or a sheep was slaughtered (in the house), the Messenger of Allah, ﷺ ordered its meat to be sent to the ladies who at one time had been friends of Khadijah. One day I asked him why did he do so, and he said: "I love all those people who loved Khadijah." [Isaba, Vol. 4, p. 283]

The Prophet ﷺ also shared gifts that he would receive with the people Khadijah (may Allah ﷻ be pleased with her) loved, in memory of her. It was reported in Al-Adab Al-Mufrad that Anas said:

> "When the Prophet, may Allah ﷺ bless him and grant him peace, was given something, he used to say, 'Take it to so-and-so. She was a friend of Khadijah's. Take it to the house of so-and-so. She loved Khadijah." [Al-Adab Al-Mufrad, 232]

The Prophet ﷺ loved Khadijah so much that even after her death, despite the passage of time and even having a number of wives in his life, his love for her only grew. His love for her was so intense even after her death that it made Aisha (may Allah ﷻ be pleased with her) jealous. Aisha reported:

> "Never did I feel jealous of the wives of Allah ﷻ's Apostle ﷺ but in the

case of Khadijah, although I did not (have the privilege to) see her." She further added that, "Whenever Allah ﷻ's Messenger ﷺ slaughtered a sheep, he said: 'Send it to the companions of Khadijah.' I annoyed him one day and said: '(It is) Khadijah only who always prevails upon your mind.' Thereupon Allah ﷻ's Messenger ﷺ said: 'Her love had been nurtured in my heart by Allah ﷻ Himself.'" [Sahih Muslim, 2435 b]

That is how much strength love within a marriage has; even after the death of his wife and after marrying other women, the Prophet ﷺ still had so much love for Khadijah (may Allah ﷻ be pleased with her) that it had the potential to incite feelings of jealousy in Aisha (may Allah ﷻ be pleased with her). With regards to jealousy, it has the potential to destroy a person and a relationship on the grounds of suspicion. This is often the result when one reaches the stage of Shagaf in a non-marital relationship where the lover is not made to feel adequate enough for the partner. Jealousy however, is promoted within the marriage so much so that even Allah ﷻ encourages it. This is a very specific type of jealousy though, which is referred to as Ghairah. The closest definition or explanation of Ghairah is protective jealousy, or an instinct within the individual to protect the beloved from the vulturous gaze of another, or from unwanted advances from another, etc. It was narrated from Abu Huraira (may Allah ﷻ be pleased with him) that the Messenger of Allah, ﷺ said:

"There is a kind of protective jealousy

that Allah ﷻ loves and a kind that Allah ﷻ hates. As for that which Allah ﷻ loves, it is protective jealousy when there are grounds for suspicion. And as for that which He hates, it is protective jealousy when there are no grounds of suspicion." [Sunan Ibn Majah, Vol. 3, Book 9, Hadith 1996]

Society has progressed into a state in which most individuals have lost their sense of modesty, and we have become unreasonably occupied with our appearances. We often wear select styles and items of clothing, and adorn ourselves to attract the attention of the opposite gender, sometimes even if we are married. This is because the definitions of love has been altered, and it is instead mistaken for lust and the fulfillment of desire. Halal love (Ishq) has become true love's forgotten creed, and people are more inclined towards short term affairs and frivolous relationships. Social networking and the sheer number of people who no longer seem to know true love's meaning, has led to people swiftly seeking to replace their partners for another without any guilt. In Islam, the concept of Ghairah is meant to reinforce this lost sense of modesty. Allah ﷻ likes it when a man feels jealous or protective over his wife, sister, and other women related to him and doesn't like other men to caste glances at them. Moreover, this goes for women as well. Allah ﷻ likes it when a woman feels jealous or protective over her husband. It is a natural feeling that Allah ﷻ has blessed us with, and the Prophet ﷺ had the most Ghairah for his wives, and his companions were known for their Ghairah as well.

To exemplify just the Ghairah of the Companions alone, Abu Huraira (may Allah ﷻ be pleased with him) once told the Prophet ﷺ about a dream he had. He said:

> "While I was asleep, I saw myself in Paradise and there I beheld a woman making ablution beside a palace, I asked, 'To whom does this palace belong?' She said, "To 'Umar bin Al-Khattab.' Then I remembered Umar's Ghairah (concerning women), and so I quickly went away from that palace." [Sahih al-Bukhari, 3242]

This is a significant example of the Ghairah of Umar bin Al-Khattab (may Allah ﷺ be pleased with him), because people feared the protective jealousy that Umar bin Al-Khattab had for his women, to such an extent that even in a dream Abu Hurairah was subconsciously aware of this.

Another example of the Ghairah of Umar bin Al-Khattab was that he even disliked it if his wives attended prayer in congregation in the Mosque. It was narrated by Ibn Umar that:

> "One of the wives of Umar (bin Al-Khattab) used to offer the Fajr and the 'Isha prayer in congregation in the Mosque. She was asked why she had come out for the prayer as she knew that Umar disliked it, and he has great Ghairah. She replied, 'What prevents him from stopping me from this act?' Another wife replied, 'The statement of Allah ﷺ's Messenger ﷺ prohibiting men from stopping Allah ﷺ's women-slaves from going to Allah ﷺ's mosques' prevents

him.'" [Sahih al-Bukhari, 900]

Therefore, the Ghairah of Umar (bin Al-Khattab) was well known, and his wives respected this Ghairah unless it was something that the Prophet ﷺ had already prohibited.

Another example of both Ghairah and Modesty between the husband and wife was the example of Asma bint Abu Bakr and Az-Zubair. It was narrated by Asma:

> "I used to carry the date stones on my head from Zubair's land given to him by Allah ﷻ's Messenger ﷺ and this land was two third forsake (about two miles) from my house. One day, while I was coming with the date stones on my head, I met Allah ﷻ's Messenger ﷺ along with some Ansari people. He called me and then, (directing his camel to kneel down) said, 'Ikh! Ikh!' so as to make me ride behind him (on his camel). I felt shy to travel with the men and remembered Az-Zubair and his sense of Ghairah, as he was one of those people who had the greatest sense of Ghairah. Allah ﷻ's Messenger ﷺ noticed that I felt shy, so he proceeded. I came to Az-Zubair and said, 'I met Allah ﷻ's Messenger ﷺ while I was carrying a load of date stones on my head, and he had some companions with him. He made his camel kneel down so that I might ride, but I felt shy in his presence and remembered your sense of Ghairah.'

On that Az-Zubair said, 'By Allah ﷻ your carrying the date stones (and you being seen by the Prophet [peace and blessings be upon him] in such a state) is more shameful to me than your riding with him.' [Sahih al-Bukhari, 5224]

This Hadith explains the sense of dignity and modesty that Asma had. She was so shy in front of men, and so careful about her husband's feelings and sense of Ghairah that she refused the Prophet's ﷺ help, even though the Prophet ﷺ was the purest of men and even though it meant bringing hardship on herself. The beauty of this example is also that it shows how much love Az-Zubair had for Asma, that even though he had a strong sense of Ghairah, he felt ashamed that he had inconvenienced his wife.

Ghairah in both men and women allows them to encourage their spouse's Haya (modesty). Modesty is a beautiful trait in both men and women, and it is an integral part of being Muslim. It was narrated by Abu Huraira (may Allah ﷻ be pleased with him) that the Prophet ﷺ said:

"Faith (belief) consists of more than sixty branches (i.e. parts). And Haya (This term 'Haya' covers a large number of concepts which are to be taken together; amongst them are self respect, modesty, bashfulness, and scruple, etc.) is a part of faith." [Sahih al-Bukhari, Hadith 9]

Moreover, it was narrated from Anas (may Allah ﷻ be

pleased with him) that the Messenger of Allah, ﷺ said:

"Every religion has its distinct characteristic, and the distinct characteristic of Islam is modesty." [Sunan Ibn Majah, Vol. 5, Book 37, Hadith 4181]

With regards to the character of the Prophet ﷺ, Abu Sa'id narrated that the Prophet ﷺ was more shy (from Haya: pious shyness from committing religious indiscretions) than a veiled virgin girl [Sahih al-Bukhari, 6119].

This is the beauty of the stage of Shagaf and how one progresses through it within a marriage. It strengthens the bond between the husband and the wife, whereas in non-marital relationships it leads to one's destruction and a loss of self-control. As explained earlier, the lover prefers death instead of living a life without the beloved. What this means is, the lover begins to lose hope in the decree of Allah ﷺ and goes as far as wishing death upon him/herself. This is illustrated by Harjeet Singh Gill in, "Heer Ranjha" when Heer has a debate with the Qazi with regards to the permissibility of a forced marriage. When she refuses to marry because of her promise to Ranjha, the Qazi threatens Heer during the Nikkah that her parents will kill her if she does not obey them. She replies:

"What is the point of saving her life now if for her broken promise she will have to suffer the fires of hell for eternity after her death, for even if she does not die today, she will die some other day. What is the good of living a life of a damned person waiting for the punishment of God after life? She would rather be killed than anything." [Harjeet Singh Gill, Heer Ranjha, pg. 11]

This passage was included in this book because it sheds light on a very significant social issue that needs to be addressed. The fact that Heer fell in love and wanted to marry someone of her choice warranted her death, according to the Qazi. This is the idea of honor killing that many cultures and societies are faced with, where young women are murdered for falling in love and transgressing in relationships, and patriarchal figures try to justify the murder under the laws of Islam. The entire purpose of this book is to prove otherwise; love is intrinsic to Islam. Murder is prohibited and Allah ﷻ says in Surah An-Nisaa:

> "Whoever kills intentionally, his punishment is hell to live therein forever. He shall incur the wrath of Allah ﷻ, Who will lay His curse on him and prepare him for a dreadful punishment." [Holy Quran, 4:93]

Moreover, in Surah Al-Maida Allah ﷻ clarifies:

> "We ordained for the Children of Israel that whoever kills a person, except as a punishment for murder or mischief in the land, it will be written in his book of deeds as if he had killed all the human beings on the surface of the Earth and whoever will save a life shall be regarded as if he gave life to all the human beings on

the surface of the Earth." [Holy Quran, 5:32]

Essentially, Allah ﷻ is saying is that whoever kills one person unjustly it is as if he has killed all of humanity, and whoever saves the life of one person, it is as if he has saved or given life to all of humanity. Moreover, the intentional and unjust killing will be met with the wrath of Allah ﷻ in the Hereafter.

I need to make reference to the significant verse in Surah An-Nisaa again to point out that, in accordance with Islam, men are the protectors and maintainers of women.

> "Men are the overseers over women because Allah ﷻ has given the one more strength than other, and because men are required to spend their wealth for the maintenance of women. Honorable women are, therefore, devoutly obedient and guard in the husband's absence what Allah ﷻ require them to guard their husband's property and their own honor. As to those women from whom you fear disobedience, first admonish them, then refuse to share your bed with them, and then, if necessary, discipline them. Then if they obey you, take no further actions against them and do not make excuses to punish them. Allah ﷻ is Supremely Great and is aware of your actions." [Holy Quran, 4:34]

Prophet Muhammad ﷺ further clarified that,

> "Every one of you is a guardian and everyone of you is responsible (for his wards). A ruler is a guardian and is responsible (for his subjects); a man is a guardian of his family and responsible (for them); a wife is a guardian of her husband's house and she is responsible (for it), a slave is a guardian of his master's property and is responsible (for that). Beware! All of you are guardians and are responsible for your wards." [Sahih al-Bukhari, 5188]

Therefore, both Allah ﷻ and his Messenger ﷺ have both made it explicitly clear that it all comes down to the male figures of the family, which includes the father and brothers, to be responsible for overseeing their families. This includes not only protecting, feeding, and sheltering them, but also guiding them to the right path.

We often forget it comes down to us as both fathers and brothers to protect and guide the women in our families, in order to preserve their honor, the same honor some are so quick to murder the women for. How often do we fail in fulfilling the rights and responsibilities that we are obligated towards our women? We owed them these obligations. We owed them a duty of care. It was commanded upon us to have protected them and guided them. If only we had done our jobs correctly and watched over them, maintained better family relationships in which our daughters and sisters were comfortable in trusting us with their daily doings and sharing secrets, that we wouldn't have had to worry about our paper-thin honors. Why is it then when the thought of honor killing comes to our minds as extremely misguided brothers and fathers, we forget to ask ourselves 'where was our honor when we abandoned the obligations prescribed upon us by the King of Kings?' What then makes us morally obligated, or even morally justified in killing the ones we ourselves were obligated to guide? Honor killings are unjust, and forbidden.

It is culture, not Islam which forbids us to love. It is cultural ideologies that maintain our women must marry within the family, or within our culture or within our tribes. It is culture which defines these paper thin thresholds of honor which we try to uphold and maintain. Islam, as previously explained, has made it clear that we, as Muslims ,can love and marry any other Muslim regardless of his skin color, race, ethnicity, social status. Allah ﷻ has absolutely no concern for the differences in race, skin color, wealth or the prestige of an individual. To Allah ﷻ the only relevant distinction among His creation is the distinction in piety. Therefore, that is what we must learn to value above anything else that we give value to.

May Allah ﷻ guide us in fulfilling our responsibilities towards our families and may we learn to love the creation of Allah ﷻ equally without prejudice based on our differences. May we learn the true value of our individual modesty, and learn to love each other to a point where we develop a protective jealousy over our spouses. May Allah ﷻ protect our relationships from our own insecurities and suspicion based on jealousy without reason.

3.7
ISHQ
(TRUE LOVE)

Perhaps the most beautiful of the stages of love is Ishq. When one reaches the stage of Ishq, he/she has perfected his love, and anything beyond this stage is madness. This is the state of mind which all lovers seek to experience, but the loss of control and enslavement to one's desires often misleads many lovers further and further away from ever experiencing this stage in love. Ishq comes with a natural satisfaction and contentment where the lover is at peace. An indicator of this is the lover's good morals and good conduct, both in public and private. The conduct of the lover is praiseworthy, especially towards the beloved. The lover has reached a state of mind in which he/she does not think of anyone except for the beloved, and his/her eyes behold nothing except for the beloved.

Compared to the earlier stages of love, the lover no longer has the need to exile himself from anyone else in order to protect his/her heart from external influences. The lover has earned the trust of the beloved, and the beloved is aware of the sincerity in the love and has responded. The lover no longer needs to cut himself off from his social connections, but may choose to do so to prioritize the beloved and to spend more time with the beloved. The significance of Ishq is that the lover is at the stage where nothing else could penetrate his/her heart except the beloved; therefore there is no need to detach from society completely.

As one progresses through the stage of Ishq, he/she is so focused on the beloved that despite being an active part of society his vision remains intoxicated with the image of the beloved. He/she is not afraid to show his/

her love, to express his/her innermost feelings in public, as the judgement of people do not affect love because there is no disgrace in the display of affection towards the beloved. The lover is put through several trials as he/she may be met with people who are far more beautiful or charming than the beloved, but this does not distract the lover because the inner beauty of the beloved means more to the lover than anything else.

> It is natural for a lover to become infatuated with someone whom he admires, with whom he desires union. But no one object in the world is so perfect as fully to satisfy the aspiration of the loving heart. This is the stumbling-block that causes every beginner in love to fall. The successful travelers on the path of love are those whose love is so beautiful that it provides all the beauty that their ideal lacks. The lover by doing this in time rises above the changeable and limited beauty of the beloved, but begins to see into the beloved's inner being. In other words, the exterior of the beloved was only a means of drawing the love out of the heart of the lover, but the love led him from the external to the innermost being of the ideal of his love. [Hazrat Inayat Khan, Spiritual Liberty, Volume V, Part IV, Chapter VI]

The complexion of the beloved, his/her figure, the eyes, the smile, and everything else which was the initial basis of attraction that the lover felt towards the beloved, now becomes secondary to the beloved's inner self. Being exposed to the inner self of the beloved, the lover is now someone of 'insight' and understands the beloved at a deeper level. This is where the telepathy between the hearts gets stronger, as one understands the other so deeply that words are no longer required to express one's desires or needs. The connection and understanding between the hearts that started in the earlier stages is now perfected.

All the aforementioned descriptions of Ishq apply within a marriage, along with the mutual intensity of affection towards one another. Ishq is reciprocal. One only reaches this stage with the blessings of Allah ﷻ, as it is a divine gift. A Sufi once said:

> "Love is a divine gift, not a thing that can be acquired by human effort without divine grace. If the whole universe wished to attract love, it could not. If it made the utmost effort to repel it, it also could not." [Sufi of the Chistiyya Order, al-Hujwiri]

Two individuals are only granted this peace and tranquility in love if they have done everything in their power to protect each other from transgression, and if they legitimated their love through marriage. It is then Allah ﷻ's promised blessing that one feels the intensity of Ishq, and one is not alone in the way he/she feels, for the beloved is also as just incomplete without the lover.

In the stage of Ishq, the lover is free from all the turmoil and anxieties that anyone would face in the earlier stages of love where he/she would have transgressed. In fact, in transgressing, the lover would never have reached the stage of Ishq as it is an ecstasy only true lovers get to taste. There is no jealousy, because

Allah ﷻ has ensured mutual trust between the spouses. There is no room for lust of anything external, as Allah ﷻ has blessed the spouses with intimacy, and the fulfillment of each other's needs between the spouses is encouraged through rewards. There is no fear of losing the beloved, as the beloved has contractually agreed to be one with the lover and Allah ﷻ has showered His blessings on this union. There is no anxiety, for the lover and the beloved are now one, and they have chosen to love one another for the sake of Allah ﷻ. There is no sorrow or grief, for there is mutual respect between the spouses. There is no impatience, for the lover and the beloved are both at peace and enjoy the tranquility of each other's love.

The stage of Ishq involves being immersed in intense love for one another, in which one is not afraid to show his/her true feelings. The examples of the Ishq between Prophet Muhammad ﷺ and his wives are especially beautiful. The love between Prophet Muhammad ﷺ and Khadijah (may Allah ﷻ be pleased with her) in particular has proven to be the most beautiful of love stories one could ever come across, as even after her death Prophet Muhammad ﷺ forever remembered Khadijah (may Allah ﷻ be pleased with her) with affection, gratitude and love. When she was alive, he took as much care of her as she took care of him.

> During her illness, he kept a nightlong vigil nursing her, comforting her and praying for her. He told her that Allah ﷻ had promised Eternal Bliss to her, and had built for her a palace of pearls in Paradise. [Sayyid Ali Asghar

Many of us feel shy or too full of pride and ego to take care of our spouse, because we don't want to show too much emotion. Men especially seem to have these macho images of themselves that they try and play off with indifference. However, in Ishq all of this disappears as the lover feels no disgrace in caring for the beloved, and this quality actually esteems him/her in the eyes of people. Can you imagine the humble nature of the Prophet ﷺ? He was the toughest of men to have undergone the hardest of trials from Allah ﷻ, and yet when it came to his love for Khadijah (may Allah ﷻ be pleased with her), he was as soft as he possibly could be, spending entire nights taking care of her and attending to her needs.

Another cultural issue and ideology that many of us are faced with is that of gender norms. We are often raised and taught to believe that some things are explicitly the job of girls, and other things are explicitly the job of boys. As we grow up, we feel as if any overlap between the duties of the different genders is somehow degrading to one's pride, and therefore many of us feel that it is degrading or emasculating for men to assist their wives in household duties. This flawed ideology is foreign in Islam though. In fact, Al-Aswad said:

> "I asked Aisha, may Allah ﷻ be pleased with her, 'What did the Prophet, may Allah ﷻ bless him and grant him peace, do when he was with his family?' She replied, 'He would do chores for his family, and when it was time for the prayer, he would go out.'"
> [Al-Adab Al-Mufrad, 538]

One may ask, what exactly does 'chores' mean? This was in fact further clarified in another instance by Hisham, who said:

> "I asked Aisha, 'What did the Prophet, may Allah 🙵 bless him and grant him peace, do in his house?' She replied, 'He did what one of you would do in his house. He mended sandals and patched garments and sewed.'" [Al-Adab Al-Mufrad, 540]

These are activities which are often associated with the duties of women in most cultures, whereas the Prophet 🙵 used to do these chores on his own. This is significant because we live in a time where many of us work from nine to five, and we come home exhausted; this is also applicable for men who come home with a sense of arrogance and dominance over the wife, especially if she is a housewife who may not work the usual nine-to-five shift. We often forget that even if the wife is not working on such a schedule, attending to the children and managing household chores is a job that requires energy twenty four hours a day, seven days a week, without any days off. The Prophet 🙵 understood this during a time when work was more intense than it is now, where many citizens were farmers or businessmen who worked outside of the typical eight-hour work day schedule. Comparatively, many of us sit at a desk all day long, and drive comfortable air conditioned cars to and from work, and yet we come home and cannot seem to spend a few minutes trying to share the household chores.

This is the beauty of the stage of Ishq; the lover doesn't care for ego or pride to come between his/her love towards the beloved. For example, the lover doesn't care if he needs to wash dishes to show his appreciation of all the hard work his wife has done at home all day, or if he needs to wake up in the middle of the night to attend to the baby who is relentlessly crying. The lover knows only one thing, he/she loves the beloved intensely, and would do whatever it takes to show his/her undying love. The lover takes steps to go beyond the call of duty to attend to the needs of the beloved, without the beloved ever having to ask. Therefore, when we find partners or develop an attraction towards another, we really need to think about these things. Does this person have the heart to love you beyond what is required of him/her to do so? Or is the person you're attracted to only concerned with what you have to offer in the relationship, and has little to give on his/her end? May Allah 🕮 teach us how to love, and how to go beyond what is expected of us in order for us to truly perfect our love for our spouses.

At any point in the earlier stages of love, whenever the lover expresses his/her love in public, he/she may begin to feel ill at ease and is afraid to be laughed at or ridiculed for being so helplessly in love with the beloved. But as one progresses to the stage of Ishq, the opinions of the outside world no longer matter. The lover is no longer ill at ease or embarrassed to be in love, and is instead entirely comfortable in expressing this love in public. The only opinion that is of any value is that of the beloved, and thus the lover expresses his/her affection openly. The Prophet 🕮 was never shy in admitting who he loved, especially his wives. Abu Uthman narrated that Prophet Muhammad 🕮 sent 'Amr bin Al As as the commander of the troops of Dhat-us-Salasil. 'Amr bin Al As said:

> "(On my return) I came to the Prophet and said, 'Which people do

you love most?' He replied, 'Aisha.' I said, 'From amongst the men?' He replied, 'Her father (Abu Bakr)'. I said, 'Whom (do you love) next?' He replied, 'Umar.' Then he counted the names of many men, and I became silent for fear that he might regard me as the last of them." [Sahih al-Bukhari, 4358]

This example illustrates that Prophet Muhammad ﷺ did not feel shy of whom he made aware of his life for Aisha (may Allah ﷻ be pleased with her), and he wasn't afraid to say it publicly, especially in her absence. Moreover, when 'Amr bin Al As thought that his question was perhaps misunderstood, he clarifies saying that he meant amongst the male companions whom did the Prophet ﷺ love? He responds, 'Her father.' This is significant because he does not respond 'Abu Bakr', which means his response is still focused on Aisha (may Allah ﷻ be pleased with her) because, even in her absence, she was still so much on his mind and in his heart that he says 'her father'. In a single response he continued to express his affection for her and his devotion to her family. It is important for one to respect the family of his/her spouse as his/her own, and for the beloved to reciprocate this. This happens naturally in Ishq, as there is no differentiation between the beloved and the lover. Allah ﷻ helps the husband and wife to truly become two parts of a single soul.

From time to time, love requires reassurance, and as honest and vocal as the Prophet ﷺ was in the absence of Aisha (may Allah ﷻ be pleased with her), he was just as vocal in expressing his love to her in her presence, and she too was equally expressive. In fact, they would often use code words to express their love playfully. It is said that:

> "She too loved him greatly in return and often would seek reassurance from him that he loved her. Once she asked him: 'how is your love for me?' He replied, 'Like a strong binding knot,' meaning that it was strong and secure. And occasionally she would ask him: 'How is the knot?' and he would reply, 'It is in the same c o n d i t i o n , a s s e c u r e a s ever!'" [Recorded by Abu Nu'aym in Hilya al Awliya (2/44), Al Shawkani in al Fawa'id al Majmu'a fi al Ahadith al Mawdu'a (no. 1180)]

In all the other stages of love, the lover is faced with anxiety, sorrow, and various kinds of hardships. In these other stages, the lover often compares his/her condition to that of the beloved and thinks that the beloved is much better off. Hence, the lover begins to envy the beloved, and believes that since the beloved is unresponsive, he/she must be much happier; this causes the lover to think, 'Perhaps if I were the beloved, I would have been much happier.' On the other hand, the stage of Ishq requires one to rise above this thought, and it is when the lover finally loves selflessly that he/she truly perfects his/her love.

One side of the lover is selfish, and this is the side that the lover must learn to overcome. The selfless lover endures all hardships, undergoes all torments, and bows in humility just to honor the inclination of his heart towards the beloved, but the selfish side always reminds the lover to look at how much happier the beloved appears in comparison. This selfish side says, 'Be happy like the beloved. Look at how the beloved is at peace in such an exalted position, and look at yourself. You've loved endlessly, and all for what? Humility and degradation?' Hazrat Inayat Khan says that these are the whispers of Satan that stop the lover from loving to his full potential.

The stage of Ishq can only happen when one overcomes all these doubts and blocks out these misleading whispers of Satan.

> "The fire of love will exalt him so that his power will even influence animals and birds; the wise and foolish will be attracted to him alike. Once he is purified, burned in the fire of love, he will become the attraction of every soul, of ever being, invisible as well as the visible. It is only the advice of satan that keeps him from that." [Hazrat Inayat Khan, Volume VII, Chapter I]

One of the ways in which the lover can be sure that he/she is at the stage of Ishq is because the way that the lover no longer cares about the state mind of the beloved, or any reciprocation. The lover simply loves for the sake of love, and for the sake of Allah ﷻ because nothing brings him more peace than loving the beloved wholeheartedly. There is neither remorse, nor regret for having loved. There are no feelings of envy towards the beloved, for the lover finds peace and comfort in simply being able to love. Within a marriage in which both spouses have the intention to love for the sake of Allah ﷻ and both are willing to honor their rights and obligations towards the other, Allah ﷻ blesses both spouses to feel mutually for each other. Therefore, both spouses are at peace and love each other selflessly; this is the ultimate blessing from Allah ﷻ and the reward of Halal love. To be able to love wholeheartedly, and to be loved wholeheartedly in return is what Allah ﷻ encourages us to purify our hearts for.

May we truly learn to keep our hearts pure from the ills of transgression, and may Allah ﷻ not only bless us with righteous spouses, but make us among the most precious of blessings for another. May we learn to love no less than what we are capable of loving, and may we be rewarded with the kind of love that is no less than how we deserve to be loved.

3.8
IBADAT
(WORSHIP AND ENSLAVEMENT)

Ibadat means to worship, and there are various kinds of worship. The first is the worship of God in heaven by those who understand Him as an entirely separate entity. Then there is the worship of a God on earth, as a god or goddess, in the form of an idol, or of some being who is considered as an incarnation of God. One of the fundamental principles of Islam as a monotheist religion is that it is focused on the existence of one God or in the oneness of God. Every Prophet taught his people the same lesson, and the Holy Quran affirms this in Surah Al-A'raf:

> "INDEED, We sent forth Nuh (Noah) unto his people, and he said: 'O my people! Worship Allah ﷻ, you have no god but Him. If you do not listen to what I say, I fear for you the punishment of a Mighty Day." [Holy Quran, 7:59]

Allah ﷻ further elaborates on this in Surah An-Nahl:

> "No doubt We raised in every nation a Rasool (Apostle), saying: 'Serve Allah ﷻ and keep away from Taghut (Satanic forces).' After that, Allah ﷻ guided some of them while deviation proved true against the others. So travel through the earth and see what was the end of those who denied Our Message." [Holy Quran, 16:36]

In Surah Yusuf, Prophet Yusuf (Peace and Blessings be upon him) also affirms this message:

> "I follow the faith of my forefathers Ibrahim (Abraham), Ishaq (Isaac) and Ya'qoob (Jacob). It is not fitting that we attribute any partners with Allah ﷻ. It is the grace of Allah ﷻ on us and on mankind (that He has not made us the servants of anyone else other than Himself), yet most of the people are not grateful." [Holy Quran, 12:38]

Not only has Allah ﷻ made clear that He is One, and that every Prophet came down with the same message of Oneness, but Allah ﷻ also defines the basis of our Creation in the Holy Quran in various chapters to worship Him alone. In Surah Az-Zariyat, Allah ﷻ says:

> "And I (Allah ﷻ) created not the jinn and mankind except that they should worship Me (Alone)." [Holy Quran, 51:56]

Moreover, in Surah Al-Isra', Allah ﷻ says:

> "And your Rabb has decreed to you that: You shall worship none but Him..." [Holy Quran, 17:23]

Not only has Allah ﷻ commanded us to worship Him alone, but He has made clear in multiple verses that assigning partners to Him is of the highest of sins. In Surah Luqman, Allah ﷻ says:

"And, lo, Luqman spoke thus unto his son, admonishing him: 'O my dear son! Do not ascribe divine powers to aught besides God: for, behold, such (a false) ascribing of divinity is indeed shirk; surely committing shirk is the worst iniquity." [Holy Quran, 31:13]

In Surah An-Nisaa, Allah ﷻ says:

"Verily Allah ﷻ does not forgive shirk (associating any partner with Him); and may forgive sins other than that if He so pleases. This is because one who commits shirk with Allah ﷻ, does indeed invent a tremendous sin." [Holy Quran, 4:48]

In Surah Al-Hajj, Allah ﷻ metaphorically describes how greatly misguided one is when he ascribes partners to Allah ﷻ:

"... whoever assigns partners to Allah ﷻ, it is as if he had fallen from the sky, and the birds had snatched him, or the wind had thrown him to a far off place." [Holy Quran, 22:31]

One of the greatest dangers of being so madly in love and recklessly progressing through the stages is that one can become enormously misguided that one may begin to worship the beloved.

Sayyid Muhammad Rizvi in "Marriage and Morals in Islam" discusses that there are two levels of love in

Islam. First, there is the love for Allah ﷻ, and then there is the love for everything else. Islam does not forbid an individual to love his spouse, children, parents, relatives, friends, and the worldly blessings that Allah ﷻ has bestowed upon him or her. In fact, Sayyid Muhammad Rizvi also sheds some light on an important topic; essentially, he discusses the ways in which people prepare for the hereafter. Some submerge themselves in the blessings of this world and completely forget the hereafter, and therefore they set themselves up for the torments and the consequences of their actions in the hereafter. Some people such as the Mystics and the Sufi's forsake this world completely for the hereafter. Lastly, he clarifies that Islam promotes a balance which is between these two extremes and that is to utilize this world for the hereafter.

Indeed there are many verses in the Holy Quran which highly praise the blessings of this world, and many other verses which strongly advise Muslims to seek the pleasures of the hereafter, and to remain in this world as mere travelers without getting attached to it. When one sees any of these verses in isolation, these verses can be used to prove either of the extreme views, that one should forsake the hereafter for this world, or that one should forsake this world for the hereafter.

There are also verses in the Quran which discuss the relationship between this world and the next, and promote a sense of balance. If one was to isolate the verses then they would contradict each other, therefore one cannot isolate these verses because they are not meant to be understood that way. Each verse is meant to compliment the other. By allowing ourselves to understand the Holy Quran in this manner, it becomes clear that we, as Muslims, are meant to utilize this world and all of its blessings to the best of our ability in order for us to prepare for the hereafter. In Surah Al-Qasas,

Allah ﷻ has made it clear:

> "Seek instead, by means of what Allah ﷻ has given you, to attain the abode of the hereafter, while not neglecting your share in this world." [Holy Quran, 28:77]

Therefore, Allah ﷻ does not want us to totally forsake this world, but the test of our lives is to learn to attain a balance. By either forsaking this world for the hereafter, or forsaking the hereafter for this world, we equally fail in attaining that balance. Allah ﷻ wants us to benefit from the blessings in this world and to love this world, but not to the extent that we forget the hereafter. In Surah Al-Jamu'a, Allah ﷻ says:

> "When you finish the Salah, then disperse through the land and seek the bounty of Allah ﷻ (go back to your normal business). Remember Allah ﷻ frequently, so that you may prosper." [Holy Quran, 62:10]

Therefore we must strive to achieve a balance between our worldly enjoyment and the obligations that Allah ﷻ has prescribed upon us, without hindering either of them. Of course there will be times when we must compromise our worldly enjoyment in order to prioritize our religious duties, such as pausing the Basketball game in order to pray Maghreb on time. The hereafter is dependent upon how obedient we are to Allah ﷻ in our worldly lives,. Therefore, we must learn to live in a way that allows us to make the best of our blessings in this life so that they help us attain rewards in the hereafter.

One is free to enjoy the worldly blessings that Allah ﷻ has given him/her. As explained in earlier chapters, the blessings of honoring one's family and kinship are so immense that Allah ﷻ dishonors those who fail to fulfill the rights and obligations of the family and the ties of kinship. Moreover, it was explained that anything an individual does for his/her spouse which could even be as simple as feeding one's spouse with his/her own hands, is considered to be an act of charity. Therefore, Islam expects love to be in harmony with the love of Allah ﷻ, and it should be based in the love for Allah ﷻ. Therefore, whatever we love must be for the sake of Allah ﷻ, and if a conflict occurs between the demand of the love for Allah ﷻ and the love for anything else, then the love for Allah ﷻ should ultimately take precedence.

In our daily lives we often have situations that arise which require a compromise that we must make, but in our love for Allah ﷻ there should be absolutely no compromise, as no other obligations or responsibilities come close to those which we owe to Allah ﷻ. In Islam, Allah ﷻ is the axis of existence, and He is the absolute truth. Worshipping Allah ﷻ is the purpose of our existence and therefore, we must always prioritize Him. Sayyid Muhammad Rizvi continues to explain this phenomenon in a metaphorical manner:

> "The moon revolves around the earth, but at the same time, it also revolves around the sun. Moreover, the magnetic relationship between the moon and the earth is a minor part of the overall magnetic force which makes the planets revolve around the

sun in our solar system. Similarly, in Islam the love between two human beings is like the relationship of the moon and the earth; and the love which a Muslim has for Allah ﷻ is like the relationship of the sun and the planets." [Sayyid Muhammad Rizvi, Marriage and Morals in Islam, Chapter Two]

Therefore the first type of love, which is the love between a man and a woman, or between an individual and his/her parents, etc. exists within the realm of the second type of love which is the individuals love for Allah ﷻ. To clarify in other words, there are two different cycles of love: the love for Allah ﷻ and the love for one's husband, wife, children, etc. The first is a wider circle within which exists the second circle of love. Therefore, the priority or the love that takes precedence is the love for Allah ﷻ, and whatever else one chooses to love should be for the sake of Allah ﷻ and should be in harmony with this wider circle of love.

Most people fail to understand this and believe that Islam forbids love. However, Islam does not forbid love for anything else as long as it is in harmony with the love for God. One's love for his wife, or her husband, or children, or anything else should not overwhelm him/her to the extent that he/she needs to forsake the love for God. In Surah At-Tauba, Allah ﷻ makes this clear when He says:

"O Prophet, tell them: 'If your fathers and your sons and your brothers and your spouses and your relatives, and the worldly goods which you have acquired, and the business in which you fear a loss, and the homes which you take pleasure in - (if all these) are dearer to you than Allah ﷻ, His Rasool (Messenger), and making Jihad (struggle) in His way, then wait until Allah ﷻ brings about His decision. Allah ﷻ does not guide the transgressors." [Holy Quran, 9:24]

In this verse Allah ﷻ goes above and beyond in defining exactly what we were discussing earlier. Instead of just mentioning spouses, parents and children, Allah ﷻ also mentions the love for wealth, worldly possessions and our businesses and livelihood. Allah ﷻ talks in a comparative manner and says that if any of us love other things or persons more than we love Allah ﷻ, then we are wrong, because such love for anything else other than Allah ﷻ can lead us on the path of disobedience, and can cause us great torment in the hereafter.

When one loves something more than he/she loves Allah ﷻ, he is almost ascribing a partner to Allah ﷻ that is worth more to him than Allah ﷻ Himself. Often such extents of love lead one into putting the beloved so high up on a pedestal, that the lover ends up worshipping the beloved. This was evident in the story of Laila and Majnun. At one point Majnun is so overwhelmed with grief and sorrow that he falls to his knees as though at prayer and he cries out, 'For God's sake, who can cure me of this sickness?' and instead of invoking God, he calls out to Layla.

"Layla, my love, my dearest heart! I am your slave, your victim: I am the hunter captured by the game! My soul cannot help but follow the mistress who owns it. If she says, 'Drink the wine of love and become intoxicated!', then I must obey; if she says, 'Become mad with desire!', who am I to argue?" [Nizami, Layla and Majnun - The Classic Love Story of Persian Literature, Chapter 7]

Majnun gets up and begins to walk away as he says his farewell to the people of the town, and once again he no longer has the strength to move and falls to his knees.

"He fell to his knees in the dust, as though in prayer, and began to impose his beloved to help him. 'Layla, I have fallen. I have fallen and I do not know what to do. Come, dearest heart, and take my hand. Reach out and touch me, for I can bear this loneliness no longer. I am yours, so come and take me: I am more use to you alive than dead... Come and enslave me, my love!" [Nizami, Layla and Majnun - The Classic Love Story of Persian Literature, Chapter 7]

It is at this stage where the lover is in extreme danger because this form of worship brings nothing to the individual but humility and disgrace in both worlds, and it is the greatest of all sins. One begins to idolize the beloved and prioritize the beloved in a way that he/she begins to forsake Allah ﷻ and His commandments. One will miss his/her prayers without remorse, but a sense of regret and remorse will overwhelm the lover if he/she is late in meeting the beloved.

In idolizing the beloved and forsaking Allah ﷻ, one lives a life that is completely opposite to the purpose of his/her creation which is to worship Allah ﷻ alone. May Allah ﷻ protect us from ascribing partners to Him, and may Allah ﷻ keep our hearts pure from such impurities, and our minds void of such obsessions. May we love Allah ﷻ above anything else in the world, and may we love everything else for the sake of Allah ﷻ.

3.9

JUNOON
(MADNESS AND BEWILDERMENT)

Junoon is the Urdu word for madness, and madness can mean different things to different people. Some tend to love madly, and some desire to be loved to the point of madness. Some find madness to be an obsession and nothing more than that, whereas some find it to be the only way to love. For some, madness is a complete loss of control, and for others madness is a blur between right and wrong in the means of attaining the beloved. Some value madness as being the extent of passion, while others fear it to be a mental illness. In the simplest terms however, for the one in love, madness is simply the inability to be understood, and for those who are not in love, madness is failing to understand. It is important to note that Junoon is a stage that does not follow a specific order, and it is entirely possible for the lover to be inflicted with Junoon at any point in time; it isn't just constricted to yearning for the beloved, but the lover can also experience Junoon even after being united with the beloved.

Junoon involves the burden of impatience within the heart of the lover. This burden becomes so unbearably heavy that the lover loses his/her strength. One can be overwhelmed with Junoon either before he/she is united with the beloved because of an intense yearning that leads to a loss of his/her senses. The lover could also be inflicted with a sense of Junoon after being one with the beloved, where any further separation from the beloved is now intolerable as the lover has yearned enough and does not want to let the beloved out of his/her sight any longer.

Junoon is excitement; it is losing one's self to his/

her passion. It is the inability to comprehend right from wrong. Junoon is extreme, intense enthusiasm where one is on the verge of lunacy in which the things he/she would do for love and the things he/she wouldn't do are both a menace to him/herself. It sounds a lot like an impairment in judgement, almost frightening to imagine, but for the lover, it is simply a state of mind in which all is justified. It involves doing anything and everything necessary in attaining the beloved, and in keeping the beloved. The lines between sanity and insanity are blurred. Junoon isn't just passion, but it is going beyond the extent to whatever passion may be.

In extreme cases, the behavior of the lover that develops an intense and unbearable longing for the beloved becomes completely insane; he/she has eyes that shed many tears, a heart that is constantly burning, and the he/she is always distracted, and may even aimlessly wander in lonely places. The lover does not know anything but the beloved, and utters nothing but the name of the beloved. In his/her madness the lover may talk to stones, grass, and inanimate objects about the beloved. Perhaps the prime example of Junoon is the story of Laila and Majnun, and particularly the person Majnun became after his separation from Laila.

> "Having lost his heart, he now lost his mind. All he could do was wander around in a trance, extolling Laila's beauty and praising her virtues to everyone he met. The more people saw him and heard what he had to say, the more insane he appeared and the more bizarre became his behavior. And everywhere the stares and the pointing fingers, the laughter and the derision, the cries of 'here comes the madman, the Majnun!'" [Nizami, Layla

Once Majnun was even seen kissing the paws of a dog. The individual witnessing this asked Majnun, "Why on earth are you doing that?" Majnun replied, "This dog has just come from the street on which Laila lives. That is why I am kissing its feet." What else can such an obsessed and insane person be called except for "Majnun"!

Majnun used to circle the street where Laila lived, reciting the following couplets:

> "I circle the walls of the house of Laila,
> Sometimes I kiss this wall, sometimes I kiss that one, It is not love for these walls that has infatuated my heart, But the love of who lives within them."

[Shaykh Zulfiqar Ahmad, Ishq-e-Ilahi, translated by Faqir Publications, pg. 77]

With all of this being well known, Majnun's parents eventually thought the best solution was to approach the parents of Laila for her hand in marriage, because she was equally in love with Majnun. Her parents responded well to this proposal by explaining that Laila too was constantly troubled with the thoughts of Majnun and even though members of their tribe would not agree to the marriage, they do not mind. Their only condition was that they needed to be convinced that Majnun was sane. On hearing this, Majnun's parents advised him to behave sensibly, and thus he agreed and they went to Laila's house.

> "The dog that used to accompany

Laila to school happened to come into the room where they were sitting. As soon as Majnun's eyes fell on this dog his emotions broke out. He could not sit in the high seat and look at the dog. He ran to the dog and kissed its paws and put all the garlands of flowers on the neck of the dog. There was no sign of reverence or worship that Majnun did not show this dog... This conduct plainly proved him insane... Laila's parents refused their consent to the marriage." [Hazrat Inayat Khan, Spiritual Libety, Volume V, Part IV, Chapter V]

Separation from the beloved for a second time brought about his separation from the rest of those he loved. He was no longer the same with his family, friends, and even with himself. All he could do was wander the streets aimlessly with no sense of direction as he was driven completely by an aching heart. He was oblivious to what people thought of him and what they called out to him. He could not see the staring eyes and the pointing fingers.

"The shell of his being had cracked, revealing the rawness of his soul. He was open, exposed, his innermost feelings and emotions laid bare. Not only had he lost Laila, he lost himself." [Nizami, Layla and Majnun, Chapter 4]

Friends, family, well-wishers, and everyone who heard of Majnun had done everything they could to try and reason with Majnun, but Junoon knows no reason! His friends explained that there are many girls who are perhaps even more desirable than Laila. They said, 'Instead of torturing your heart and turning it into a shrine for the one you cannot have, find someone who will comfort it instead. Forget Laila, let her go!' But those who are not in love cannot understand the intense fire that the lover has burning in his/her heart for the beloved, and thus his friends had absolutely no idea how intense Majnun's love for Laila really was. It is true that those who have never experienced such pain cannot understand it, nor can they council against it, for it would be equivalent to mocking a pain one has not endured.

Eventually, Majnun reached the point where he could not tolerate the company of others. He left everyone and ran away deep into the desert, unaware of where he would end up. All he did was cry, "There is no power except for the power of God," and he desired nothing more than to put himself at the mercy of his Lord and the desert wastes.

> "For Majnun, good and bad were no longer distinguishable; for him, what was right and what was wrong could no longer be known. He was a lover, and love knows no laws... He was not even aware of himself; it was as though he had ceased to exist, as though his name had been erased from the book of Creation, causing him to be forgotten. His heart was crushed, his flame of life had all but gone out, the bird of his soul had lost its will to live and now lay, fluttering helplessly in the dust, waiting for death to overtake it." [Nizami, Layla and Majnun, Chapter 7]

Junoon is as if the lover loses his/her mind, but it is

308

completely justified to him/her, for it is simply the intensity of the love he/she has for the beloved. It knows no reason, nor does it understand or subjects itself to any laws. But it brings about great humility both in this world and in the hereafter, for one totally abandons everything for the worldly beloved. In abandoning the world, one also forgoes all obligations bestowed upon the individual, especially his/her spiritual obligations. The more one loses sense of himself, the more he also loses consciousness of Allah ﷻ. As fascinating as Junoon may have sounded, this is where it gets frightening. However, if Junoon for the worldly beloved can bring about humiliation, imagine how must esteem and honor Junoon for the One True Beloved could bring in both the world and in the hereafter!

Communication with Allah ﷻ is done through Prayer (Salah) and Du'a. Imagine if one becomes so attached to Allah ﷻ through regularly conversing with Him during prayers, that being late for a prayer constitutes as a type of separation from Him. Imagine going completely out of your mind, and having tears in your eyes in being even a minute late for your prayer. Imagine how much Allah ﷻ would love the sentiment in which your heart and mind become overwhelmed just because you are late to appear in front of Him. The world may call you mad, or the world may even console you and say it's okay if you are a few minutes late because religion has been made easy for you, and Allah ﷻ will forgive you. But imagine the intensity and the Junoon in your love for Allah ﷻ that it drives you to be completely unaware of what is reasonable and what is not in this case, and you may even pray in the middle of the street or wherever you may be. Imagine how much love Allah ﷻ would have for you. This lover of Allah ﷻ would be considered mad in the world, but the heavens will know of his passion and his commitment towards Allah ﷻ. Humility in love towards a worldly beloved is accounted for in the Hereafter, but whatever humility you face towards the path of Allah ﷻ is rewarded for abundantly.

The story of Prophet Yusuf (Peace and Blessings be upon him) and Zulaikha is a perfect example to illustrate some of the points discussed in this chapter. The story of Prophet Yusuf (Joseph) (Peace and Blessings be upon him) and Zulaikha is an example of the consequences of beauty in this world. Prophet Yusuf (Peace and Blessings be upon him) was the second last son of Prophet Yaqub (Jacob) (Peace and blessings be upon him) and he was a man with many gifts, including the gift of prophecy and immense beauty. His beauty was able to captivate the attention of anyone and because of this, Yusuf (Peace and Blessings be upon him) had a great influence on his father and anyone else that he met. This made his elder brothers extremely jealous, and they conspired to throw him into a well.

After some time, a group of merchants who were passing by found Yusuf (Peace and Blessings be upon him) in the well as they were drawing water, and they pulled him out. The merchants were extremely fond of him because of his beauty, and decided to sell him as a slave. Yusuf (Peace and Blessings be upon him) was purchased as a slave by the chief of Misr (Egypt), who made him his personal attendant.

Zulaikha, the beautiful wife of the chief became attracted to the youthfulness and charm of Yusuf (Peace and Blessings be upon him) as soon as she laid eyes on him for the first time. Every-day her attraction towards him grew stronger and stronger, and she regarded him as not a mere slave, but rather as a king.

Zulaikha became so consumed by Yusuf (Peace and

Blessings be upon him) that she experienced a sense of Junoon. She lost all sight of what was right and what was wrong, and began losing control of herself. She was so overwhelmed with desire that she had no idea of what to do and how to proceed when he was around.

> "And (it so happened that) she in whose house he was living (conceived a passion for him and) sought to make him yield himself unto her; and she bolted the doors and said, "Come thou unto me!" (But Yusuf) answered: 'May God preserve me! Behold, my master has provided me with good residence. Should I betray his trust? Such wrongdoers shall not prosper.'" [Holy Quran, 12:23]

There are many versions of this story that have been passed down from generation to generation and changed through verbal communication over the years. Allah ﷻ, through the Holy Quran, narrates only some of the necessary details with regards to the lessons one is to take from this story. The rest of the story has been passed down and recorded through various sources and narrated by Sufis. In *Spiritual Liberty, Volume V, Part IV, Chapter II*, Hazrat Inayat Khan explains that Zulaikha admired Yusuf (Peace and Blessings be upon him) and played with him, and they became more intimate every day until a spell of passion overcame Yusuf (Peace and Blessings be upon him).

> When the shadow of passion fell upon the soul of Yusuf, Zulaikha happened to think of covering the face of the idol, which was in her room. This astonished Yusuf and made him ask her, 'What doest thou?'

She said, 'I cover the face of my god that teeth us with his eyes full of wrath.' This startled Yusuf. He was the vision of his father pointing his finger towards heaven. Yusuf said, 'Stay, O Zulaikha, of what hast thou put me in mind! The eyes of thy god can be covered with a piece of cloth, but the eyes of my God cannot be covered. He seeth me wherever I am.' [Hazrat Inayat Khan, Spiritual Liberty, Volume V, Part IV, Chapter III]

Yusuf (Peace and Blessings be upon him) was reminded of God in a moment of vulnerability and passion, and thought of His wrath; by doing so, he regained control of his own desire. In Surah Yusuf this is illustrated though the following verse:

"And, indeed, she desired him, and he desired her; (and he would have succumbed) had he not seen (in his temptation) an evidence of his Sustainer's truth: thus (We willed it to be) in order that We might avert from him all evil and all deeds of abomination - for, behold, he was truly one of Our servants." [Holy Quran, 12:24]

Allah ﷻ says in the Holy Quran, that Yusuf (Peace and Blessings be upon him) had control over his desires because Allah ﷻ Himself had shielded him from committing the sin because Yusuf (Peace and Blessings be upon him) was a righteous slave. His righteousness would not allow him to further transgress. But at this point, Zulaikha was completely blinded by her own passionate desires and did not listen to Yusuf (Peace and

Blessings be upon him). She continued to advance towards him without desisting upon request, and when he still refused, she became overwhelmed with anger. She cursed him and reminded him of his status as a slave. Upon being cursed, he rushed to leave the room, at which point Zulaikha caught him by the neck and tore his garment. At this very moment, the chief entered the room and was amazed at the sight. Immediately, Zulaikha took the opportunity to hide her fault and said Yusuf made an attempt to lay hands on her and she was trying to protect herself.

> "And they both rushed to the door. In order to stop him she caught his shirt, and as a result she ripped his shirt from behind. At the door they met her husband. Seeing him she cried: 'What punishment does someone who intended evil against your wife deserve except imprisonment or a painful chastisement?'" [Holy Quran, 12:25]

This enraged the chief who gave orders that Yusuf (Peace and Blessings be upon him) should be taken as a prisoner and be held captive for life. Yusuf (Peace and Blessings be upon himself) then tried to explain:

> "Yusuf said: 'It was she who attempted to seduce me.' At this - one accusing the other - one member of her own family bore witness saying: 'If his shirt is ripped from the front, then she is speaking the truth and he is lying. But if it is ripped from behind, then he is speaking the truth and she is lying." [Holy Quran, 12:26-27]

"And when (her husband) saw that Yusuf's shirt was ripped from behind, he said to her: 'It is one of the tricks of you women! Your trick was mighty indeed! O Yusuf, say no more about this, and you (O my wife) seek forgiveness for your sin, for you were indeed the wrongdoer." [Holy Quran, 12:28-29]

Rumors began to spread and the friends and relatives of Zulaikha began to take an interest in her attraction towards Yusuf (Peace and Blessings be upon him); this put Zulaikha in a difficult position.

Zulaikha became annoyed at the rumors because people could not understand her uncontrollable attraction towards Yusuf (Peace and Blessings be upon him). One day, she invited all of her friends and relatives, and gave them all a fruit and a knife. She told them to cut the lemons when she commands them to, and then she called out to Yusuf (Peace and Blessings be upon him). When he came out, she told them to cut the fruits, but everyone was so mesmerized by the overwhelming beauty of Yusuf (Peace and Blessings be upon him) that instead of cutting the fruits, they cut their fingers.

"When they saw him, they were so amazed that they cut their hands and exclaimed spontaneously: 'Good Lord! He is no human being; he is but a noble angel.'" [Holy Quran, 12:31]

"She said: 'Well, this is he about whom you blamed me. No doubt I seduced him, but he escaped. If he doesn't do what I say, he will certainly be thrown into prison and be disgraced.'" [Holy Quran, 12:32]

Some accounts of the story claim that Zulaikha's husband ordered for Yusuf to be imprisoned for life without hearing him out. The Quran testifies that upon being threatened by Zulaikha, Yusuf (Peace and Blessings be upon him) chose prison for himself.

> "Yusuf said: 'O my Rabb! I would rather go to prison than that to which they invite me; and unless You ward off their cunning snare from me, I may, in my youthful folly, feel inclined towards them and become one of the ignorant. Thereupon his Rabb granted his prayer and warded off their cunning snare from him; surely He hears all and knows all.'" [Holy Quran, 12:33-34]

> "For, presently it occurred to the nobleman and his household - (even) after they had seen all the signs (of Yusuf's innocence) - that they might as well imprison him for some time." [Holy Quran, 12:35]

While Yusuf (Peace and Blessings be upon him) was in prison, Zulaikha became overwhelmed with sorrow and repentance. Years passed and the pain consumed her entirely. She was constantly tormented by opposing sides of her conscience, and the guilt of her own beloved being thrown into prison on her account almost took her life away. After the death of her husband, she became even more lonely and fell into great depression.

All she did was long for Yusuf (Peace and Blessings be upon him), and it was as if the entire world was a vessel for her to communicate with in order to feel the presence of Yusuf (Peace and Blessings be upon him). The wind that she felt against her skin was the breath of Yusuf (Peace and Blessings be upon him). The night was as if he had closed his eyes, and day-light was as if he was awake. Every sound, every touch, and every whisper from every direction brought news of her beloved, Yusuf.

On the other hand, despite being in prison, Yusuf (Peace and Blessings be upon him) was adored by the other prisoners, and his presence made the prison into a sort of comfortable heaven for all the prisoners. Yusuf (Peace and Blessings be upon him) would interpret dreams whenever asked, and he would tell stories which helped to pass the time. He never blamed Zulaikha; in fact, he too had fallen in love with her and as the days passed, he too was deeply consumed by her thoughts. Despite the depth of his love for Zulaikha, he was firm on his principles and he did not, even for a moment, regret pushing her away because no act of transgression was worth engaging in, once he was reminded of the fear of God. [Hazrat Inayat Khan, Spiritual Liberty, Volume V, Part IV, Chapter III]

Many years passed, and Zulaikha and Yusuf (Peace and Blessings be upon him) longed for each other greatly, but both continued their lives in separation. One day, the Pharaoh dreamt a dream which alarmed him, but no one could interpret his dream.

"One day the king of Egypt said: 'I saw seven fat cows in my dream which were eaten up by seven lean cows, likewise I saw seven great ears of corn and seven others that were dried up. O chiefs! Tell me the meaning of my dream if you can interpret the dreams.

They answered: '(This is one of) the most involved and confusing of dreams, and we have no deep knowledge of the real meaning of dreams.'" [Holy Quran, 12:43-44]

One of the Pharaoh's servants advised him of Yusuf's (Peace and Blessings be upon him) gift of interpreting dreams. The Pharaoh sent someone to Yusuf (Peace and Blessings be upon him) with a message of his dream, and the interpretation given by Yusuf (Peace and Blessings be upon him) served as wise counsel which relieved the Pharaoh of his worries.

"The king said: 'Bring this man to me.' When the messenger of the king came to Yusuf, Yusuf said: 'Go back to your king and ask him (first to find out the truth) about those women who cut their hands - for, behold, (until now it is) my Sustainer (alone who) has full knowledge of their snare." [Holy Quran, 12:50]

"(Thereupon the King sent for those women; and when they came,) he asked: 'What was it that you hoped to achieve when you sought to make Yusuf yield himself unto you?' The women answered: 'God save us! We did not perceive the least evil (intention) on his part!' (And) the wife of Yusuf's former master exclaimed: "Now has the truth come to light! It was I who sought to make him yield himself unto me - whereas he, behold, was indeed speaking the truth!'" [Holy Quran, 12:51]

When Yusuf (Peace and Blessings be upon him) learned of this, he said, 'I asked this so that my former master may be aware that I had no intention to betray him, and it is Allah ﷻ who saves the righteous from committing such sins, and it is Allah ﷻ who does not let the treacherous succeed.' In return, the Pharaoh ordered for Yusuf (Peace and Blessings be upon him) to be released and made him chief, thereby giving him power and honor.

> "And the king said: 'Bring him unto me, so that I may attach him to my own person.' And when he had spoken with him, (the king) said: 'Behold, (from) this day thou shalt be of high standing with us, invested with all trust." [Holy Quran, 12:54]

Hazrat Inayat Khan continues to explain that one day Yusuf (Peace and Blessings be upon him) and his group of assistants and advisers were riding by the place where Zulaikha had decided to spend the rest of her life in misery. On hearing the sound of the horses, many people ran to see who was passing, and called out, 'It is Yusuf, it is Yusuf!' On hearing the name, it was almost as if Zulaikha was brought back to life and desired to see him once more. She called out for him, and people managed to get him to stop. He failed to recognize her for she was no longer her youthful self; she was struck by utmost misery and sorrow to the point she was completely unrecognizable. He asked, 'What desirest thou of me?'

> She said, 'Zulaikha still has at the same desire, O Yusuf, and it will continue here and in the hereafter. I have desired thee, and thee alone I will

desire.' Yusuf became very convinced of her constant love, and was moved by her state of misery. He kissed her on the forehead, and took her in his arms and prayed to God. The prayer of the Prophet and the appeal of long-continued love attracted the blessing of God, and Zulaikha regained her youth and beauty. Yusuf said to Zulaikha, 'From this day thou becomest my beloved queen,' and they were then married. [Hazrat Inayat Khan, Spiritual Liberty, Volume V, Part IV, Chapter III]

According to Sayyid Abul Ala Maududi in "Tafhim al-Qur'an - The Meaning of the Quran", there is a specific purpose of the inclusion of the story of Prophet Yusuf (Peace and Blessings be upon him) and Zulaikha in the Holy Quran. One of the most important lessons is as follows:

"Whatever Allah ﷻ wills, He fulfills it anyhow, and man can never defeat His plan with his counterplans nor prevent it from happening nor change it in any way whatever. Nay, it often so happens that man adopts some measure to fulfill his own design and believes that he has done that very thing which would fulfill his design, but in the end he finds to his dismay that he had done something which was against his own and conductive to the Divine purpose." [Sayyid Abul Ala Maududi, Tafhim al-Qur'an - The Meaning of the Quran, Surah Yusuf]

When the brothers of Yusuf (Peace and Blessings be upon him) threw him into the well, they thought that he may have died. In doing so, for a while they may have been convinced that their plan was successful. In actuality, all they did was pave the way for the divine purpose of making him the ruler of Egypt. Similarly, Zulaikha had sent Prophet Yusuf (Peace and Blessings be upon him) to prison thinking she got her revenge, but she only provided him the opportunity to become the ruler of Egypt.

> "Moreover, the story contains other lessons for those who intend to follow the way of Allah ﷻ. The first lesson it teaches is that one should remain within the limits, prescribed by the Divine Law, in one's aims and objects and measures, for success and failure are entirely in the hands of Allah ﷻ. Therefore if one adopts pure aims and lawful measures but fails, at least one will escape ignominy and disgrace. On the other hand, the one who adopts an impure aim and unlawful measures to achieve it, shall not only inevitably meet with ignominy and disgrace in the Hereafter, but also runs the risk of ignominy and disgrace in this world.
>
> The second lesson it teaches is that those who exert for the cause of truth and righteousness and put their trust in Allah ﷻ and entrust all their affairs to Him, get consolation and comfort from Him, for this helps them face their opponents with confidence and

courage and they do not lose heart, when they encounter the apparently terrifying measures of the powerful enemies. They will persevere in their task without fear and leave the results to Allah ﷻ." [Sayyid Abul Ala Maududi, Tafhim al-Qur'an - The Meaning of the Quran, Surah Yusuf]

Moreover, in the context of our discussion, Prophet Yusuf (Peace and Blessings be upon him) refused to transgress despite the mutually passionate desires between him and Zulaikha. The Quran does not provide an explanation of what happened to them after Prophet Yusuf (Peace and Blessings be upon him) was released from prison and eventually became the ruler of Egypt, but from stipulating around the various narrations, and especially that of Hazrat Inayat Khan, one can conclude that surely if someone is meant to be with you, no matter what trials and tribulations you may be faced with, the two of you will end up together. One doesn't have to transgress and go against the laws of Allah ﷻ in order to secure him/herself a spouse, but what is meant to be will inevitably find its way. If Allah ﷻ has willed for something to be, no power on earth can undo it. From the account provided by Hazrat Inayat Khan, Prophet Yusuf (Peace and Blessings be upon him) and Zulaikha were finally united and their union was blessed by Allah ﷻ through marriage.

In the state of Junoon one may be furiously inclined towards fulfilling his/her passionate desires, but right when the lines between right and wrong become blurred, it is that much important for one to remind him/herself of the consciousness of Allah ﷻ in order to prevent transgression. May Allah ﷻ protect us from losing our minds to a beloved other than Allah ﷻ. May Allah ﷻ protect us from facing humility at the hands of His creation. May we all become so attached to Allah ﷻ that we experience a sense of Junoon in wanting to fulfill our duties and obligations towards Him. May we become so immersed in the love for Allah ﷻ that we passionately follow in the footsteps of His beloved Prophet Muhammad ﷺ, and may our love and the very madness in our love for Allah ﷻ take us to Paradise.

3.10
MAUT
(DEATH OF THE SELF)

The word Maut means 'Death' in Arabic and Urdu, and in love it can mean several things. As a starting point the beloved is independent of the lover, and for the beloved to exist he/she does not require anything from the lover. On the other hand, the lover depends on the beloved, and begs of the beloved for nothing but the beloved him/herself. The lover reaches the point of self-annihilation, and loses a sense of their own self completely, and instead gains a sense of identity and everlasting life in the beloved.

This is the stage of love in which the lover negates all the attributes of him/herself, and identifies him/herself by the very essence of the beloved alone. For example, it is said that Majnun was once making sketches of Laila, and then began to erase the sketch and instead drew a sketch of himself. Someone remarked, 'What kind of love is this where one erases the face of the beloved?' to which Majnun replied, 'If you cannot find Laila in me, then draw her again. If you cannot find me in Laila, draw me again.' Therefore, one reaches a point where the existence of him/herself is made manifest by the existence of the beloved, and one ceases to acknowledge a separate or independent existence. For example, one wears what the beloved would like to see him/her wear; one styles his/her hair according the tastes of the beloved; one eats what the beloved would eat; one greets others in ways similar to how the beloved would greet others. Essentially one's likes and dislikes are now the same as the likes and dislikes of the beloved.

Hazrat Inayat Khan describes Maut to be entirely different. He describes it to mean a life that is lived without ever experiencing love. The very effect of love is pain, and when there is no pain, there is no love. Anyone who claims to not have experienced the agonies of love is not a lover, and his claims of ever being in love are false. Love comes with agony and anxiety, whereas marriage is its cure. However, even within the marriage there is lots of hard work and commitment involved and at times it will hurt, but this very hurt brings the spouses closer as long as both are determined to overcome the barriers between them. Hazrat Inayat Khan says:

> "Those who have avoided love in life from fear of its pain have lost more than the lover, who by losing himself gains all. The loveless first lose all, until at last their self is also snatched away from their hands. The warmth of the lover's atmosphere, the piercing effect of his voice, the appeal of his words, all come from the pain of his heart. The heart is not living until it has experienced pain. Man has not lived if he has lived and worked with his body and mind without heart. The soul is all light, but all darkness is caused by the death of the heart. Pain makes it alive." [Hazrat Inayat Khan, Spiritual Liberty, Volume V, Part IV, Chapter IV]

The pain and sorrow of love is something that continual and does not end. The lover is in some sort of pain in the presence and in the absence of the beloved. When the beloved is present, the lover fears his/her eventual or potential absence. In the absence of the beloved, the lover is in pain due to the longing for the presence of the beloved. Maut is living an entire lifetime without ever experiencing the nectar of love, without ever knowing what it means to long for the beloved. If one lives an entire life without experiencing pain, then he never has the pleasure to understand what joy and happiness truly means. One needs to understand what pain is in order to know happiness.

The real essence of happiness, joy, and pleasure are only known to the lover alone. The individual who has never loved and has not experienced the agony and the torments of love only know these words by name and not in actuality.

> "It is like the difference between a man and a rock. Man, with all life's struggles and difficulties, would rather live as a man than become a rock, which no struggle or difficulty could ever touch. For even with struggles and difficulties the joy of living is immense. With all the pains and sorrows that the lover has to meet within love, his joy in love is unimaginable, for love is life, and its lack is death." [Hazrat Inayat Khan, Spiritual Liberty, Volume V, Part IV, Chapter IV]

The agony in being separated from the beloved is indeed a torment that only a lover knows, and therefore finally being united with the lover is a happiness that only a lover can ever experience. Anyone else can know of it through words, descriptions and poetry, but even then it'll be of little relevance to them personally. Indeed, simple joys such as buying a car one desired may bring joy, but such joys are nowhere near in comparison to the joy one experiences when he/she can finally embrace the beloved. Allah ﷻ knows of this longing, for He has created us with these weaknesses, and He knows exactly the kinds of torments that our hearts endure in love. Therefore, He has commanded us to withhold and endure, and to do whatever we can to make our love Halal. There is a kind of pain that consists of transgressing with the beloved, and eventually pushing him/her further away from you and experiencing depression from the withdrawal. Or there is the kind of pain one can experience by trying to gain control over his/her feelings and keeping a safe distance away from the beloved, in order to control one's heart from temptation. There is great pain in avoiding the object of your love, to lowering your gaze and protecting the beloved from any thoughts that may humiliate you in front of your Lord. Allah ﷻ values this, and He has commanded this of you in order to bless you with the ultimate happiness when the beloved is finally yours, and when you are finally united with the beloved in marriage.

It happens every so often that two people meet, they become mutually attracted to one another, they begin told desire and crave each other physically and intimately, and after the fulfillment of the desires they are empty again. Even if they were to marry, they would feel just as unfulfilled and unsatisfied because they did not endure any separation or feel intense longing, and they did not feel the pain a lover would feel in wanting to protect and preserve his/her love. Therefore, they don't truly understand or experience happiness in being in the company of the beloved.

Now, imagine a situation in which your heart felt inclined towards a woman, and her kindness was something that you wanted in your life. Her compassion towards her parents and her siblings was something that attracted you. You asked her if you could pursue her through asking her parents for her hand in marriage, and she agreed. Imagine the torment of staying away from her, and avoiding her in order to protect her and yourself from any transgression. Imagine longing for her, night and day, and praying for her safety. Imagine spending your nights wondering what she might be thinking at that moment, or if she would be asleep. Imagine the countless scenarios in your mind of how your first conversation as spouses would be like. All that is great pain and the longing is unbearable. Simultaneously, the woman that you asked and have pursued is now just as curious about the outcome of this proposal. She is just as excited towards wanting to start a new life and having someone as a companion. She too spends her nights imagining what your conversations would be like; she too longs to get to know you better. Can you imagine the amount of happiness, the overwhelming joy and excitement in your heart when you finally sign the Nikkah, and you now belong to each other? Can you imagine how beautiful that moment would be for the both of you? Only some are able to experience that moment in all its beauty, because only some are true Disciples of Ishq. Only some respect the sacredness of love and go to all the extents to keep it Halal without tainting it with illicit acts of transgression. Disciples of Ishq start off as two individuals in love, with the aim of achieving oneness; for that is what the purpose of love is. Hazrat Inayat Khan also affirms this by stating:

> "Man's greatest enemy in the world is his ego, the thought of self. This is the germ from which springs all evil in man. Even the virtues of the egoist turn into sin, and his small sins into great crimes. All religions and philosophies teach man to crush it, and there is nothing that can crush it better than love. The growth of love is the decay of the ego. Love in its perfection entirely frees the lover from all selfishness, for love may be called

in other words annihilation. 'Whoever enters the school of lovers, the first lesson he learns is not to be.'" [Hazrat Inayat Khan, Spiritual Liberty, Volume V, Part IV, Chapter VI]

He further clarifies that in order for us to love selflessly and wholeheartedly, we must learn to kill our ego. Ego is the enemy of love, and it stops the self from loving to his/her full potential. The ego is akin to an antibiotic that is capable of destroying or weakening one's feelings of love. Therefore, Maut does not need to be a total annihilation of the self, but rather of very control of one's ego, which then allows the lover to put the beloved before him/herself.

Shaykh Zulfiqar Ahmad provides another perspective on what Maut means. He says that the ultimate consequence of metaphorical love is the separation of the lover and the beloved and thus, disgrace in this world and the Hereafter. Whoever is in love with creation will have to separate or be separated from his beloved one day. And, whoever loves Allah ﷻ will be united with Him one day. For Shaykh Zulfiqar Ahmed, Maut is the end of love, as it is the ultimate consequence.

> "At the time of death, the true reality of life becomes manifest before everyone. All infatuations end. All illusions fade. This is the final end of metaphorical love. Whoever wishes to lead a successful life must abstain from it." [Ishq-e-Ilahi, Shaykh Zulfiqar Ahmad, translated by Faqir Publications, pg. 80]

His analysis is limited to the love that is metaphorical, or love for the sake of beauty and pleasure of the fulfillment of one's desire. It is true that when one loves for the sake of his/her desire and pursues another for the fulfillment of that desire, there is nothing but disgrace for him in both worlds. Even if one attains the beloved and spends a lifetime together, separation is the ultimate end.

We are the Disciples of Ishq, who believe in nothing but Halal love. We love solely for the sake of love itself, and for the sake of Allah ﷻ. Therefore, the opinion of Shaykh Zulfiqar Ahmed is of value to us, because we agree with it, to the extent that love for the sake our desires leads to humiliation. However, we follow the example of Prophet Muhammad ﷺ and his love for Khadijah (may Allah ﷺ be pleased with her) and his love for all of his other wives. These are the examples of love that we focus our lives around, and this is what we pray Allah ﷻ bestow us with out of His endless kindness and mercy.

We also know that in Halal love, Maut doesn't mean an actual death of the self, but rather ad eat of thinking that we only have an obligation to our own dreams, goals, and aspirations, because we now have those of the beloved to be committed to as well. In a marriage, it involves going out of our way to aid and support the beloved in and accepting his or her goals as our own. As discussed in the earlier chapters, Khadijah (may Allah ﷺ be pleased with her) was a beautiful example of this, as she invested her resources, both tangible and otherwise, in Islam because she knew of, and accepted as her own, all of Prophet Muhammad's ﷺ aspirations and dreams. This is what the idea of Maut signifies in a Halal union. It is the commitment towards one another as if both are one.

For us as Disciples of Ishq, love is not metaphorical, because it does not revolve around the desire for beauty and sexual relations. Instead, we seek to legitimate our love through marriage as soon as possible. We want Allah ﷻ to bless our union with our beloved, and we want this love to take us to Paradise. Allah ﷻ has promised in Surah Ar-Ra'd that:

> "... Those who are patient in adversity out of a longing for their Sustainer's countenance, seek the pleasure of their Rabb, and are constant in their prayer, and spend on others in secret and openly out of the sustenance We have provided for them, and repel evil with good - they are the ones for whom there is a home of the hereafter: the Paradise of perpetual bliss: they will enter into it along with their righteous forefathers, their spouses and their descendants. The angels will come to welcome them from every side saying, 'Peace be upon you for all that you steadfastly endured in the World. No! How excellent will be the fulfillment in the hereafter!'" [Holy Quran, 13:22-24]

Allah ﷻ has promised that those among us who are righteous and patiently endured the hardships of the world shall enter Paradise with their parents, spouses, and children. That is the goal of the Disciples of Ishq, not only to enter Jannah with our spouses, but to build a lifetime together by helping each other to earn the blessings that Allah ﷻ will be most pleased with in the hereafter. Moreover, in Surah Ya-Sin, Allah ﷻ says:

"Behold, those who are destined for paradise shall today have joy in whatever they do: they and their spouses will be in shady groves reclining on soft couches, [only] delight will be there for them, and theirs shall be all that they could ask for." [Holy Quran, 36:55-57]

Allah ﷻ promises this to us again in Surah Az-Sukhruf:

[And God will say:] "O you servants of Mine! No fear need you have today, and neither shall you grieve - [O you] who have attained to faith in Our messages and have surrendered your own selves unto Us! Enter paradise, you and your spouses; you will be made happy." [And there] they will be served with trays with golden dishes and golden goblets, and they shall have everything that their souls can desire and all that their eyes can delight in - and it will be said to them: "Now you shall abide therein forever." [Holy Quran, 43:68-71]

Therefore, while it is true that the transgressors and the ones who loved for the sake of their illicit desires will be humiliated in both worlds, the outcome will be completely different for Disciples of Ishq. For those that followed Allah ﷻ's commands in this lifetime and upheld the ties of kinship, feared Allah ﷻ, remained patient and righteous towards one another and fulfilled the duties and obligations owed to one another, they shall be reunited in Jannah. Disciples of Ishq do not believe in the concept of 'till death do us part,' but, rather 'death will give us an eternal start.' Indeed the time in Paradise will be endless, and we will be truly immortal and united with those we love for an eternity.

May Allah ﷻ aid us in loving our spouses wholeheartedly and in building our lives together in a way that pleases Allah ﷻ. May we protect our spouses from anything that displeases Allah ﷻ, and may we be among the righteous couples who shall be greeted by the angels at the gates of heaven. May we be among the righteous for whom death will give an eternal start. May our love take us to Paradise.

SECTION FOUR

4.1
ISHQ-E-HAQIQI
(DIVINE LOVE)

Dr. Alireza Nurbakhsh explains that human love begins with an encounter, and the same love holds true for divine love. Without an encounter with the divine, there can be no divine love.

> "One cannot engage and participate in divine love through descriptions of the divine alone - even if they happen to be the 'right' sort of descriptions. An encounter with the divine love is the precognition of divine love." [Dr. Alireza Nurbakhsh, Sufi Journal, Issue 81, 2011]

The encounter with the divine may happen suddenly through an ordinary experience in the world such as the smile of a friend, hearing a melody, grasping the meaning of a love poem, kindness from a stranger, or sincere contemplation of the favors bestowed upon mankind by Allah ﷻ. One can even ignite this love through contemplation of the attributes of Allah ﷻ, and find that each attribute provides unlimited reasons for which to love Him. Once this encounter happens, one begins his/her journey on the path of divine love. Dr. Nurbakhsh explains that what makes our love divine is not what we love, but the way we love it.

> "This may sound contradictory. On the one hand I have suggested that an encounter with the divine is the precondition of love and on the other hand I am proposing that what makes

our love divine is the way we love, not what we love. Why should a divine encounter be necessary if it is only the manner of our loving that makes our loving divine? Moreover, if we are capable of encountering the divine to begin with, why not characterize divine love in terms of such an encounter?" [Dr. Alireza Nurbakhsh, Sufi Journal, Issue 81, 2011]

He explains that the encounter with the divine is essential for us to be able to fall in love with Him. Such an event does not happen outside this world, or through some divine miracle, but the individual's encounter with the divine can happen anywhere, through anything, and at any time. Each object in this world manifests the divine, and therefore Allah ﷻ is everywhere. Once the encounter happens, the lover realizes that the divine permeates everything. This is significant because instead of loving one particular person, divine love becomes the love of everything. It is different from human love because of its unconditional nature.

As demonstrated through the progression of various stages of love, at some point the lover falls out of love with the beloved. The nature of human love is that it eventually demands to be loved in return. Human love is a reciprocal relationship between two people based on mutual expectations, and these could even be expectations of lust and the fulfillment of those desires. When the desire is not met, the lover seeks it elsewhere. If the lover is mistreated by the beloved, and the progression through the stages of love leads the lover into understanding that the beloved does not meet his/her expectations, the lover falls out of love and looks for another who may better fulfill his/her needs. The beauty of divine love is that it is not necessarily reciprocal; it does not change or diminish in the face of harshness or indifference from the True Beloved, Allah ﷻ. In fact, the love for Allah ﷻ changes the way we look at the entire world.

Under normal circumstances, it was described in the stage of Shagaf that the lover begins to take the likes and dislikes of the beloved to be his/her own. The lover may begin to view the friends and family of the beloved as his/her own as well. However, Dr. Nurbakhsh continues to clarify that another way in which divine love differs from human love is the indiscriminate or all-encompassing nature of divine love. Normally in our love for others, we begin to feel indifferent towards some people and it may even be possible for our hearts to hate. But divine love requires a 'burning heart' through which the lover's heart cannot find it in itself to hate or to be indifferent to anyone.

> "It is as though divine love erases any thought and feeling of indifference or hatred that we may have towards others. This is the essence of compassion. The one who is in love with the divine wants others to be happy and free from suffering regardless of who they may be." [Dr. Alireza Nurbakhsh, Sufi Journal, Issue 81, 2011]

Another way in which divine love is different from human love is that, in the former, the lover is selfless in relation to his/her beloved.

> "In ordinary love, it is customary for the lover to desire his or her beloved only insofar as the beloved can satisfy the lover's needs and desires. Here the

lover is motivated by what makes him or her happy, not by what the beloved may want. But in divine love priority and importance are given to the beloved; the lover wants only what the beloved wants." [Dr. Alireza Nurbakhsh, Sufi Journal, Issue 81, 2011]

In Surah Al-Imran, Allah ﷻ says:

"If misfortune touches you, (know that) similar misfortune has touched (other) people as well; for it is by turns that we apportion unto men such days (of fortune and misfortune); and (this) to the end that Allah ﷻ might mark out those who have attained to faith, and chose from among you such as (with their lives) bear witness to the truth - for Allah ﷻ does not love the unjust and the wrong-doers." [Holy Quran, 3:140]

What Allah ﷻ seems to be saying in this verse is simply that He keeps alternating the days (good and bad) among mankind, so that Allah ﷻ can distinguish between the true believers and those who are wrong-doers, since the true believers will trust in Allah ﷻ no matter what. Even if Allah ﷻ takes away from the true believers what they love, their true love for Allah ﷻ will remain unaffected. This is the selflessness of divine love as opposed to any other love. But, do we not at times become restless, despite having utmost trust in Allah ﷻ? Do we not sometimes feel despair and become overcome by utmost sadness?

Shaykh Zulfiqar Ahmed believes that all this is a part of love. The state of the lover who loves Allah ﷻ is also affected by the changes in life. Allah ﷻ is deliberately alternating time, and the lover is met with both the good and the bad times.

> "Like the tides of an ocean, the tides of life are perpetually changing. At times life is stormy; at other times life is calm. At times everything appears to blossom; at other times everything appears dismal. At times a person feels close to his Lord; at other times he feels distant. At times there is vitality; at other times there is listlessness. At times there is sickness; at other times there is health. The human condition never remains the same."
> [Shaykh Zulfiqar Ahmad, Ishq-e-Illahi, translated by Faqir Publications, pg. 37]

Therefore, at times the lover is happy, and at other times he/she is sad. At times there is affection and grace from the Beloved, and at times there is anger and reproach. At times there is fervor and excitement, and at other times there is peace and contentment. However, no matter what the circumstances may be, a true lover always remains pleased with Allah ﷻ.

Many have turned away from metaphorical beauty, and have changed their direction toward the true beauty of Allah ﷻ, for no love in the world could be as satisfactory as divine love. In "Ishq-e-Illahi", Shaykh

Zulfiqar Ahmad tells the story of a man who once lived in a Muslim kingdom. He was a very handsome man who fell in love with the local princess as he would often see glimpses of her because he worked in the ruler's palace. Against all odds, he managed to get his message of love conveyed to the princess. She had already heard praises of how handsome he was, and so she also fell in love with him. They would often exchange messages and share their feelings of mutual affection, but could not find a way to meet inside the palace. The princess thought of a plan and sent a message to her beloved informing him that the ruler greatly respected pious people.

The princess suggested that if her beloved were to leave his job, live on the outskirts of town, and engage himself in piety and worship for some time until he gained popularity, then she would be able to go out and meet him without restraints. He did as suggested and settled near the edge of the town. The man adopted the Sunnah of the Prophet ﷺ as his way of life and became occupied in remembrance (dhikr) and contemplation (fikr) of Allah ﷻ.

It didn't take long for him and his piety to become well known among the people, and he devoted himself in the worship of Allah ﷻ completely. The princess had been anxiously waiting for this opportunity, and took the first opportunity to ask her father (the ruler) for his permission to see this 'holy man' so she could ask him to make Du'a for her. When she arrived at the edge of town, and entered his house, she asked for her entourage to remain outside.

When her old admirer saw her, he said, 'Sister please go outside. How did you enter without permission?' The princess reminded him that she was the same one whose beauty had enchanted him and whom he had desperately ached to meet in private. She had finally come to see him so they can be alone together. He turned his head away from her and said, 'I am sorry sister, that time has gone. I had chosen this life of piety in the hope of meeting you. But now my heart abounds with the love of the True King. I desire not to even look in your direction.' [Paraphrased from Ishq-e-Illahi]

This story is very similar to the story of Heer Ranjha in which both came up with a plan in order for them to transgress. Similar to how Ranjha became a Yogi in his desire to transgress and be one with Heer, the man in this story also turned to the One True Divine, but the love for the Divine could not lead him to transgress. Such is the encounter with the divine, it can happen at any time, and when it happens, the love for Allah ﷻ is so overwhelming and incomparable with the love for anything else in the world that one simply lets go of the world.

Shaykh Zulfiqar Ahmed tells another story of Hadrat Abdullah bin Mubarak who became infatuated with a beautiful girl in his youth. One day, she asked him to wait outside of her house at night so she could come to see him alone as soon as she got a reasonable opportunity to do so. He stayed awake the entire night, shivering in the cold, but she did not come out as promised. When the call to prayer (Adhan) was heard in the morning, he could not help but feel humiliated and disgusted with himself, and he was overcome with remorse and sadness at his lack of judgement. He thought to himself, 'If only I had spent the whole night awake in the worship and remembrance of Allah ﷻ, I would have received some portion of his mercy and blessings.' Hadrat Abdullah bin Mubarak then made sincere repentance, and obtained a religious education, passed through the stages of purification of the self and heart, and became a leading scholar in the field of Hadith. [Paraphrased from Ishq-e-Ilahi]

An individual is not capable of truly loving Allah ﷻ if his compassion has not been awakened to the beauty of the earth. Someone once came to a Sufi and asked to be his disciple. The Sufi asked, "Have you ever loved anyone in life?" The man said, "No." The Sufi responded, "Then go, and love someone, and then come to me." Since some people's hearts have not been able to attach to the favors and the creation of Allah ﷻ, many great teachers and masters have had difficulty in awakening the love for Allah ﷻ in such people. To explain this, Hazrat Inayat Khan gave the example of a disciple who had been under the discipleship of a spiritual guide for a very long time, but could make no progress as he was not inspired. This got to a point where he had become so disheartened that he felt himself to be misfortunate, and thought of giving up. The spiritual guide suggested that he cease the spiritual practices for a time and live comfortably without thinking too much about his misfortune. Everyday the spiritual guide sent him good food, and on the last day of his stay, the food was delivered by a fair young woman who put the tray down and immediately left. Her beauty was so immense that the disciple could think of nothing else. He longed to see her again, and his longing only increased every minute. He became so preoccupied by the thought of her that he forgot to eat, he couldn't sleep, and all he could do is weep. After some time when the spiritual guide visited the disciple, he was immediately inspired.

> "There are two worthy objects of love: on the lower plane man, and on the higher God. Every person in the world first learns to love on the lower plane. As soon as the infant opens its

eyes it loves whatever its eyes see, whatever seems to it beautiful. Later there comes the love for what is permanent, for what is unchanging, which leads to the ideal of God. But then the man is already fixed in such a difficult position in life that there is a struggle between the one and the other. The idol pulls from one side and the ideal draws from the other side, and it is only the rare one who rises above this difficulty." [Hazrat Inayat Khan, Spiritual Liberty, Volume V, Part IV, Chapter IV]

Love for any one person, no matter what extent it reaches, will always remain limited. Perfection in love lies in its vastness. Sufis say, "The tendency of love is to expand, even from one atom to the whole universe, from a single earthly beloved to God." Therefore, the love for the human being is incomplete, but it is needed to begin with. One simply cannot love God without love for His creation.

"Love creates love in man and even more with God. It is the nature of love. If you love God, God sends His love evermore upon you. If you seek Him by night, He will follow you by day. Wherever you are, in your affairs, in your business transactions, the help, the protection and the presence of the Divine will follow you." [Hazrat Inayat Khan, Spiritual Liberty, Volume V, Part IV, Chapter IV]

One of the greatest lessons from Sheikh Abdul Qadir Jilani, the Honorable jurist based in Baghdad, and the founder of the Qadiriyya Sufi Order, is that if you simply abandon the world and submit to your Lord, He'll ensure that the world will be at your feet. Everything you loved, including the luxuries, the wealth, and the people, will be returned to you. The people that you loved, cried over and chased after shall cry over you and chase after you, but by then your heart will already be attached to something far greater.

Sheikh Abdul Qadir Jilani explains that one of the most frequent complaints that we, as humans, have with regards to what we love, is that we are most often taken away from the object of our love due to several reasons. These reasons may include losing someone to death, or due to an illness, grudges, and even conspiracies or misunderstandings. He explains that if this is the case, then you are very fortunate, for Allah 🕌 wants you for Himself, whereas you still wish to belong to His creation. Sheikh Abdul Qadir Jilani actually advises such individuals to become a broken vessel that would only be able to hold the love for Allah 🕌, and anything else would simply slip through its cracks. As long as you continue to choose things above Allah 🕌, He will break you at the hands of those things. But if you submit to Allah 🕌, and prioritize Him above all else in your life, all of existence shall be placed within your reach and at your disposal. This includes all your relations, your objects of love, your wishes, wealth, desires and all the luxuries that you crave/ these will be yours for the taking, but they will no longer mean as much to you, in comparison to your love for Him. As long as you prioritize these worldly things, they will have the power to hurt you. Once you choose to abandon them for the sake of Allah 🕌, they will chase you. Everything that you love will hurt you, other than the love for Allah 🕌. Therefore, attach yourselves to Allah 🕌 and all else will be granted to you without the effort of you having to chase it.

One of the ways in which we may encounter our Lord is through heartbreak, because in searching for peace and tranquility, somehow we allow ourselves to stray away from the very Source of Peace. It is only when we hurt as if we are beyond repair that we finally come back to the only One who is able to repair us. It is almost natural for us to return to Him, as if it's a built-in navigation system for when our soul feels lost. Heartbreak is possibly one of the hardest things to understand and to come to terms with. Since we progress through the stages of love in a way in which we experience so much hardship, is why many have described the love for anything other than Allah ﷻ to be a psychological sickness. The lover's desire to be one with the beloved affects the mind to such an extent that he becomes afflicted with intense sadness, to the point where he can no longer function in his daily routines. The love for Allah ﷻ is a natural cure to this psychological illness. Therefore, sometimes heart break comes to us as a blessing in which Allah ﷻ ordains to us a means of coming back to Him for the sake of cleansing our heart.

The next paragraph is extracted from a piece of advice that I recently gave to a very special friend of mine, and I wanted to include it in this book for my readers to also hold dearly.

Every night you sit there for hours on end and you wonder, and the only question that ever seems to come to mind is, "Why?" And no matter how much thought you put into it, and no matter what perspective you look at it from, it simply ceases to make any sense. "Why did he/she leave?" You were perfect, and believe me, not ever, not even for a split second do I doubt that you were anything less than perfect. You were the dream. You were everything a person craves in another. You were understanding, patient, compassionate, and most of all you loved unconditionally. You are the epitome of everything humanity was meant to be like. Why then would he/she choose to let you go? That's the thing with the universe and its doings. We build imaginative heavens around people which inevitably turn into realities of hell that haunt us for what seems like an eternity. But what if I was to tell you that no matter what your imaginative heaven may have resulted in, Heaven itself, in all its Grace, indeed has a plan for you? What if I were to tell you that it was written for him/her to make the biggest mistake of his/her life, in order to prevent you from making yours? It may not mean anything to you right now, because that still does not answer your, "Why?" But I ask you to trust me. One day, your heart will be ready, and as soon as it is, what has been taken away from you will be replaced with someone who will mean so much more to you, that you'll never ask yourself, "Why?" again. I understand that it still doesn't mean much at all, and in this very moment as you read this, every fiber of your being wants to fight back and to say that you don't want it replaced. But trust me, the answer to your "Why?" will make you glad that you asked that question in the first place.

If you find yourself asking these questions, trust in Allah ﷻ. We've already established that nothing happens without the will of Allah ﷻ. Therefore, both your inclination towards the beloved and your separation from him/her had a purpose. Perhaps its purpose was to teach you a lesson you may not have otherwise learned without submitting your heart to the beloved, or perhaps the separation itself is meant to be a lesson to either you or to the beloved. Leave it to Allah ﷻ, and let Allah ﷻ take care of it. In the meantime, attach your heart to Allah ﷻ

completely. There are absolutely no mistakes in the unraveling and the unfolding of life, and wherever life takes you is exactly where you are supposed to be, whether you are alone or alongside the beloved.

Each of us has a purpose in each other's lives, and some of us are simply meant to help another attach to the True Beloved, Allah ﷻ. Sometimes you meet someone and he/she is only meant to be a temporary change in your life, a means of guidance that Allah ﷻ has sent for you to be inspired by and to be lead on to the path of Allah ﷻ. Perhaps our hearts become attached to this individual, and even their absence works wonders in our lives, and especially in the ways we attach to Allah ﷻ in memory of such an individual. Patience is the ultimate lesson to any ache that Allah ﷻ bestows upon us.

In Surah Al-Baqara, Allah ﷻ clearly tells Prophet Muhammad ﷺ what He intends for us in this life:

> "And most certainly We shall try you by means of fear and danger, hunger, loss of wealth and worldly goods, or you as the individual in your lives or the fruits (of your toil) but give glad tidings to those who are patient in adversity - who, when calamity befalls them, say, 'Verily, unto Allah ﷻ do we belong and, verily, unto Him we shall return.'" [Holy Quran, 2:155-156]

In order for us to grasp the concept and significance of this verse, it is important to focus on what it says individually. The verse is essentially Allah ﷻ saying:

1. Do not, for a moment, be mislead into believing that this will not happen to you. I will certainly put you through a trial of any of these sorts in your life time:
   1. A trial of fear and danger
   2. A trial of hunger
   3. A trial of loss of wealth and worldly goods
   4. A trial directed to you individually in your lives
   5. or I will try you with the fruits of your toil.
2. I give glad tidings to those who have been patient
3. To be patient is to learn that you belong to Me, and to Me you will return.

[Extracted from the Friday Sermon by Shaikh Musleh Khan on 'Our Struggle and Hardships' given at the Islamic Institute of Toronto on 11/05/2016]

A significant challenge that we face in our lives is when we are met with struggles and hardships. We are constantly on the pursuit of happiness and when we find whatever makes us happy, we try to maintain that for as long as we possibly can. For example, if we think a new job will make us happy, we will pursue that job and do any thing in our power to get that job; once we have the job, our goal will be to keep it for as long as it makes us happy. Imagine wanting a car so bad that you do whatever you can in order to save up money for it, and then you finally purchase that car. You feel happy, you take care of that car and you maintain it, and you keep it for as long as it makes you happy. We engage in relationships and make friends with this same idea in mind. If the company of someone makes us happy then we try and become their friends to ensure that we can be happy in their presence for as long as we possibly can. That is what most people define life to be; the pursuit of happiness.

Sometimes in life though, we are faced with things that we have no control over. Imagine being absolutely happy and content with life, and one day as you go through your daily routine Allah ﷻ sends down a struggle, hardship or a trial for you. Naturally, you'd complain. You'd think to yourself, "How come I didn't see this coming?" and eventually you'll blame yourself and say, "What did I possibly do or not do to deserve this?" Allah ﷻ answers these questions throughout the Holy Quran, but especially in Surah Al-Baqara.

In this verse, Allah ﷻ explicitly says that you will be tried. There are many words used in the Holy Quran to signify being tested and put through trials, but the word used specifically in this verse refers to the kind of trial that is absolutely unavoidable. There is nothing you can do to divert it or to escape from it. You cannot say to yourself that, 'Perhaps if I had done this, I would not have been tried in such a way; or perhaps if I hadn't done that, then things would have been another way.' This is a test or hardship that is destined to you regardless of the decisions you've made in your life; it is a trial that you cannot avoid. In certain parts of the Quran, Allah ﷻ has explained why He chooses to test us in such a way, and it is because He wants to see which one of us will still perform righteous deeds. He emphasizes not on which one of us will do more than the other, but simply which one of us will remain righteous in times of hardship. It is easy to be righteous and patient in good times, but many of us fail to be sincerely devoted in worshiping Him during times of hardship. Therefore, in verse's 155-146 of Surah Al-Baqara, Allah ﷻ says in order to determine who will remain sincerely devoted to Him, He will test us in any of the 5 categories:

1. A trial of fear and danger
2. A trial of hunger
3. A trial of loss or subtraction of wealth and worldly goods
4. A trial directed to you individually in your lives
5. A trial of the fruits of your toil.

Allah ﷻ has used many words to describe fear in the Holy Quran, but in this verse he has specifically chosen the Arabic word 'Khauf'. This word signifies the immediate or initial fear that one responds in the state of fear. For example if Allah ﷻ intends for an earthquake to happen before you, (may Allah ﷻ protect us) that initial fear or immediate response is what Khuaf is. Some people would stand still and become paralyzed, and others would scream and shout for help. Allah ﷻ is essentially saying that there will time a time in our lives where we will be put in a state of fear, so that when it confronts us, we'll have an immediate reaction. In other words, when we see it, we will recognize it. For some of us, just the thought of such a trial will bring us to the verge of tears. May Allah ﷻ protect us, and make our trials easy for us. May Allah ﷻ give us strength.

In terms of the second category mentioned above, when we think about being tried with hunger, we restrict it to the understanding that Allah ﷻ will withhold His provisions from us and take away food. It is important to realize that the verses in the Quran require deep reflection and contemplation, and we must not look at them as superficially or wrongly restricting the meaning of such deep verses to just one thing. We need to reflect on how these verses are relevant to our own lives. When Allah ﷻ says that He will test us with food, it could also mean an abundance of food. For some of us, He may withhold his provisions during a time where we experience difficulties in business and cannot afford the grocery items that we would normally purchase. For others, it could mean that Allah ﷻ increases them in provision in order to test them, for example with regards to whether or not they waste food. Perhaps some of us are in a position to feed the needy and share our food. Jabir reported that Prophet Muhammad ﷺ said:

> "Food for one (person) suffices two, and food for two (persons) suffices four persons and food for four persons suffices eight persons." [Sahih Muslim, 2059d]

Therefore, some of us may have enough to share with others but we may refuse to do so. That could be our test. Some of us will have such an abundance of food that we will waste more food than we actually eat. What we do with these provision that Allah ﷻ has given to us could be our test.

In the next part of the verse Allah ﷻ says specifically that He will subtract from our wealth. He didn't use the same wording earlier for food, which meant that it could mean either a subtraction or an increase in provisions; but in this case, Allah ﷻ was specific in saying that He will test us with the subtraction of wealth itself. Scholars say that the eloquence of this verse is tremendous, and they say that Allah ﷻ uses the word 'subtraction' with regards to wealth because a human being is never truly poor. We always have blessings that we often do not even count. Therefore, we cannot restrict wealth to being only of monetary value. The ability to see is wealth; the ability to hear is wealth; knowledge is wealth; setting goals and being able to achieve them is wealth; the ability to stand on our two feet is wealth; the ability to use our hands is wealth; the ability to think on our own and make our own decisions is wealth. Allah ﷻ has given us so many blessings in the form of wealth that we often fail to regard as wealth, and He says that He will make these blessings to be a trial for us.

This is significant because we need to pay attention to our lives and reflect on what wealth means to us. If we consider wealth as money, then if we experience a hard time and lose our jobs, that means Allah ﷻ could be testing us in this way. For others, wealth could even simply mean the ability to walk and stand. When I personally reflected on this part of the verse, I was brought to tears because I felt as if Allah ﷻ tested me with the wealth of mobility. In fact, I started writing this book after an incident that led me to be diagnosed with a lower back injury referred to as Sciatica. It was due to the compression of a spinal nerve root in my lower back caused by a herniated disk. Sciatica took away my ability to sit, stand or even walk comfortably for almost eight months. During this time, I was strictly confined to my bed. Contemplating on this made me realize that we take a lot of the wealth that Allah ﷻ has given us for granted, and Allah ﷻ can simply take it away all at once. Therefore, it is important to individually reflect on what these verses mean to you in your personal life, and allow these reflections to humble you. Allah ﷻ will certainly test you to see if you will show gratitude for what you still have, instead of complaining and allowing the hardship to lower your faith in Allah ﷻ.

Allah ﷻ also says that He will test you as an individual, and this is often misinterpreted to be restricted strictly to the impact we as individuals may have on someone else life. It is important to remember that this verse also requires thought and reflection. It could mean different things, and one of those is that Allah ﷻ may send someone in our lives that will be a means of great hardship to us. Allah ﷻ may test us through a group of people, or someone in particular, who will be a struggle in our lives. For some, this could mean that it is a spouse or a beloved who may be a source of hardship; for others it could be a group of people such as in-laws or neighbors.

Many of us have probably been in a situation where we allowed ourselves to get close to someone, and we gave our heart to them, and Allah ﷻ decided for them to be our hardship. The way in which Allah ﷻ blesses us with hardships is in itself very interesting. Allah ﷻ has said in Surah Al-Sharh:

> And, behold, with every hardship
> comes ease: verily, with every hardship
> comes ease! [Holy Quran, 94:5-6]

The beauty of this verse is that many scholars have taken it to mean that Allah ﷻ has promised ease with every hardship twice; in other words, for every endured hardship we will be rewarded twice. This could mean different things, and one of the explanations that some scholars have given is that we will be rewarded for the hardship in this world, and also in the hereafter. One can be sure that no hardship will go unrewarded.

Falling in love, or having the inclination of our heart towards someone, is a means of immense sorrow and hardship. Allah ﷻ knows this, and as long as you experience those hardships for the sake of Allah ﷻ, He will reward you. For example, if you are attracted to a beautiful woman, and you take every step possible in order to not transgress or flirt with her, and you instead pursue her as a spouse, then the stress and anxiety that you experience will somehow be rewarded in this world and in the hereafter.

There might be a situation where Allah ﷻ will test you through a certain individual, and you might become emotionally inclined towards this person; however, the purpose of them being in your life will strictly be to guide you towards Allah ﷻ. Perhaps Allah ﷻ intended for you to pray and seek Him through your separation from this individual. Allah ﷻ will reward you for that hardship. It often happens that our Emaan (faith) might be very low, but in order to avoid losing someone we love, we naturally turn to Allah ﷻ in remembrance and in prayer. Throughout such long days and restless nights, our faith becomes revived, and for a period of time we become steadfast in hoping that Allah ﷻ will fulfill our needs. That was our test, and that revival of our faith was Allah ﷻ's purpose. Therefore, the beloved was simply the means of bringing us closer to Allah ﷻ.

For others, it could mean a test to/for them individually. One day they may wake up with a cough, and upon getting tested they may learn that they have been diagnosed with lung cancer. (May Allah ﷻ give us all good health, and give us His complete cure.) It could also mean that Allah ﷻ will put you through a trial in which He intends for you to be a means of aid or assistance to someone else. Perhaps someone in your life will be in great need, and Allah ﷻ will have made you a means of their sustenance or support. If you then refuse to share the provisions that Allah ﷻ blessed you with in abundance, and refuse to acknowledge that responsibility, you would therefore fail the test Allah ﷻ bestowed upon you.

Lastly, Allah ﷻ says He will test us with fruits. When Allah ﷻ says this, He refers to the various seeds that eventually grow into provisions in our life. Essentially, the fundamentals and principles that we instill in others that eventually prosper and grow, are the fruits. An example is the education you give to your children, and you can then proudly see where that education leads them. Scholars have looked at this to also mean children that have passed away. Some of us have children (May Allah ﷻ give them a long life and make them the most righteous among us all), and when they are growing up, they can bring us immense pleasure. Imagine how happy you'd be to see your child progress through school, and get his/her first award, and then graduate and even attain his/her first scholarship. It brings the parent immense joy, and this is something that Allah ﷻ may test us with. He may take away our children through an accident or an illness, and that could be our test. (May Allah ﷻ give us patience). In some situations we see that the parents are very humble and very righteous, but perhaps the child made the wrong friends and went on a totally different path. That could also be Allah ﷻ's test.

Many scholars and teachers have found the next verse to be incredible. In delivering his Friday Sermon, Shaikh Musleh Khan also referred to this verse to be incredible. Allah ﷻ says:

> "...but give glad tidings to those who
> are patient in adversity..." [Holy
> Quran, 2:156]

This is incredible because the Arabic word that Allah ﷻ
uses is "Bash-shir" which literally means
"Congratulations or Glad Tidings". Sheikh Musleh Khan
explained it as a verb used to describe when one takes
marbles and scatters them all over the floor. In other
words, Allah ﷻ is sending congratulations and good
tidings to everyone for being patient. Allah ﷻ just told
us five categories in which we will be put through an
immense trial, so why are we being congratulated?
Someone may have lost a child, or a spouse, or a parent,
or a job. So what is there to be congratulated about? We
must remember, there is wisdom in hardship.

The purpose of these trials is to teach us to be
patient, and if patience is the one thing we learned
through whatever hardship Allah ﷻ put us through in
our life, He says "Congratulations, Glad tidings to you."
Allah ﷻ congratulates the ones who are patient for
learning the lesson that He intended for us to learn
through the hardship. The verse continues:

> "...but give glad tidings to those who
> are patient in adversity - who, when
> calamity befalls them, say, 'Verily, unto
> Allah ﷻ do we belong and, verily,
> unto Him we shall return." [Holy
> Quran, 2:156]

This means that those who are patient will have learned,
"We belong to Allah ﷻ, and to Allah ﷻ we shall return."
The word Allah ﷻ uses in Arabic for calamity is

'Musibah' which refers to a man who shoots an arrow that always hits its target. Musibah is the arrow that, even if it is shot in the opposite direction, somehow always finds its target. Therefore when a calamity or Musibah is destined to you, it will surely come to you and it will not miss you regardless of where you are. May Allah ﷻ give us strength to withstand such trials, and may we learn the lesson that Allah ﷻ intends for us to learn.

Allah ﷻ says that the patient among us will learn that we solely belong to Allah ﷻ, it is to Him we will return. Thus, the lesson for us to learn out of every hardship and trial is to confront ourselves amidst the sorrow and affirm to ourselves that everything is the way it is supposed to be; essentially, there is absolutely nothing you could have done differently to have changed the calamity that has struck you because it was destined to you. The Prophet ﷺ has said that no hardship goes unrewarded, as the road to Paradise is surrounded by hardships, and the Fire is surrounded by desires. [Jami at-Tirmidhi, Vol. 4, Book 12, Hadith 2559]

Moreover, in the Hadith transmitted by Yahya b. Sa'id on the authority of Qatada, Prophet Muhammad ﷺ said:

> "(The believing servant) finds relief from the troubles of the world and its hardships and (gets into) the Mercy of Allah ﷻ." [Sahih Muslim, 950b]

Therefore, no matter what trial we are faced with, we must be patient. Love is a trial that Allah ﷻ puts us through via another individual. It is perhaps one of the hardest tests to endure, for one truly has the ability to lose his/her senses. But, if Allah ﷻ takes someone away from you, it means that you must observe patience, for you are being tested. You must affirm that you, yourself, are owned by Allah ﷻ. This always helps to put things into perspective. For example, earlier we imagined that we bought a brand new car that made us tremendously happy, and our goal was to hold on-to this car for as long as possible in order to prolong the happiness. Imagine, as soon as you drive the car out of the dealership, you get into an accident and the car is now damaged, and perhaps you sustained a minor injury. You can either be upset about it, or you can accept Allah ﷻ's decree and remind yourself, "To Allah ﷻ I belong, and to Allah ﷻ I shall return".

May we understand our purpose on earth and the meaning of our lives, and stay focused on the humbling idea that we do not even belong to ourselves, but instead we belong to Allah ﷻ. Therefore, whatever happens which is beyond our control, is the doing of Allah ﷻ. We must respect and accept the doings of Allah ﷻ, for there is divine reasoning behind it. When we learn to accept this, we begin to show gratitude towards our Creator and begin to live with a sense of humility in our life. For example, the new car that we bought; wasn't solely because of our own hard work. Indeed, we made an effort, but it was Allah ﷻ that made it easy for us. It was Allah ﷻ that provided the opportunity, and increased us in wealth in order for us to be able to afford the car. Perhaps the accident was meant to humble us, or perhaps it was a calamity which Allah ﷻ put us through in order to save us from an even bigger calamity at some point in our lives or even in the Hereafter. Similarly, when we fall in love, it was Allah ﷻ that made our heart inclined towards the beloved. Perhaps we disrespected the blessing that we were being given and transgressed, and now we are being held accountable for it. Or, perhaps the person wasn't meant to stay in our lives for long, and he/she was only meant to serve as a lesson. Maybe the beloved was supposed to be a means of learning humility and patience. We must make Du'a, but in the end there are things which are far beyond our control and we must accept the Qadr (decree) of Allah ﷻ. If it is yours, or if Allah ﷻ intends it to be yours eventually, it will not miss you. If it isn't yours, and if Allah ﷻ doesn't intend for it to be yours, no power on earth could bring it to you regardless of your efforts. To Allah ﷻ we belong, and to Allah ﷻ we shall return. May Allah ﷻ give us patience and strength to get through the various struggles in our lives.

Often when we become heart broken, we begin to blame love. We begin to think and express ideas such as: there is no such thing as love, love is fake, it does not exist, and it is merely an illusion. To certain extents, we might be convinced of all this, but we forget the fact that just because the love did not reciprocate or did not last, this doesn't mean that it wasn't real. Everything about you is real. The fact that you were able to love is proof that it was real; the lesson here is that if one could love the wrong person so much, imagine how much love he/she is capable of having for the right person! But if the lover blames love for his/her pain, then he/she will also eventually move onto blaming him/her own self. The lover begins to think that he/she will never be loved by someone else, or he/she will never be able to love someone else again. This may have even happened to you. Maybe you loved with all your heart, and it still didn't work out well; for a moment you may have felt furious thinking that love isn't real and it was all an illusion. Maybe you met someone at some point in life and they said, "I cannot love another human again because I've been disappointed in it once. I'd rather love my pet cat; or dog better because they will not disappoint me like the last person I loved." Maybe you met someone who said, "I love money; it is all you really need in life. It is the only friend that ever comes to my rescue. The money that I have in my bank does more for me than anyone has ever been able to do, then why should I not love money?" We must trust that these are actually the words of the heart broken.

One of the most beautiful explanations of love according to the Sufi thought as brought forth by Hazrat Inayat Khan, is that love has created beauty so that it may be able to love. This really makes you think, and once you grasp the idea of this, it truly makes you feel content with yourself and the beauty of Allah ﷻ and His Creation. Allah ﷻ is love; that is why He is called the Creator. The lover alone has the power to create, and all that which He creates is for the purpose of receiving His love.

Allah ﷻ is beautiful because He has created beauty. If there was no beauty in Him, there would have been no beauty in His manifestation. Subhan'Allah! Similarly, He has created us to be able to reflect our own beauty into the manifestations of ourselves. If there was no beauty in the thought of the poet, he/she could not have written a beautiful verse. If there was no beauty in the thought of the artist, he/she could never have painted a beautiful picture. It is impossible to see the beauty in the heart of the poet, or the writer, or the painter except in the beauty of whatever he/she has created; in the poem, in the painting, in the sketch, etc. It is not only the poem, the painting and the sketch that is beautiful, but the heart of the writer or the artist was beautiful to begin with.

> "Consequently we become able to see
> the beauty not only in manifestation,
> but also before it was manifested; and

before it was manifested it existed in love. In other words, we can see that the beauty was hidden in love; beauty is hidden in love, and the beauty that love has before it to love is its own beauty. Therefore, to whatever extent beauty is beautiful, so is love beautiful; even more so, for the Creator is more beautiful than the thing He has created." [Hazrat Inayat Khan, Volume VII, In an Eastern Rose Garden, - Love, Harmony and Beauty]

When we begin to understand this, it becomes obvious that the lover is incomparably vaster than the object he loves.

"The real love, the real beauty, is in the lover. The object that he loves is much smaller, although for the moment the lover is not aware of the difference. The lover thinks, 'You are the object before which I bow. You are the object of which I think day and night, before which I am helpless. You are the object that I admire, that I adore.' Yet he does not realize the vastness of his love, and indeed, strictly speaking; love is vaster than the lover." [Hazrat Inayat Khan, Volume VII, In an Eastern Rose Garden, - Love, Harmony and Beauty]

This shift in perspective makes one realize that it was not the beloved that instilled love inside of you; in fact, the love was always there. The intensity of love that you felt was only the love that you were created with, and the object of your love is what brought forth those feelings.

Now imagine you're in love with someone and you give them your attention. So, you put them on the pedestal in which you completely disregard all their flaws, and they become the epitome of perfection in your mind. Maybe you even love them with the expectation that they'll love you back, and that you'll live happily ever after. Unfortunately, things do not go as planned, and now you're heart-broken. For a while, you will certainly hurt, but eventually, as we have discussed through the course of this book, you'll come to terms with it all. When one is attracted to another because of beauty, and after a short moment of heart-break he/she falls out of love, it is because the lover was only in love as long as the beauty remained his ideal. Therefore, after a period of time when the heart is ready to listen to reason again, you will begin to let go of whatever ideals you originally held on-to with regards to the beloved. You will then find another object of attention who is perhaps more beautiful in ways only you can understand, and this becomes the new ideal. The pedestal on which you placed the previous object of your love no longer qualifies for the same position in your heart, because once you begin to notice the flaws in the previous love, you are no longer blinded. Essentially, heartbreak offers you clarity. The beloved no longer proves to be what you expected, because you unreasonably placed them in a position which they could not realistically live up to simply because of a face, or figure that you may have been initially attracted to. Therefore, you learn to raise the standards of your love, and begin to value the things that the beloved lacked that someone else may have. From this moment on, the love that you already have inside you, despite believing at some point that you'll never be able to love again, causes you to idealize the new beloved in your thought and imagination, and you continually add to the beauty of the manifestation which is the new beloved.

This is how Allah ﷻ has created us, to be able to

love. Some of us are materialistic, and therefore we appreciate material beauty. This is not our fault, and it's completely normal for an individual to admire what directly appeals to him/her. Some of us may prefer the beauty of mind, virtue, personality, good manners and that is what will attract us; namely, a beautiful personality, and a sympathetic presence. Others may be inclined towards someone who we find to be an ideal of inspiration, peace of mind, and joy. However, we mustn't forget that if Allah ﷻ has intended our love to be a lesson, then it is a lesson that we will inevitably experience and hopefully learn from. If you love someone simply for a beautiful face and a soul that does not reflect the same beauty, then Allah ﷻ will teach you how to love someone with a less attractive face but beauty that is so immense at their heart.

There is immense beauty in Allah ﷻ, and therefore it is evident in all of His creation. What may seem unattractive to you, may be the most beautiful thing that someone else has ever known. The perception of beauty has to do with one's personal evolution. Hazrat Inayat Khan explains:

> "He who is of lower evolution cannot love a higher object. But a person of higher evolution can love the lower as well as the higher... Hatred is found in the lower grades of evolution, not in the higher; and the higher the evolution develops, the less the hatred and prejudice become. As high as one sets one's ideal, so high does one reach, and it is by raising the standard of beauty step by step that one rises up and up into the highest heaven." [Hazrat Inayat Khan,

This is how some of us can raise our ideal to the height that we are able to love Allah ﷻ, who is The Formless and above all goodness and virtue. These are the ones amongst us who may have loved a worldly beloved for the wrong reasons; in being broken, Allah ﷻ allows us to learn exactly what qualities, and the type of beauty, that we should actually be looking for. Allah ﷻ is the source of all beauty, and once someone is able to understand that, he/she is unable to stop himself from loving Allah ﷻ. When Allah ﷻ becomes your beloved, you reach a point where just the simple acknowledgement of an attribute of Allah ﷻ will move you to tears. Simply hearing a word of truth will move you to tears. These are the people who will feel Allah ﷻ when they listen to the sounds of instruments, and love Him for granting them the sense of hearing. They will feel Allah ﷻ in the winds, and love Allah ﷻ for granting them the sense of touch. Even merely standing before a beautiful painting, they will be able to see Allah ﷻ. While being lost in a crowd amidst hundreds of faces, they will only see the harmony of His creation, and they will love Allah ﷻ. Once your beloved is Allah ﷻ, you will see a vision of the beauty of Allah ﷻ in everything: the desert, the sea, the sky, the earth, in light, and in darkness, in every color and every texture; in every blur and every spec of clarity.

In order to attain true love for Allah ﷻ, one must establish certain principles in his/her life. The foremost condition of attaining love for Allah ﷻ is to sincerely crave such love. All the stages of love that we discussed in the previous chapters are equally applicable for the love of Allah ﷻ.

In the stage of Ulfat, one's heart becomes inclined towards the beloved. Imagine if the Beloved is now Allah ﷻ. One does not have to worry about the Beloved loving him/her back, because Allah ﷻ loves us all equally and individually. Indeed, He has already bestowed favors of His love upon us abundantly. Allah ﷻ loves us unconditionally, and His mercy and benevolence is always available to us. Allah ﷻ says in Surah Al-Mu'min:

> "And your Lord said: 'Invoke me (i.e. believe in My Oneness and ask Me for anything) I will respond to your (invocation). Verily, those who scorn My worship (i.e. do not invoke Me, and do not believe in My Oneness) they will surely enter Hell in humiliation!" [Holy Quran, 40:60]

Allah ﷻ, our true Beloved has already commanded us to call him whenever we need Him, and He promised to respond to us. Unlike the worldly beloved, you do not need to chase Allah ﷻ. Some people believe in Allah ﷻ only as their Creator. Essentially, they think Allah ﷻ created them, and then Allah ﷻ simply stepped away from His creation. Others have true faith in Allah ﷻ. They acknowledge that Allah ﷻ is their Creator, but they also acknowledge that Allah ﷻ is always there, and never for a moment does He leave His creation unattended. Allah ﷻ says that He is whatever you expect Him to be. If you believe that He has left you unattended, you will miss His presence in your life. If you have faith that Allah ﷻ is always there, He will show you His signs beautifully. One does not have to chase Allah ﷻ, for Allah ﷻ is the Beloved that chases you, if you truly believe. Abu Hurairah reported Allah ﷻ's Messenger ﷺ as saying that Allah ﷻ, the Exalted and Glorious, thus stated:

> "I am near to the thought of My servant as he thinks about Me, and I am with him as he remembers Me. And if he remembers Me in his heart, I also remember him in My heart, and if he remembers Me in assembly, I remember him in assembly, better than his (remembrance), and if he draws near Me by the span of a palm, I draw near him by the cubit, and if he draws near Me by the cubit, I draw near him by the space (covered by) two hands. And if he walks towards Me, I rush towards him." [Sahih Muslim, 2675 a]

Therefore if you walk towards Allah ﷻ, He will run towards you.

The stage of Unsiyat in Divine love is also true friendship; the strong attachment between you as the lover and Allah ﷻ as the Beloved. As long as you are sincere and loyal in your love towards Allah ﷻ, He reciprocates this love tenfold. Whatever Allah ﷻ does is incomparable, and so is His love. Look at all that Allah ﷻ has given you out of His unconditional love. You have the wealth of sight, hearing, speech, touch, you have parents, siblings, and friends to give you company. You have water to relinquish your thirst, and food to sustain yourself. Simply look around you, and all you will see are bestowals of unconditional favors from your true Beloved. Imagine how Allah ﷻ will reciprocate when you truly live up to the obligations and duties that He has prescribed to you.

In the stage of Mavaddat, one leaves everything for the beloved, and yet he/she is faced with hardships and agony. But, do you remember the lesson from Sheikh Abdul Qadir Jilani in the beginning of this chapter? He literally advises the individual to become a broken vessel that would only be able to hold the love for Allah ﷻ, and anything else would simply slip through its cracks. As long as you continue to choose things above Allah ﷻ, He will break you at the very hands of those things. But if you submit to Allah ﷻ, and prioritize Him above all else in your life, all of existence shall be placed within your reach and at your disposal. As long as you prioritize worldly possessions, they will have the power to hurt you. Once you choose to abandon them for the sake of Allah ﷻ, they will chase you instead.

That is the beauty of loving Allah ﷻ as compared to anyone else. If you leave everything for a man or a woman, it will never be appreciated, and it will only instill pride and ego in your worldly beloved. But if you leave everything for Allah ﷻ, He gives you the world in ways that you never even imagined, and yet it would mean nothing in comparison to the intensity of your love towards the Lord of the Worlds. Truly, Allah ﷻ reciprocates far beyond the extent of what we could ever imagine.

In the earlier chapter regarding the stage of Hawaa, Ibn Arabi was quoted:

"All human beings have Hawaa for a different beloved. Allah ﷻ commands His servants to direct this Hawaa to Him." [Srecko Horvat, The Radicality of Love, Publication by John Wiley & Sons]

Hawaa means to fall, and Allah ﷻ commands us to fall for nothing and no one except Him. In "The Dispraise of Hawaa", Ibn Qayyim Al-Jawziyyah states that Allah ﷻ will give shade to seven, on the Day when there will be no shade but His. It was Narrated by Abu Hurairah that the Prophet ﷺ said:

"(These seven persons are) a just ruler, a youth who has been brought up in the worship of Allah ﷻ (i.e. worships Allah ﷻ sincerely from childhood), a man whose heart is attached to the mosques (i.e. to pray the compulsory prayers in the mosque in congregation), two person who love each other only for Allah ﷻ's sake and they meet and part in Allah ﷻ's cause only, a man who refuses the call of a charming woman of noble birth for illicit intercourse with her and says: 'I am afraid of Allah ﷻ', a man who gives charitable gifts so secretly that his left hand does not know what his right hand has given (i.e. no body knows how much he has given in charity), and a person who remembers Allah ﷻ in seclusion and his eyes are then flooded with tears." [Sahih al-

Bukhari: 660 or Vol. 1, Book 11, Hadith 629]

Imam Jawziyyah (may Allah ﷻ have mercy on him) explains that these people deserved the shade because of their opposition to al-hawaa. Therefore, for those who devote themselves to Allah ﷻ and become overwhelmingly inclined towards Him, Allah ﷻ reciprocates by aiding them on the Day of Judgement by saving them from punishment. As described in the earlier chapters, in the stage of Hawaa the lover would do anything for the beloved, because he/she wants to spend his/her entire life in obedient devotion to the beloved by dedicating all that he/she has to him/her. Despite this devotion, there are times when the lover gets nothing in return but humility and agony. On the other hand, it is truly beyond our comprehension, the way in which Allah ﷻ will reward us if we devote our obedience to Him and Him alone as our true Beloved.

In the state of Shagaf, one experiences extreme passion and jealousy if the beloved diverts his/her attention away from them because of insecurities. However, in showing extreme passion for Allah ﷻ and jealousy of Allah ﷻ, one commits him/herself entirely in pleasing Allah ﷻ unconditionally. One is always consciously aware of Allah ﷻ and his/her actions are always reflective of this consciousness. Shaykh Zulfiqar Ahmad wrote that one of the most distinct sign of the sincere lover of Allah ﷻ is that he does not care for anything other than his Beloved, Allah ﷻ. In the Shariah, just as loving Allah ﷻ is an act of worship, so too is having disdain for anything other than Allah ﷻ. Just as one would empty his/her heart for anything other than

368

the beloved, a sincere lover of Allah ﷻ only has space for Allah ﷻ in his heart. One may fall out of love for the worldly beloved and become distracted by the beauty of another person, but the heart of the lover who is immersed in the love of Allah ﷻ loves no one else in such a manner. Shaykh Zulfiqar Ahmad refers to the story of a man who once saw a beautiful woman and exclaimed, 'I am in love with you and want only you!' She replied saying, 'My sister is far more beautiful than me, in fact she's coming right behind me.' As the man turned to look behind her, the woman struck him on the head with her shoe saying, 'You liar! If you truly loved me, then you would never have looked in any other direction.' When one has the sincerest love for Allah ﷻ in his heart, there is absolutely nothing that can distract the lover from looking in another direction, except for the direction of Allah ﷻ.

One who experiences Ishq is referred to as an Ashiq. Shaykh Zulfiqar Ahmed describes that the first characteristic of a sincere Ashiq is a pale and yellow complexion, as intense spiritual training and abundant devotions often have such an effect. Moreover, a sincere lover of Allah ﷻ can be recognized by the nature of his/her being. A lover of Allah ﷻ is blessed with radiance on his/her face and a noble demeanor, such that even a stranger can recognize his love for Allah ﷻ upon seeing him. Sincere love for Allah ﷻ comes with a natural blessing that even though the lover is modest, anyone can recognize the sincerity of his/her love towards Allah ﷻ at first glance. It is said that hearts are attracted to a sincere Ashiq as strongly as metal is attracted to a magnet. The second characteristic of an Ashiq is deep sighs of longing, due to separation from Allah ﷻ. The third characteristic is that the lover's eyes remain wet with tears, as the restlessness of the heart is released through the eyes. One is always brought to tears through feelings of gratitude and appreciation for the blessings that Allah ﷻ has bestowed upon him/her. The fourth characteristic is eating modest amounts of food. A sincere Ashiq does not succumb to gluttonous pleasures; rather he/she eats merely to get by. The fifth characteristic is to speak little, because a person whose inner soul converses with Allah ﷻ has no desire to engage in idle conversation and only speaks out of necessity. The sixth and most significant characteristic of the Ashiq is to sleep little. His/her nights are spent in the remembrance and worship of Allah ﷻ, because Allah ﷻ is closest to the earth during the night.

One needs to actively seek the love for Allah ﷻ, as it is a treasure, and one must make firm intentions in his/her heart to acquire true love for Allah ﷻ. The friends of Allah ﷻ have gone as far as sacrificing all worldly pleasures in their devotion to Allah ﷻ in order to secure a beautiful afterlife.

It is imperative to recognize that the lover of the material world can never become a lover of Allah ﷻ, because there will always be excuses that will come between him and Allah ﷻ. As long as one continues to give importance to worldly benefits, the fulfillment of those worldly benefits will always come between the love for Allah ﷻ. Every desire must be removed from the heart until it is empty, except for the desire to genuinely love Allah ﷻ. Moreover, one needs to continually recite the Tahlil which is 'La ilaha lilal'Lah' which means, 'There is no Diety but Allah ﷻ, and no one and nothing is worthy of worship but Him'. Shaykh Zulfiqar Ahmad explains that this is important because it annihilates all false deities that may reside in one's heart. [Shaykh Zulfiqar Ahmad, Ishq-e-Illahi, pg. 103] Lastly one should engage in constant reflection (fikr) of Allah ﷻ in which one imagines that the spiritual blessings of Allah ﷻ are descending into his/her heart. One should deeply contemplate the attributes of Allah ﷻ, and the vastness or the ultimate extent to which each attribute could possibly extend. However, one can never truly grasp the vastness or the extent of Allah ﷻ's Majesty, for there is no end to it. In everything that Allah ﷻ is, whether it is being Merciful, Full of Bounty, and Mighty, Allah ﷻ is endless and unimaginable. However, one can still love Allah ﷻ within the limitations of his imagination and his common sense through understanding the attributes of Allah ﷻ.

I would like to summarize this discussion with the following quote:

> "He who loves because he cannot help it is the slave of love, but he who loves because it is his only joy is the king of love. He who, for the sake of love, loves someone who falls short of his ideal is the ruler of love. And he who can seal his heart full of love in spite of all attraction on part of the beloved is the conqueror of love." [Hazrat Inayat Khan, Spiritual Liberty, Volume V, Part IV, Chapter IV]

May Allah ﷻ give us the strength to seal and protect our

hearts full of love inspite of the overwhelming attraction on the part of our beloved. May He aid us in legitimating our love through marriage. May we become conquerors of love, and love for the sake of Allah ﷻ. May we learn to love nothing more than our love for Allah ﷻ. May Allah ﷻ guide us all and make it easy for us. May Allah ﷻ bless us all immensely for our efforts in keeping our love Halal. May we love Allah ﷻ enough to accept His decree unconditionally.

A NOTE FROM THE AUTHOR

"O Allah ﷻ! Send your blessings and peace on Muhammad ﷺ, our Master, and on his Progeny and his Companions in the amount equal to the total number of letters in the Holy Quran and let each letter carry thousands of blessings and salutations with it." - Durood-e-Quraani

It brings me great peace and pleasure in knowing that one day I too will no longer be among the people in this world, but I will have left behind this book with all of its lessons for those who come after me, so that they may be guided. The quest for knowledge is regarded as being equivalent to having the knowledge and sharing it. May we all benefit from this book equally. Abu Umamah (may Allah ﷻ be pleased with him) reported:

> The Messenger of Allah ﷺ said, "The superiority of the learned over the devout worshipper is like my superiority over the most inferior amongst you (in good deeds." He went on to say, "Allah ﷻ, His angels, the dwellers of the heaven and the earth, and even the ant in its hole and the fish (in water) supplicate in favor of those who teach people knowledge." [Riyadh as-Salihin, The Book of Knowledge, At-Tirmidhi, Book 13, Hadith 1387]

Moreover, Abu-Darda (may Allah ﷻ be pleased with him) reported:

> The Messenger of Allah ﷺ said, "He who follows a path in quest of knowledge, Allah ﷻ will make the

path of Jannah easy to him. The
angels lower their wings over the
seeker of knowledge, being pleased
with what he does. The inhabitants of
the heavens and the earth and even
the fish in the depth of the oceans
seek forgiveness for him. The
superiority of the learned man over
the devout worshipper is like that of
the full moon to the rest of the stars
(i.e., in brightness). The learned are
the heirs of the Prophets who
bequeath neither dinar nor dirham but
only that of knowledge; and he who
acquires it, has in fact acquired an
abundant portion." [Riyadh as-Salihin,
The Book of Knowledge, Abu
Dawud and At-Tirmidhi, Book 13,
Hadith 1388]

It then becomes clear that for every reader who picks this
book up with the intention of attaining knowledge, the
angels and the inhabitants of the heavens will be pleased
with him/her. May every page benefit you in developing
a stronger consciousness of Allah ﷻ, and may it give you
an increased sense of confidence in your worship and
Du'a. May your newly found understanding of love
inspire many more around you, and may its practice lead
you to Jannah. May the knowledge you attain through
this book add to your deeds in the Hereafter, and may
the distribution of this book add to my deeds in the form
of ceaseless charity.

Abu Hurairah (may Allah ﷻ be pleased with him)
reported:

The Messenger of Allah ﷺ said,

"When a man dies, his deeds come to an end except for three things: Sadaqah Jariyah (ceaseless charity); a knowledge which is beneficial, or a virtuous descendant who prays for him (for the deceased)." [Riyadh as-Salihin, The Book of Knowledge, Muslim, Book 13, Hadith 1383]

Therefore, I would humbly request that no matter when this book falls in your hands, the message in this book would indeed remain timeless whether I remain among you or not. May this book be a means of Sadaqah Jariyah (ceaseless charity) for me. May I be rewarded every time this book is shared with another. Moreover, If I have been able to make even the slightest bit of a difference in your lives, please keep me, my family, my beloved, the family of my beloved, and each and everyone of those mentioned either in the text of this book or in the acknowledgements, in your prayers. May we all be united under the protection of the Prophet's ﷺ umbrella on the day of judgement, and may Allah ﷻ raise us in ranks and make us among those He is most pleased with.

The discussions in this book have been a major part of my life and philosophy, and I have sincere hopes that this book may have a special place in your lives, and that it may mean something significant to you all as well. Ibn 'Uthaymeen (may Allah ﷻ have mercy on him) explained that if any individual has a proper understanding of what he is calling people to, it makes no difference whether he is a great scholar, or a seeker of knowledge who is a hard worker, or an ordinary Muslim whose knowledge of a particular issue is clean and certain. May you all benefit enough from this book to share this knowledge among yourselves and your families. It was narrated by 'Abdullah bin 'Amr (may Allah ﷻ have mercy on him):

"The Prophet ﷺ said, 'Convey (my teachings) to the people even if it were a single sentence, and tell others the stories of Bani Israel (which have been taught to you), for it is not sinful to do so. And whoever tells a lie on me intentionally, will surely take his place in the (Hell) Fire." [Sahih al-Bukhari: 3461, or Vol. 4, Book 55, Hadith 667]

The Prophet ﷺ advised us to convey from him, even if it is a   single sentence. He did not stipulate or discriminate among us based on whether the individual should have vast knowledge, rather he made clear that the individual be certain of his knowledge and not be one who is ignorant. Therefore, I encourage you to continue seeking knowledge of your religion beyond this book and strengthen your beliefs, and convey that knowledge to people. May Allah ﷻ reward you for all your efforts, and further aid you in seeking His pleasure.

I have written this book through various struggles that I've been faced with. "Disciples of Ishq," took a long time to compile, and in writing all that you hold in your hands, some days I experienced unexplainable happiness while on other days I was at my lowest. Therefore, the lessons in this book have made me realize some of my own mistakes, and even the mistakes that those closest to me have made as well. We often become inclined towards another individual, and allow our hearts to become attached to them in various ways in the hopes of legitimating these attachments one day. Our intentions may be the purest of intentions, but it does not justify the attachment.

The day our attachments are legitimated through marriage could be a month from now, or a year from now, or it may never even come as the next moment in time isn't even promised to us. A lot happens in between, and a lot of it has the potential to cause us great anxiety and grief such as the struggle with convincing our families to accept the partner of our choice. Many have failed at this stage, and have been so severely attached that it left both individuals heartbroken. Nothing is guaranteed to go as planned, and therefore Allah ﷻ has asked us to keep our guard up and try to legitimate our love or inclination towards the beloved through marriage first. The moment we allow ourselves to get attached to someone outside of a marriage regardless of our intentions, we inevitably put that guard down. This allows us to become vulnerable to Shaytan, and our own Nafs, along with our own vulnerabilities and weaknesses. The anxiety and grief that we inflict upon our own hearts is never worth it, because Allah ﷻ has forbidden it. Yet we justify our attachments, and these attachments always lead to the same lesson: it shouldn't have happened in the first place. Therefore, it is better to be comfortable in one's solitude than to be hurting over a mistake that Allah ﷻ has forbidden.

With that being said, it does become increasingly difficult for all of us to be alone as we progress through our lives and as we begin to age. We see that the friends we grew up with are getting married, our cousins are perhaps all married, and some of the friends that we used to know in high school even have children! But here we may be alone and unaware of who we are going to marry. I understand the struggle. I know the questions you ask yourselves, and I know how hard it is to be waiting. But after reading all this and understanding the significance behind the philosophy of Halal love, I ask you to promise yourself never to settle. I ask you to be patient, no matter how long it takes. I want you to remember that the author of the story of your life is Allah ﷻ, and He has written it beautifully and with purpose. You are the answers to someone's sincerest Du'a. You are the fulfillment of someone's prayer. Somewhere out there, someone longs to finally meet you and they drop to Sujood and make Du'a to Allah ﷻ to keep you safe. So I humbly ask you to guard your Emaan (faith), lower your gaze, preserve your Haya (modesty), attach your hearts to Allah ﷻ so when the time for fulfillment finally comes, it would have been worth the wait. Do not lose hope in Allah ﷻ's timing. Remember, what is yours will find you, for never could it belong to anyone else. You don't have to settle, you don't have to compromise your modesty to secure a spouse, you don't even have to go out actively looking for a spouse either. The universe is subject to the will of Allah ﷻ, and as long as you choose to observe the guidance of Allah ﷻ and His Messenger ﷺ, Allah ﷻ will ensure that the universe will conspire to bring you to what is yours at the right time. If lightening cannot strike without His permission, and if the wind cannot carry leaves without Him knowing, what is yours will not move towards you until it is in accordance with His timing and His will.

My dearest sisters and brothers in Islam, this will require you to be vigilant and to maintain control over your comfort zones. Keep your guard up and do not be too trusting. Your modesty is precious, and it is yours to guard and you need to enforce a safe distance between yourself and whoever your heart may become inclined towards. If a man is truly in love with you, or genuinely interested, he will fight the world for you without you having to compromise your modesty and your comfort space. Similarly, if a woman is truly in love with you, she will do everything she can to help you in legitimating that love.

We live in a time where love seems to have lost its meaning, and members of society are constantly competing for attention. For example, many young females that grow up in these societies feel the need to compromise their modesty in order to secure a relationship. If you need to compromise your morals and your modesty in order to get a guy's attention, he is not meant for you. So it is important to maintain and enforce a comfort zone. It is important to protect yourselves from premarital attachments with the opposite gender. This is important because we end up attaching ourselves to people, and we invest our time and feelings in them and they eventually reveal their true intentions which are often other than marriage.

Remember your worth and stand firm on Nikkah if anyone claims to love you. Words are easy to use, and many of us are gifted with putting together words which can win hearts over. Therefore, be careful not to allow anyone to lure you into sticking around and investing your time and emotions on the mere promise of a marriage. It is not worth attaching yourself to someone on the promise of a year from now, or a month from now because the next moment isn't even promised to us. If two individuals are attracted to one another and make the mutual intention to get married, surely, Allah ﷻ will make it easy for them. If it is meant to be, it will be made easy for you without having to fight for it because Allah ﷻ will bless you for your intentions. Many relationships end up being complicated and full of pain and anxiety because we hold on and justify it with excuses of a promise of eventually being married, at some point in time. If it is meant to be, it will be regardless of your attachment. Your name was written with someone before you were even born, and you truly don't have to force the wrong pieces to fit with yours.

Similarly, my dearest brothers in Islam, refrain from misleading women with false intentions and do not engage in forbidden relationships. It is equally important for all of us to protect our hearts from attachments which are not meant to be for us. It is always important to remember that the woman you engage in premarital activities with is potentially the honor of another man who can promise her marriage. Therefore, do not mislead her into believing you will marry her. Allah ﷻ tests you with the wrongs that you have done, and you will eventually be made to realize the extent of the damage that false promises and misleading intentions can do, perhaps through your sisters or daughters. May Allah ﷻ protect them. We must be patient and work on protecting ourselves and trying to make us worthy of the kind of woman we want to be with. If you yearn for a righteous wife, become the man that deserves such a blessing, and Allah ﷻ has already promised you in Surah An-Nur that good women are for good men.

> "[In the nature of things,] corrupt women are for corrupt men, and corrupt men, for corrupt women - just as good women are for good men, and good men, for good women." [Holy Quran, 24:26]

If you truly fall in love with a woman, protect her from engaging in haram (forbidden/illicit) activities with you, and help her guard her modesty. Instead of promising her marriage at some point in time, make sure you are ready and then make your intentions before Allah ﷻ and ask for His help. Make every possible attempt at marrying her as soon as possible, before your attachments strengthen. If you cannot marry her, let her go for the sake of Allah ﷻ. If she is meant for you,

Allah ﷻ will unite you when the time is right. If not, Allah ﷻ will mend both hearts beautifully as He has promised to aid you in anything done for the sake of Him.

If you are married to someone who wasn't of your choice, love her for the sake of Allah ﷻ or you will be cursed and be held liable for every trouble you inflict upon her. She is yours to protect and you are her protector. Keep an open mind and be flexible with adjusting to the new relationship. Allah ﷻ has intended it to you, and perhaps there is immense good in it if only you allow yourself to grow in the marriage. Everything you do for each other will be an act of charity, and not only will it be rewarded by Allah ﷻ but it will increase love between you. One progresses through to the stage of Ishq through marriage, and if you make every attempt at it, Allah ﷻ will aid you.

If you have not loved, may true love find you in the most beautiful of ways; and when it does, may your love be the purest of kinds like that of Prophet Muhammad ﷺ and Khadijah (may Allah ﷻ be pleased with her). May you honor and protect your beloved from any transgression that may displease Allah ﷻ, and may the doors of marriage open for you with ease so you may legitimate your love. May the togetherness of you and your beloved be blessed by Allah ﷻ, and may your union be a means for you to become closer to Him in love and devotion. May your marriage be a way for you and your families to enter Jannah, and may you be blessed with children who will be a source of great joy and happiness. May Allah ﷻ protect your marriage from the whisperings of Shaytaan, and any external harms. May Allah ﷻ give you the strength to live together in justice, equity, love and mercy.

May we all become Disciples of Ishq. May halal love no longer remain true love's forgotten creed. May it be the only other love that penetrates through the hearts of mankind besides the love for his kin, and the incomparable love for Allah ﷻ.

Lastly, may Allah ﷻ reward all the respective authors that I've referenced within this book. May their struggles be made easy, and may they find peace and comfort in the Hereafter. More specifically, I owe an enormous amount of gratitude to the Alim Foundation and the Arabic Playhouse for their creation of alim.org which made the Holy Quran and its translations easily accessible in English. I am also equally thankful to the entire team at Understand Quran Academy for helping me broaden my knowledge and perspective of the attributes of Allah ﷻ. Moreover, I am indebted to the creators of sunnah.com for creating the first online, authentic, searchable, and multilingual database of collections of Hadith from our beloved Prophet Muhammad ﷺ, which served as an incomparable aid to the compilation of this book. May Allah ﷻ reward the entire team behind each organization immensely for their efforts in making the Holy Quran, Hadith and authentic Islamic Knowledge easily accessible and for all their efforts which have helped me in ways they'll probably never know. It is primarily through these sources that I have personally checked and verified the references to the Hadith, and translations of the Holy Quran used in this book, and I have done so to the best of my ability in order to ensure that I am personally confident in the credibility of the information that I've passed on to you. Allah ﷻ knows best.

May Allah ﷻ also send His peace and blessings on our beloved Prophet Muhammad ﷺ, his children and his companions in the amount of the total number of letters in this book every time one of you decides to read it, and may each letter carry thousands of blessings and salutations with it.

CPSIA information can be obtained
at www.ICGtesting.com
Printed in the USA
LVOW13s1447180518

577683LV00017B/559/P